ULSTER'S UNCERTAIN
DEFENDERS

ULSTER'S UNCERTAIN
DEFENDERS

Protestant Political, Paramilitary
and Community Groups and
the Northern Ireland Conflict

Sarah Nelson

APPLETREE PRESS
SYRACUSE
UNIVERSITY PRESS

Published and printed by
The Appletree Press Ltd
7 James Street South
Belfast BT2 8DL

British Library Cataloguing in Publication
Data
Nelson, Sarah
Ulster's uncertain defenders. — (Modern
Irish Society, ISSN 0263-595X)
1. Political parties — Northern Ireland
2. Protestants — Northern Ireland —
Political activity
I. Title   II. Series
322.4′2′09416   JN1572.A979
ISBN 0-904651-99-1
ISBN 0-904651-89-3 Pbk

Published in the United States by
Syracuse University Press
1600 Jamesville Avenue
Syracuse
New York 13244-5160

ISBN 0-8156-2418-2

Cover: 'The Twelfth' by Rita Duffy

9 8 7 6 5 4 3

Manufactured in Ireland

Contents

Acknowledgements

It would be impossible to mention everyone who has helped me to write this book. Most of the people who feature in its pages were as generous with their time as they were with their hospitality. I should like to thank everyone who put up with my questions: though they may not agree with my conclusions, I hope they will feel the book has some value. I am especially grateful to those people in political parties, paramilitary groups (including loyalist prisoners) and other organisations who gave continuing help over several years. They may prefer to remain anonymous but are remembered with appreciation.

Many people in the academic profession gave me advice, information and encouragement. My greatest debt is to Professor Richard Rose of Strathclyde University, whose patience, tolerance and confidence in my ability helped me overcome many problems and setbacks.

I should also like to thank Professor John Whyte and Professor Cornelius O'Leary of Queen's University; staff and research fellows at the University's Institute of Irish Studies, especially Professor David Miller; Professor James Cornford, Dr J. R. S. Wilson, Frank Wright, Tom Hadden, John Darby, Maurice Hayes, Professor Bill van Voris, Professor J. Bowyer Bell, John Bayley and Ron Wiener.

Mr Ronald Adams generously gave me access to his personal collection of Ulster ephemeral political literature. Among journalists who gave me their time and advice I am especially grateful to David McKittrick and Alan Murray. On the secretarial side Mrs Margaret McGlone and Miss Pat Smyth kept me going with their continuing help and humour.

I want to thank the people I stayed with while I was researching the book for their generosity and patience. The support and encouragement of my own family was greatest of all, and is appreciated in the same degree.

Abbreviations

CONI	Community Organisations Northern Ireland
CRC	Community Relations Commission
DUP	Democratic Unionist Party
IRA	Irish Republican Army
IRSP	Irish Republican Socialist Party
LAW	Loyalist Association of Workers
NICRA	Northern Ireland Civil Rights Association
NILP	Northern Ireland Labour Party
RUC	Royal Ulster Constabulary
SDLP	Social Democratic and Labour Party
SRA	Shankill Redevelopment Association
UCAG	Ulster Community Action Group
UDA	Ulster Defence Association
UDR	Ulster Defence Regiment
ULA	Unionist Labour Association
ULCCC	Ulster Loyalist Central Co-ordinating Committee
ULF	Ulster Loyalist Front
UPA	Ulster Protestant Action
UPL	Ulster Protestant League
UPNI	Unionist Party of Northern Ireland
UPV	Ulster Protestant Volunteers
UUUC	United Ulster Unionist Council
UVF	Ulster Volunteer Force
UWC	Ulster Workers Council
VPP	Volunteer Political Party
VUP	Vanguard Unionist Party
WCDC	Workers Committee for the Defence of the Constitution
WDA	Woodvale Defence Association
WRVS	Women's Royal Voluntary Service

Introduction

Who are the loyalists of Ulster? To many outsiders they are 'the voice of unreason, the voice of illogicality'.[1] They are loyal to Britain, yet ready to disobey her; they reject clerical tyranny, yet oppose secularism; they proclaim an ideology of freedom and equality, except for Catholics; they revere law and authority, then break the law. And they refuse to do the rational, obvious thing.

Thus Irish nationalists have asked: 'Why do they not accept their Irish identity?' Socialists have asked: 'Why do they not side with their natural allies, the Catholic working class?' Liberal democrats have sighed in frustration: 'Why are they so anachronistic—can they not forget the past and stop fighting about religion?'

This bewilderment, distaste or outrage seems to have discouraged outsiders from even trying to study and understand the loyalists of Ulster. Northern Irish Catholics have attracted far more attention from authors and scholars, and have also written more about themselves. Until the mid-1970s little research was done on the role of Protestant extremists in the latest Ulster conflict, despite their well-publicised involvement in the disturbances. As the weary inhabitants of Bogside or Ballymurphy were aware, everyone in the research and journalism business was 'doing the Catholics'.[2]

Thus a vicious circle was created. There was little material which gave the means of understanding how one group of people saw its own actions as rational, how it made sense of the political world and resolved the contradictions of its ideology. This itself perpetuated the irrational stereotype and kept alive mutual hostility between loyalists and the Press or 'intellectuals'.

This book is about Ulster Protestants, some of whom were actively involved in loyalist political, paramilitary or workplace groups while others lived in areas of strong loyalist tradition. In recent times, that tradition has been identified with a number of familiar political positions.

It has not described those who gave unequivocal loyalty to governments at Stormont and Westminster. Rather, it has been associated with Protestants who have opposed concessions to the Catholic minority, condemned links between Northern Ireland and the Irish Republic, and resisted Westminster's attempts to enforce political change.

Though they have disagreed about the limits of justified resistance, they have all seen loyalty to elected governments as conditional. In their view, Stormont and Westminster governments have been disloyal to the Protestant ideals they were founded to uphold, and must be re-called to the 'true' principles of their 'glorious past'.[3]

This book looks at political beliefs and expectations which people from a loyalist tradition derive from their upbringing in Ulster, which shaped their reaction to the civil rights movement and the civil disturbances in Northern Ireland from the late 1960s onwards. It examines the background and motivation of some people who joined action groups including political, paramilitary, workplace and community organisations. It also looks at how groups and individuals changed over time in response to new events and experiences. The book concentrates on three particular time-periods: the first widespread outbreak of urban violence in August 1969; the suspension of Stormont in March 1972, and its aftermath; and the consequences of the Ulster Workers' Council strike which brought down the power-sharing Executive in May 1974.

Much of the book is based on interview material, so it is heavily concerned with subjective reality—with the perceptions of those involved in the conflict. What value can this kind of study have? First, I would suggest that any general explanation of the Ulster conflict is inadequate if it does not take account of subjective reality.

There have been many attempts to provide general explanations of the divisions in Northern Ireland. These have been prescriptive as well as analytical—about solutions, as well as causes. For instance they have sprung from different Marxist analyses; from two-nations theory; from traditional Irish nationalist theory; from concepts of race and ethnicity; from social psychology theory etc.[4] But they have often failed to consider issues and problems raised by the participants' states of consciousness.

Frank Burton, for example, has shown how left-wing analyses have ignored the complexity of Northern Ireland in order to maintain the plausibility of their theoretical position. Failure to take account of subjective or mediated reality has produced glaring omissions and simplifications, and has led writers to press for unrealistic solutions which exaggerate the radicalisation of the Catholic working class. Burton concludes that any general explanation which analyses economy and social structures must be able to fit the subjective reality into its framework, just because social consciousness is the active process in the determination of political struggles.[5]

There is perhaps particular need for studies which look at this aspect of Ulster Protestantism, just because they have been so thin on the ground until now. The potential value of such studies has already been suggested by work like that of the anthropologist Rosemary Harris, whose study of a rural community in the 1950s gave many insights into poor Protestants' relationships with Catholics and with their own social superiors.[6]

Another reason to study the thinking of people from a loyalist tradition is that, since the late 1960s, they have faced an upheaval that has been more mental than physical. While Catholics bore the brunt of physical suffering, their beliefs about themselves, their sense of identity, and their conviction that their demands were justified, was more often strengthened than weakened by the events triggered by civil rights.

In contrast, many Protestants found their political world collapsing around them. Their beliefs, their very political and social system, were questioned on a world stage, while each political reform (culminating in the suspension of Stormont) seemed to remove another plank from the structure they were defending. How did people adjust mentally to this often fast-moving process? How did they make it tolerable or comprehensible, and how did it affect their political behaviour?

Lastly, there is more reason to study subjective reality than the hope of bridging gaps in general explanations or providing a new angle for the interest of research students. Conflicts and solutions are played out by real people; to examine their feelings and experience is to re-state the importance of people, not as pawns in a historical process but as actors who respond to and influence events. It gives some sense of what it is actually like to live through a time of violent conflict and change.

It must be stressed that this is not some definitive study of the loyalist mentality (even if such a straightforward thing existed!). First, the study was confined to the Belfast area. Despite its importance historically, politically and in terms of population (it has been called 'the cockpit of Ulster politics') one should be cautious about generalising from Belfast to other parts of Northern Ireland. The city has some distinctive historical characteristics, some of which are touched upon in this book.[7] In particular, class conflicts within the Protestant community have stronger roots than elsewhere in Ulster.

Secondly, this book is not a blow-by-blow account of events within loyalist groups up to the present time which can be used to predict either the next leadership battle in the Ulster Defence Association

(UDA) or the definitive way loyalist groups will jump politically in the future. The research on which it is based ended in the mid-1970s but I hope and believe that it can do more than simply contribute to a history of the civil disturbances. The feelings and experiences of people in conflict—as Frank Burton has shown us—are interesting and important; they are worth recording and deserve to be. If we judge them out of date we are also rejecting everything our historians and our novelists have given us.

Some of the findings suggested by the research clash with popular wisdoms about Ulster loyalism:

1. That it is equipped with a clear Ulster nationalist ideology, that its adherents take a purely cynical, self-interested view of the British connection, and that they are prepared to fight Britain and set up their own state if Westminster defies them.

Events after Stormont's suspension in 1972 showed that even those Protestants who came closest to this image (Vanguard's political wing) were unwilling or unable to back their threats with action, while other loyalists were openly unhappy with Vanguard's line. Again, loyalist groups accepted Westminster's rejection of the majority Convention report in 1976. So while Protestants might well turn to armed struggle if they were pushed towards a united Ireland, the great majority have accepted, however grudgingly, the loss of their parliament and subsequent direct rule.

The book further suggests that few Protestants have a clear and distinct sense of Ulster nationhood or can articulate just what an Ulster identity is. Most loyalists have complex and ambivalent feelings of identity, in different situations, a sense of 'Ulsterness', 'Britishness' or even 'Irishness' may dominate.

For most loyalists, expressions of feelings for Britain are not just cynical exercises. While some have gained a more realistic sense of modern British feelings towards them, others still believe Britons will one day recognise them as allies, and cling to a sentimental (some would say maudlin) attachment to Britain. Abandoning this belief often means losing a sense of self-worth which has been built on the idea that Ulster Protestants are vital to the mother country, her staunchest defenders through history. To consider that this may be untrue is to challenge the point of past sacrifices, to invite the disturbing question: 'Who am I then, and where do I belong?'

2. Another popular wisdom has it that loyalists possess a militantly racist and supremacist ideology about Catholics.

Only a minority, mainly middle class, are racist in the sense of seeing Catholics as inherently inferior. Of course folk beliefs about difference (and clues for identifying someone's religion) exist, but their importance as bars to friendship or co-operation can be exaggerated.[8] It was not because some SDLP politicians 'looked like Catholics' or had large families that some Protestants were ill disposed towards them. A conviction that Catholics have been made disloyal (by a scheming church or Irish Republican Army (IRA)), along with memories of physical hostilities are more divisive than beliefs about character differences. They also provide excuses for carrying out, or tolerating, discrimination.

Far from feeling superior, many Protestants feel inferior to Catholics in political and verbal skills. The very people who repeat clichés about Catholic reluctance to work or subservience to the Church will often envy what they see as Catholics' ability to 'get on', and their greater capacity for independent social and political action. Protestants lack confidence as a community: the phrases used about Irish unity suggest few can even picture a situation where they will not be annexed, repressed or submerged: 'Six into twenty-six won't go.'

Working-class Protestants also tend to see themselves as a disadvantaged community (in comparison with the British), whose loyalty has forced extra sacrifices on them and not rewarded them with extra benefits.

3. A third popular wisdom suggests that loyalist ideology readily justifies violence, and that loyalists glory in such violence.

Encouraged by the 'public band' tradition (and by historic tolerance in high places), some loyalists have felt totally justified in taking the law into their own hands. Yet there have been variations in, and limits to, the violence: between 1969 and 1975 there were no concerted, sustained killings of British forces, and only one period of widespread, random, anti-Catholic killings.

This is neither to diminish Protestant responsibility for violence, nor to dismiss the suffering and intimidation faced by many Catholic people. Rather, it is to suggest that Protestants, perhaps even more than Catholics, put constraints on their own gunmen's freedom; and that only fear of imminent moves towards Irish unity has made populations willing to tolerate widespread violence.

This theory may gain some support from the level of Protestant violence from 1975 until the present. Under the direct rule administration it has been lower than many observers of loyalist politics expected, given recurring high levels of republican armed action, occasional civilian atrocities and events like the IRA hunger strikes, which raised bitterness between the communities.

Nor has increasing poverty and unemployment among Protestants provoked the sectarian attacks which, some analysts of Northern Ireland have long told us, are inevitable during times of economic hardship.

The book suggests that most Protestants find extra-legal violence hard to rationalise. Belief in their respect for the law is a crucial means of distinguishing themselves, morally and politically, from republicans. Illegal violence has to be redefined as defensive action or the unfortunate result of provocation; otherwise responsibility is just denied as long as possible. Even loyalists do not on the whole glory in violence and the pre-emptive tradition—as some of their own songs would suggest— but are reluctant to confront the implications of what they do. In that sense, self-deception is more noticeable than gleeful pride in Protestant attitudes to violence.

Critics might suggest that many Protestants have overcome their qualms about acting beyond the law by condoning violence where it was committed in some type of official uniform. That would be fair comment on some of the people in this book, and was a source of anger among Protestant paramilitaries. They felt their 'respectable' loyalist critics were hypocritical in condemning them, while supporting a 'third force' under politicians' control.

4. According to a fourth folk wisdom, working-class Protestants are the most extreme members of their community.

Some research has already challenged the view that working-class Protestants vote for the most extreme election candidates.[9] The book shows that the most influential members of loyalist parties were middle class, and that they often had more extreme views on Catholics, on the Union or on economic matters than did members of the UVF and UDA.

What is clear is that people of different backgrounds have expressed their beliefs through different means. Political activists often wanted force used against those they saw as the enemy, but did not wish to take that action themselves. At times they rationalised or encouraged violence by others, as did wider populations, if only by looking the other way. Attitudes among politicians and the public were as symptomatic of real political conflict in Ulster as was the violence of the paramilitants: all reflected and perpetuated the conflict and each affected the others' freedom of action.

There are also various reasons, besides extremism, why people in areas where guerillas operate may sympathise with or fail to denounce them. They may support some of the militants' grievances because they have shared them (e.g. army searches, lack of proper judicial process). Conflicts of loyalty are much increased by personal knowledge of the militants. The man of whose actions they disapprove may be their son's best friend, or their neighbour. While outsiders judge violent people for what they do, insiders must also judge them for the kind of people they know them to be. The picture has been similar in Catholic areas, as Frank Burton sensitively shows. Mental conflicts mean popular support has fluctuated between the state and extra-legal groups, producing a complex relationship between population and guerillas.

5. It is said that only backwoodsmen, psychopaths or those with abnormal hostility to Catholics join loyalist groups.

Throughout the time-period studied, each loyalist group attracted different kinds of people. Some were stereotyped backwoodsmen content to devoutly follow a leader, others were ambitious, articulate people who were discontented with traditional parties or had class grievances against the 'fur coat brigade'. The nature of membership was also closely linked to the wider political situation. When most Protestants tolerated the regime, as in the late 1960s or later 1970s, loyalist groups (especially paramilitaries) drew in more deviant personalities. When large sections of the Protestant population were alienated and highly anxious about the future (as in 1972 and 1973), armed groups attracted many young men who were broadly representative of their class and age group.

6. Loyalism is said to be monolithic. On this view internal differences have been unimportant and politicians, workers and paramilitaries have formed a frightening united front, ready to crush Catholics and moderates if the opportunity arose.

Yet differences and disputes beset loyalist groups throughout, no more so than when there was supposed to be unity under the 'Vanguard umbrella'. Even the UWC stoppage was not really an example of active co-ordination among the different wings of loyalism. Rather, most loyalist politicians stood reluctantly aside, and temporarily allowed others to take over a leadership they quickly made every effort to reassert.

There were differences between groups: in particular between new and traditional ones. The conflict brought out class tensions which had always existed, but which had been suppressed. Mutual suspicion, even hatred, took up a great deal of people's time and energy.

There were also differences within groups. These could happen when one organisation represented different historical strands. For instance the Independent Unionist element in Paisleyism could clash with the messianic, fundamentalist one on social issues and internal democracy. Dissension could also occur when a group lacked tradition to guide policy. The rapid growth of the UDA and LAW quickly forced their leaders to ask what their long-term goals were to be. Where different people saw different possibilities, where one man was often unable to enforce his will, the groups tended to become multifunctional. Sometimes factions co-existed uneasily, sometimes open conflict erupted.

7. Many people have believed loyalist paramilitary groups would carry out a coup if they could, and were willing and able to take over the country.

On the contrary, most paramilitants distrusted the political world and lacked the self-confidence to take part in it. Even a UDA leader could believe, 'You couldn't have bricklayers running the country, or someone like me—could you?' Often they were not even sure what kind of country they were fighting and killing for.

8. It's often assumed that loyalists could move from planting a bomb one day to going on strike the next, to standing up in parliament the next.

Ireland is meant to have a tradition in which people move easily between soldiering and politics, between extra-legal and legal worlds. Certainly some people have managed to hold the proverbial gun in one hand and the Bible (or order paper) in the other. But most people in this book had unhappy experiences when they tried to move among political, military and community roles, and the Protestant population put strong constraints on such movement. The experience of the UVF in 1974 is perhaps the most striking in this respect, as Chapter 14 suggests.

9. Many people take for granted that traditional loyalist ideology is diametrically opposed to traditional nationalist and republican ideology.

Certainly there are important and well-publicised differences. But similarities that have strongly affected people's behaviour and political expectations have tended to be ignored. The view of politics as a zero sum game where compromise equalled weakness or betrayal was strengthened by experience of the Stormont regime. Alienation from what many Britons see as moderate, indeed natural, ideas about politics has not been confined to the most bigoted and prejudiced.

Secondly, sections of both religious communities have been influenced by conservative ideologies of the social order, which extol the virtues of imposed discipline and submission to the group and stress obedience to authority figures.

This has profoundly affected the way people think of themselves and their social superiors. Indeed the power structure of each community may influence the behaviour of its members as much as the conflict *between* communities may do.

Many people in this book were absorbed in the struggle either to reassert old Protestant hierarchies or to break through them. For instance, the accounts of community group activity reveal a series of tentative steps towards self-assertion. Others who broke through the brick wall of traditional attitudes and practices found they had walked into a fire.

The book also calls in question some Protestant myths about themselves, e.g. that they are free and equal and subservient to no-one, that they are proud individualists, or that they are much too moral and law abiding to commit the sort of brutalities done by certain republicans.

This book considers the concept of change, and how we may define it. Is wholesale change—like Shankill people embracing Irish nationalism—the only meaningful kind? Is voting behaviour the basic criterion, or does the fact that the UDA have sat down with the IRA at housing conferences, that Vanguard members have held talks with the Social, Democratic and Labour Party (SDLP), suggest some basic shift in their political views? Faced with questions like this, observers have often drawn the conclusions that tally most obligingly with their own analysis of the Ulster conflict. But this study tries to suggest there were many different levels of social and political change in groups and communities. It also suggests, that on an individual level, it was often former hardliners whose political views went through the most radical transformation as a result of their experiences.

Research methods

As this book draws on the approaches of political science, sociology and social anthropology, it may either be a masterpiece of fine interwoven strands or a hotch-potch of the misunderstood and the misapplied. This was the background to the research: after taking a social science degree I spent a year (1971–2) as an unqualified social worker in Belfast. I was assigned to the Shankill area when I became interested in Ulster loyalist politics.

The experience was a useful one for a research student, in several ways. It gave an outsider time to become aware of differences in political culture between Ulster and mainland Britain, and gave some background knowledge of Protestant communities and organised groups. It eased problems of acceptability in certain areas of Belfast and brought direct experience of a particularly violent period of the Troubles, with events like 'Bloody Sunday', the suspension of Stormont, the Vanguard rallies, the birth of the UDA, 'Bloody Friday'. Social work often involved direct contact with people who had suffered heavily from the effects of communal violence.

It also clarified my ideas about what kinds of research questions might be useful. For instance, the importance of conflicts within the Protestant community seemed clear for in 1972 class tensions were beginning to surface openly. The inadequacy of models that portrayed whole communities as sick or bigoted, or individual militants as psychopaths and fanatics, was also suggested by personal contact with local populations.

In general, while there was no shortage of theorising about Ulster loyalism, there was a lack of detailed information on either the feelings of loyalist communities about the Troubles, or about the organised loyalist groups that were springing up with a range of initials that could baffle many observers.

My main aim when I began the research in 1972 was to gather information about activists in political parties, paramilitary groups and workplace groups which described themselves as loyalist. For instance: What was their social and political background? Why did they join the group, and what was their role in it? What did they see as the main political issues, what did they think about these, and how did they perceive other parties to the conflict? How had their views and actions been affected by experience of the conflict?

I felt that the open-ended interview method would at least reduce the danger of imposing my own political and cultural assumptions on people and would also allow them to talk about ambivalent feelings instead of, say, having to tick boxes asserting that they either felt 'British' or 'not British'.

The interviews were carried out between January 1973 and June 1976, during a number of fieldwork visits to Belfast. The decision to include community groups was taken after I began the research. Though they did not fit neatly into the research framework, being avowedly non-sectarian rather than loyalist, I came to feel that no discussion of the experience of change would be adequate without including them, especially since a number of loyalist groups took up community action activity after 1972. Changes in political views and self-perceptions very often showed through at the community action level rather than the party political one. And the very existence of community groups suggested some Protestants saw another alternative to the gun or the ballot box and no longer saw the other organisations featured here as adequate to their needs.

I supplemented the interviews with research on written material produced by these groups, such as election literature or news-sheets, and with observation of political meetings, HQ activity, etc. As the research progressed I found there were a number of difficulties about treating these activists in isolation, without reference to views and assumptions held by much wider groups in the Protestant community. Detailed discussion of such views seemed important at certain points in the book—to give a sense of perspective, to explain the constraints populations sometimes put on their activists, and to emphasise points at which it seemed there were basic differences between the way outsiders and Ulster people thought about issues. The complexity of people's assumptions about discrimination was one example.

Research problems

Particular difficulties are mentioned at points in the book but I should make some brief points here:

1. I met few problems of personal acceptance, and most people were keen to talk about their views and experiences. Several things facilitiated this, including my sex and my Scottish origins; a widespread feeling that nobody was interested in the Protestant viewpoint, and a strong wish to explain it; the fact that I was not researching across the divide and perhaps giving information to enemies; relative lack of suspicion in Protestant areas about Government or army spies, etc.

Problems of access arose much more from the structures and security of particular groups. In some, it was hard or impossible to find that magic representative sample. Membership figures and other statistics might be unknown or unavailable. Nor was it possible to develop a single method of contact. Problems of security and trust in para-military groups, for instance, meant one had to rely on a personal passing-on system. Relations with such groups could be broken and have to be re-established; contacts could be and sometimes were deposed, imprisoned, or even assassinated.

I spent many years trying to find a telephone number for the Democratic Unionist Party and trying to get myself invited to party meetings. Officials of the Loyalist Association of Workers proved as elusive as their organisation. They always seemed to live in remote, unknown places, and attended meetings round the clock.

2. Since the research was done between 1973 and 1976 problems about recall and retrospective judgments happen when people talk about earlier times. These problems can be reduced, for instance by checking written material or by comparing the accounts of several people. But they cannot be eliminated altogether and observers can only make the best fallible judgments they can.

Inaccuracy is not always a negative thing, though. It can give valuable information, especially about the experience of personal change. When people redefine their past beliefs, why do they feel they ought to have believed a particular thing in 1966 or 1970? And why do many people assume interviewers want to hear them express particular sentiments? Confronting such questions may lead observers to a better understanding of the pressures and influences people in conflict have faced over time.

3. Social researchers who make contact with groups whose behaviour is criminal, socially deviant, or politically unacceptable to many people, have always faced accusations of partisanship. Students of the modern Ulster conflict have been no exception, so the issue must be confronted here.

I share neither the religious nor the political views of the people in this book. Nor would I wish my research to be used as moral justification for discriminatory or violent behaviour by people of a loyalist perspective. While the 'post-nationalist position' which has developed in recent years has provided some welcome re-assessment of entrenched wisdoms, uncritical acceptance of loyalist behaviour seems to have replaced past hostility among some theorists and writers.

I wrote the book in the belief that different groups in society should have an accurate picture of what others are actually like, and what they believe: especially in conditions of civil conflict, where segregation hinders understanding but does not prevent factions and governments adopting policies towards each other which have far-reaching human consequences. I also believe that if one wants to know what people are like and what they think, there is no substitute (not even the most elaborate theoretical framework) for meeting, observing and listening to them.

This view has not been shared by the counter-insurgency theorists who have greatly influenced official security policy in Catholic working-class areas, nor by certain republican socialists who have urged their followers to smash the loyalists: while political moderates who lament the power of myths and shibboleths often see no need to test their own by contact with the people they condemn.

While pontification from a distance has been acceptable to many shades of political opinion, conclusions formed through contact are bound to fail the validity test of one group or another. Social researchers must accept this, and often the criticisms will be more than valid. But those who believe that to associate with people is to agree with them, or that to explain is to sympathise, are surely bad sociologists and worse logicians. What they usually mean is that they do not like the people who are being explained, and they do not like the research findings, because they clash with their own opinions.

Social researchers are not, or should not be, in business to confirm the prejudices of governments or other parties to a conflict. Their purpose should not be to fudge social reality but to increase understanding of it. The aim of this book then, is to explain and inform, rather than to excuse or justify.

PART ONE

TO THE PRECIPICE

In August 1969 the storm-clouds that had been gathering over Northern Ireland finally broke, as serious communal violence erupted on the streets of Belfast and Derry. From now on, Protestant politics was to be a politics of division and strife. A community that had seemed united for so long argued fiercely about the very definition of what was happening: were they seeing a British sellout to the Republic, a take-over bid by the IRA or Church of Rome, or a painful modernisation, fought by bigots, that would drag Ulster into the twentieth century?

They disagreed about definitions of themselves: What did it mean to be British, Irish, Northern Irish or Protestant? They took different views of Catholic intentions, and of how far the minority could be trusted with political power. Class tensions and resentments within the Protestant community began to be openly expressed, and the civil rights slogan, '50 years of Unionist misrule', was increasingly heard from the lips of working class loyalists.

People also disagreed about what means should be used to pursue political beliefs. Some turned their backs on political parties and joined paramilitary groups, workplace organisations or community groups. Along with political parties, such groups also began attracting people who had never been involved in political activity before—whose social and political life had traditionally been controlled by certain elite groups in Ulster society.

People did not react to the Troubles in some sort of vacuum. Their responses were heavily influenced by the beliefs and assumptions with which they had grown up in Northern Ireland. Lack of socialisation into certain ideas could also affect their reactions. For instance, if Protestant workers showed confusion about class issues and class concepts it was not because they were somehow more stupid than workers in other countries, but because they had grown up under a social order which, by and large, discouraged people from thinking and talking about such notions, and denied them the everyday experience of exercising control over important areas of their lives.

If the roots of people's reactions can be found in beliefs expressed or encouraged by the Northern Ireland regime before 1969 so, we may speculate, can the roots of some divisions. A genuinely united community does not fragment into a dozen pieces under the impact of political crisis.

On the surface, Ulster Protestant politics was remarkably monolithic for most of the regime's history. Between 1920 and 1969 the Unionist Party never won fewer than 32 out of 52 Stormont seats. Its main rival among Protestants, the Northern Ireland Labour Party (NILP), gained its peak representation of 4 seats in 1958. Again, at the first Stormont election in 1921, the Unionists gained 66.9 per cent of the vote; in 1969 they won 67.4 per cent.[1]

But tensions lurked beneath the surface, especially on social and economic issues, as (for example) the Independent Unionist tradition suggests. Again, both the beliefs and methods of modern protest groups have links with the past. Ultraloyalist factions sprang up sporadically throughout the regime's history, especially in times of economic crisis. Communal street conflict and vigilantism, as writers like Andrew Boyd[2] have shown, have a long history in Belfast. Furthermore, modern protesters have often been consciously aware of past developments and have deliberately drawn parallels in the attempt to legitimise their actions.

1

Ulster Protestant Politics 1920-69: Constitutional and Religious Issues

Ulster and Britain

When the British army arrived on the streets of Belfast in August 1969, Protestant Ulster people had certain expectations about how the British administration would behave towards their province. These were rooted in their past understandings of what it meant to be British and loyal, and what were the proper relations between Stormont and Westminster. What had experience given them to believe?

Between 1920 and 1969, debate between Stormont and Westminster had centred more on financial issues than constitutional ones. The kinds of moral and political questions that confronted Protestants after 1969 seldom arose, or could be avoided. They did not have to choose between loyalty to something called Britain or something called Ulster because they were easily able to think of themselves as good Britons *and* good Ulstermen.

Conflicts about loyalty were avoided mainly because the British chose neither to alter Northern Ireland's constitutional position, nor to intervene in internal Stormont affairs, though clause 75 of the Government of Ireland Act* gave them authority to do so. The principle of non-intervention came to appear the natural order of things, and Protestants grew used to Stormont governments exercising full control over internal affairs—the things closest and most important to them. British non-intervention also encouraged them to assume Westminster accepted, even condoned, Unionist policy, and did not consider it un-British.

It is true that before 1920, Protestants had put different emphasis on

---

* Notwithstanding the establishment of the parliament of Northern Ireland or of anything contained in this Act, the supreme authority of the parliament of the United Kingdom shall remain unaffected and undiminished over all persons, matters and things in Northern Ireland and every part thereof.

the meaning and value of Union. Some of their internal conflicts about this after 1969 could be seen as having roots in much earlier struggles.[3] Lord Carson avoided emphasis on religion, preferring to stress the material benefits of Union. For him the fight for Ulster was a fight to retain the integrity of the British Empire. In this patriotism and love of Empire Protestantism, as the torchbearer of liberty, played an important role—but not as a repressive anti-Catholic force.

To others, religion was crucial: the Union was a bulwark against a rampant Catholicism which, being itself political, must be fought by politicised Protestantism. Their loyalty was to a country which took seriously the rejections of Catholic doctrine in its coronation oath.

But Unionist support for Carson's open defiance of Westminster did not prove that a coherent Ulster nationalism existed, nor that Unionists were admitting disloyalty. The six county settlement was not won after a campaign for a Northern Ireland government, but accepted as a second best solution. In 1912 Protestants believed that Westminster was abandoning Ulster to the nationalists, that Westminster was being disloyal both to the Empire and the Protestant faith. So the formation of a Provisional Government seemed the only alternative to losing both the Union and everything else Protestants thought Home Rule would destroy (religious freedom, physical and economic security).

Another reason why Unionists were able to side-step accusations of disloyalty was that those whom Carson called 'the best in England' supported their stand: many wealthy and powerful English people sanctioned the Unionist rebels. These were people whom many beyond their own caste regarded as principled and patriotic, and as good judges of moral questions. They lent moral authority to the Unionist stand. Modern Protestant rebels have, of course, lacked this support and source of supposed legitimacy.

So this earlier conflict between Ulstermen and Britons did not produce some coherent Ulster Sinn Féin ideology that equipped the next generation. Rather, it produced a lingering distrust and suspicion of British administrations, which was likely to intensify in any future conflict between Westminster and Stormont about the way Protestants ran their regime. Sir James Craig (later Lord Craigavon) acted on this mistrust in seeking maximum control over policies most vital to Protestants, such as security and the franchise. He and his successors found that the British did not press their own stipulations when these were ignored or overturned: for instance, when Craig abolished proportional representation in local and Stormont elections. When various groups protested to the British about anti-Catholic discrimination or repressive security laws, they were told these matters were the concern of the Northern Ireland parliament.

Thus neither Westminster nor Stormont seemed to feel that the Union involved identical policies and regulations by the two parliaments. By implication, there was nothing un-British about a regime that carried through the draconian Special Powers Act.

The only exception to the policy rule was the social services, as Unionist Minister Edmund Warnock stated in 1945: 'I am not aware of any undertaking... that our legislation should proceed step by step on matters other than those connected with the social services'.[4]

Ulster faced some of the most severe social and economic problems in western Europe, yet the regime had minimal powers of taxation. Several times Craig's government found itself verging on bankruptcy, which threatened the regime more effectively than the IRA, and undermined propaganda claims about the economic benefits of Union. Thus Unionist governments spent much of their time trying to make Westminster fulfil as many fiscal duties as possible. After a long struggle, the principle of parity got *de facto* recognition during Andrews' wartime administration. Westminster acknowledged, 'the Imperial authorities will give sympathetic consideration to the case for special measures regarding any service in which Northern Ireland has leeway to make up in order to attain equality of standard with the United Kingdom'.[5]

This new commitment could be put at risk if Stormont diverged too much from British social and economic legislation. Thus most of the new welfare state policies were grudgingly passed by the conservative-minded Unionists at Stormont, while the same party at Westminster often opposed them. This only emphasised the distance between the two groups: for most Ulster Protestants, their Westminster group was neither familiar nor relevant. It was one step removed from their political world.

The significance of the subtle change in the idea of Union, which step by step had brought about, was that it opened the way for some basic rethinking of the Ulster–Britain relationship. The parity debate made popular the notion of equality of standards. Accepting step by step also meant accepting mutual obligations: Unionists were tacitly admitting that British responsibility for Ulster's economic health called for a response that went beyond support in the event of war, or such traditional loyalist 'proofs' of their allegiance to things British.

Soon reforming Catholics and Protestants were to demand that principles of equality in one policy area (the social services) should apply throughout the political system: they called for 'full British rights, full British standards'. O'Neill's supporters also held that being British meant behaving like modern British people.

For most Protestants, these were unfamiliar if not revolutionary notions, which neither Stormont nor Westminster governments had previously upheld. At the same time, Unionist MPs were unprepared for arguments about constitutional questions, and unused to justifying the Protestant political position. They knew how to argue about money, and they knew how to say 'this issue is an internal matter': in any war of words on a bigger stage, they were doubtfully equipped for the Protestant front line.

Ulster and the Irish Free State/Irish Republic

For most of the time between 1920 and 1969, relations between Northern Ireland and the 26 county state were such as to encourage several Protestant perceptions of Southern intentions. Broadly speaking, these were of: *physical hostility* to Protestants and a wish to remove them by force or by the marriage laws; *cultural separateness* from Protestants (Gaelic, Catholic, anti-British); *political designs* on Northern Protestants ('the takeover'); *economic* impoverishment; *religious dominance* over political life ('Home rule is Rome rule'). Apparent changes were examined from the basis of these beliefs: it was not just 'have they changed', but 'can we believe them when they say they have changed?'

When all Ireland lay under British rule, Unionists could feel both Irish and British. But the 1916 rising seemed to them a shameful act of treason against a country in the throes of devastating war, indicating what kind of people the rebels must be. With the great Sinn Féin successes of the 1918 election a new kind of Irishness was proclaimed that could never find accommodation with the Irishness of someone like Carson. It drew its self respect from independence from Britain and elevated a culture that was Gaelic and Catholic. Left wing elements of the movement merely fuelled Unionist fears of Bolshevism, rather than hopes of non-sectarian political policies. The reprisals and counter-reprisals in the countryside provided yet more atrocity stories and strengthened Protestant beliefs that the nationalist movement threatened both their lives and their property. Many years later, Ulster Protestants could ask this author: 'Will you Scots take us in when they drive us out?' They had a certainty about their fate that did not brook talk of 'if' or 'perhaps'.

The strained relations of the 1920s were much exacerbated after Eamon de Valera's Fianna Fáil party won power in 1932. Fianna Fáil's first preoccupation was Britain rather than the North: repudiation of the 1921 treaty, and the symbols of subjection that went with it.

But the process could not leave the North unaffected. The tariff war of the 1930s hit hard at a time of severe economic difficulty while the anti-British climate of the time gave growing offence to northern loyalists. This reached its peak with Ireland's declaration of neutrality at the outbreak of war in 1939. Meanwhile, Protestants found substance for their claim that home rule was Rome rule. Enforcement of the *Ne Temere* decree (which stated that children of a marriage between a Catholic and a Protestant were to be brought up as Catholics) was one undoubted factor in the decline of the Southern Protestant population from about 220,000 in 1920 to 208,000 in 1926 (to 120,000 in 1961). Divorce was banned in the Free State in 1925 and literary censorship introduced in 1929.

The 1937 Constitution was drafted in consultation with Catholic church leaders, embodied Catholic views on church–state relations, marriage and the family, and recognised 'the special position of the Holy Catholic Apostolic and Roman church'.[6] The Constitution also claimed jurisdiction over the whole of Ireland, and coincided with an intensified antipartitionist campaign by Southern politicians. Speaking in England in 1938, de Valera offered the Unionists a federal arrangement, to which Craigavon replied 'I can only reiterate the old battle cry of Northern Ireland—no surrender!'

The entrenched mutual perceptions were not necessarily devoid of respect. The leaders in each regime understood each other well in one sense, because they each held principles on which they could not budge. Each expected the other to go on behaving in the same way, and so did their supporting populations. Each intractable assertion of principle produced its mirror image: so Craig's famous boast that 'we are a Protestant parliament and this is a Protestant state' was answered a year later by de Valera's 'since the coming of St Patrick ... Ireland has been a Christian and a Catholic nation ... she remains a Catholic nation'.[7]

Between 1948 and 1951, during which time the 26 counties declared itself an independent republic, de Valera brought the antipartitionist campaign to many foreign countries. Brookeborough responded by undertaking an international speaking tour in defence of Ulster's position.

Changed economic circumstances provided the basis for movement from these deeply entrenched positions. Southern protectionism had failed to prevent large scale unemployment and emigration, which reached a new peak in the 1950s. In trying to escape from stagnation by moving towards free enterprise planning programmes, Fianna Fáil also cautiously began moving away from ideological traditionalism about the North. In 1963 the Taoiseach (Prime Minister), Seán Lemass, stated that the Northern Ireland regime existed with the support of a majority in that area. He represented a new generation of Southern politician who saw two advantages in the 'kid glove' approach to Irish unity. First, that improved relations might bring great economic benefits to both parts of Ireland; secondly, that unity was more likely to come after a period of mutual trust and co-operation that was based on recognition of existing constitutional realities.

Here he was saying something novel: that material things mattered more than the immediate ending of partition, and that some matters were amenable to compromise and negotiation. The 'good' Irishmen and women could work with people who opposed their political aspirations, without betraying those very ideals which made them Irish: they could also be both Irish and European.

A Northern generation was emerging which shared Southern politicians' views on materialism and cosmopolitanism. For Terence O'Neill's supporters, basic reappraisals of traditional views on the South were essential: not just because of the material benefits that could result, and the inroads being made by the ecumenical movement, but also because old enmities contradicted the moral ideals of political modernism. Traditionalism spoke for people who remembered every quarrel; who feared and opposed political change, whose political world stopped at their own shores. There was no room in this for the cosmopolitan whose interest was not in the past, but the future.

The Catholic minority

F. S. L. Lyons writes of the 1920s: 'In this generation there could be no real work of conciliation—all attitudes had to be related to whether or not the state was to continue in being'.[8] Unionist attitudes towards Catholics remained consistently hardline till the mid-1960s, in the sense that no substantial group advocated, or considered possible, measures that would integrate the minority as fully allegiant citizens. Thus there were no fierce divisions of the kind that rent Protestants after O'Neill came to power. If Protestants differed, they did so over the degree of threat Catholics posed, the kinds of measures that should be taken to counter that threat and the extent to which Protestants had a right to preferential treatment by the regime.

The fierce strife in the North that preceded the founding of Stormont (232 people died in 1922 alone) left a legacy of bitterness and mistrust on both sides. Protestant fears about their physical fate under Catholic rule were reinforced by historic beliefs about the lawlessness and ferocity of the native Irish.[9] The 1920s troubles ensured that future generations of Protestants would have a store of folk memories about the physical hostility of Catholics, which any new crisis was likely to re-awaken.

Given the political climate, Unionists and Nationalists were likely to become disillusioned quickly if any efforts at conciliation seemed to fail. A vicious circle emerged, where Catholic politicians, who alternately entered and withdrew from Stormont, were encouraged by despair to embrace the very attitudes of which Unionists accused them: determined antipartitionism and hostility to virtually every measure proposed at Stormont.[10] This gave Unionists a justification for continuing inflexible attitudes. Sporadic IRA campaigns had the same effect, and kept reminding Protestants that some Catholics would resort to arms to overthrow the regime.

Hardline policies also benefited the Unionist Party by drawing the religious battle lines as sharply as possible and reducing any socialist threat. The abolition of PR hit Labour and Independents much harder than the Nationalists. During the 1930s, of course, Unionist politicians were repeatedly accused of formenting sectarian strife to break up Protestant–Catholic alliances on social issues, especially after the Belfast sectarian riots of 1935.

The other advantage to Unionists in taking hardline positions was that it kept them in favour with influential Protestant groups. Some of these groups shared characteristics with loyalist groupings that emerged in the 1960s.

One of the most powerful and influential pressure groups was the Orange Order. Its influence has caused prolonged debate in academic and political circles. What is important here is the general direction of its influence in Ulster: towards an active, assertive and politicised Protestantism.[11] For the Order, Protestantism was the most important thing the regime was defending, so it stood against both secularisation and non-sectarianisation of that regime.

The Unionist Party largely conformed to the Order's views. It bowed to their protests over the Lynn Committee's education plans in 1924 and upheld Christian precepts in social life (even children's swings in Catholic areas were dutifully locked on Sundays). The party supported the Order's opposition to admitting Catholics into Unionist membership. Several times it also lifted bans on Orange processions in Nationalist districts.[12] This meant supporting a certain interpretation of democracy which some loyalist groups were to proclaim in modern times: that a minority should respect the symbols of a majority regime which had a right to parade them where it wished. In contrast, flaunting of minority symbols was provocative and undemocratic.

Other groups, too, considered that Protestants had a right to preferential treatment. Many of Ian Paisley's modern supporters have come from a tradition which believes liberality to Catholics increases the power of a monolithic and aggrandising Church that enslaves the body and soul of human beings.[13] For such people, maintenance of Protestant truth depends on its constant reassertion (e.g. through street preaching) and on suppression of Catholic doctrines. These believers were an important element in groups like the Ulster Protestant League (UPL, founded 1933) and Ulster Protestant Action (founded 1959). But these did not confine themselves to religious issues. Arising during economic recession, they also demanded job reservation for Protestants and drew much support from shipyard men, unemployed and marginal workers.

The third issue that concerned ultraloyalists was law and order. The notion of the 'public band',[14] where Protestant citizens grouped together to defend themselves against the native Irish, had left an impact on sections of Protestant opinion. The shipyard workers who expelled Catholics from the yards in 1920 were declaring that unofficial groups had a right to take armed action against the 'rebels', and should not be punished by a Protestant government. Many modern loyalist paramilitaries have believed likewise.

Unionist governments often supported, by word or deed, demands for preferential treatment or discrimination. After the UPL called for job reservation Brookeborough made his famous speeches advocating giving jobs to 'good Protestant lads and lassies' over the heads of Catholics, '99 per cent of whom are disloyal'.[15] At other times politicians called for the liquidation of local Catholic electoral majorities, funds to prevent Catholics buying Protestant property, and the 'fixing' of election boundaries. In other words they reaffirmed that the regime existed to serve a sectional interest. Unionist leaders also seemed to condone the actions of Protestant rioters, legitimising the idea of the 'public band'. For instance Sir James Craig told loyalist shipyardmen who had expelled Catholics in 1920: 'Do I approve of the action you boys have taken in the past? I say yes'.[16] The point about statements like this is that they created expectations in certain Protestants, which persisted into modern times, about what was tolerable behaviour and what response their Government would make to loyalist initiatives.

Some Protestants openly protested at offensive utterances by politicians. This does not mean they agreed with future O'Neillite Unionists that Catholics could be won over to the regime. Rather they saw no need for Unionism to be openly sectarian and inflammatory. They felt the law would be brought into disrepute if extra-legal excesses went unpunished, and hoped that bigotry could be eradicated by more education. The Progressive Unionists,[17] a few business and professional men who challenged Craig at the 1938 election, wanted reform in agriculture, housing and employment. They also obliquely attacked Government policy towards Catholics, calling for 'a fair chance for the citizens of Northern Ireland to share in its government'. The group, who were decimated in the emotional election after the new Free State constitution was passed, also represented people who disliked a definition of 'democracy' that involved flouting the sensitivities of political opponents. As one former Unionist candidate put it: 'I didn't canvass in RC areas, what would have been the point? It would only have been provocative and hostile. They had their views and I had mine—no hard feelings'.

The extreme end of positive views towards Catholics lay in the socialist tradition. In a sense socialists were beyond the bounds of conventional Ulster politics since they were not merely advocating more liberal outlooks in the context of existing divisions. They were actually telling people that the real divide was not between religions but between 'the poor who have no bread and the rich who have a surplus'.[18] On the whole, the Unionist Party tried to claim that such people were simply pursuing traditional republican goals by devious, deceptive means (as in the slogan 'If you want a Catholic for a neighbour, vote Labour'.)

A signal for the kind of divisions that rent Unionists after O'Neill's accession was the clash between Lord Brookeborough and the attorney general, Brian Maginess, in 1959. The issue was admission of Catholics to the Unionist Party. Proposing admission, Maginess said: 'To shed our parochialism is not to deny our inheritance. Toleration is not a sign of weakness, but proof of strength. To broaden our outlook means no weakening of our faith.' Brookeborough replied: 'There is no use blinking the fact that political differences in Northern Ireland closely follow religious differences... the Unionist Party is dedicated to the resistance of these aims' [an all-Ireland republic]... there is no change in the fundamental character of the Unionist party or in the loyalties it observes and preserves... if that is called inflexible then it shows our principles are not elastic'.

In his positive view of compromise and his implicit hint that Catholics could actually be won over to working for their old enemies' party, Maginess foreshadowed the O'Neillites, just as Brookeborough provided the phrases for their future loyalist opponents. The stage was set for a battle in which words would play as vital a role as other kinds of weapon.

Consequences for the political culture of Northern Ireland

Protestant politics and ideology have been discussed as if they were quite distinctive from Catholic politics and ideology. But we cannot understand the traditional political world of Protestants properly without considering some values and expectations held by both religious groups. These tended to be mutually reinforcing and thus especially tenacious. They made the ideas of O'Neill and the civil rights movement seem, not eminently moderate, but almost revolutionary: an alien input into an historic, reassuring set of beliefs about what politics itself meant.

Insofar as Unionists and Nationalists had similar ideas, this was partly because they really were alike in some respects (e.g. in their social conservatism). Another reason was that when Nationalists might have chosen to behave differently, they were either forced into playing the game[19] or resigned themselves in despair to it. The Unionists were the winners in 1920, they made the rules after that, and did their best to enforce them. By seeking constantly to portray politics as a zero sum game, a battle between only two irreconcilable groups, they often forced Nationalists to conform to their intransigent stereotypes and become a mirror image of their opponents.

These actual or enforced similarities strengthened certain assumptions about politics among the population, which we can summarise and illustrate with people's own recollections.

(1) Democracy as majority rule: Democracy is not about the rights of minorities. The legitimacy of Northern Ireland rested on Protestant

claims about the democratically expressed wishes of the bulk of its citizens. Central to the Nationalist case for Irish unity was the argument that a minority in the North was blocking the democratic wish of most Irish citizens for unification.

(2) The supremacy of absolute, non-material values: The constitution is the key issue; other things (like economics) are of secondary importance. So an old Sandy Row shipyard worker recalled: 'What did politics mean? Flags, parades, the red, white and blue: that's what you remember.' Politics is a battle over things which cannot be divided, but only won or lost.

(3) Hence politics is a zero sum game: What Catholics gain Protestants must lose, and vice versa. Each side is thus expected to work for its own: this may be regrettable but it is the way things happen. Nor does one expect politicians of the other side to work in one's interest. So immediately a huge range of issues becomes 'political', from allocation of houses down to the appointment of a council gardener. Protestants as well as Catholics complain loudly of discrimination, but each side expects it to happen. Indeed, they find it hard to imagine a world without it.

(4) Politics is a predictable world: This reassuring predictability counteracts the tension and insecurity of Ulster, with its suppressed frustrations and hostility. Politics is predictable because issues are simple and straightforward, and each religious group behaves as one expects it to do. One can usually work out by a head-count who will win in a certain area, and whether or not it is even worth fighting the seat. Stormont politics is gladiatorial, and unreal in the sense that outcomes are already settled. It is an arena for the ritual restatement of ideals, where politicians reassure the public that nothing has changed nor lost its clarity.

(5) Refusal to compromise is a sign of honesty and integrity: Thus in all my discussions with former Stormont Unionists I never heard hostility expressed towards Nationalist members, but only compliments. They were 'straight, principled and honest', and you knew where you stood with them—in fact, they thought very much like those who were paying the compliments. In contrast people who sought compromise were quickly regarded as turncoats, weaklings or dangerous characters fired by personal ambition. People who did not fit in (like Socialists and Independents) were suspected of pursuing the old political goals by devious means.

(6) But greater honesties create lesser dishonesties. Over the major

issue there can be no foul play or compromises, but because the struggle is so vital the end justifies the means outside the letter of the law. These in turn tend to become habits. Gerrymander, personation and the 'dead vote', described coyly as 'a disgrace' by many people, are still the stuff of electoral politics. Skilful use of these is a source of pride to constituency activists. Minds are concentrated on the minutiae of political life in a world where grand political outcomes are tediously predictable. Some people find it hard to believe that other countries do not behave in exactly the same way. In contrast, British political life is characterised by relative honesty in election procedures, and flexibility on major political issues. Indeed most Governments since the Second World War (with the notable and interesting exception of Mrs Thatcher's Conservative administration) have made a positive virtue of their desire to compromise and seek the middle ground.

(7) For those who do not want to play the sectarian game or who seek basic changes in Ulster politics, a political career is unattractive and prospects for achievement are poor. Stormont gives little challenge to intellectual or political skills: it has even accommodated people who found it difficult to understand the basic procedures of the House. Members sit for many years, politics has a stagnant quality and most members do not need to be responsive to their constituents' needs in order to be re-elected.

A long-serving Unionist senator and a former Liberal MP illustrate some of the assumptions above but take very different views of those assumptions.

(a) 'The old time politicians were like gladiators—like Horatius on the bridge. The Nationalists had some fine debaters, they fought their corner and we fought ours and everyone knew where they stood. Old X now, straight as a gun-barrel. But I don't understand all this talk now about horse shoe assemblies ... how would you know which side people were on?

'Things aren't the same now—so much bitterness. In the old days, it was a bit of a game. We had some really fierce debates, but still talked to each other afterwards. I think people went into it from a sense of duty, not like now, all this professionalism and playing to the gallery.'

(b) 'Neither side liked me being there (at Stormont). One told me he didn't mind a decent Nationalist, but someone who was masquerading under false colours ... The standard of debates was pretty appalling ... it was also very much a part-time place, and so predictable ... the

Nationalists would go on again about the B Specials and old Y would pop up regular as a cuckoo clock saying they were the finest force in the world. The Labour MPs worked very hard indeed. They wanted to be the official Opposition, but the Unionists refused to recognise them. The 'real' opposition, as they saw it, was on the Border—everything else was a nuisance, an irrelevancy.'

What happened after O'Neill came to power was that some Protestants and Catholics began saying new things about the very basics of politics, not just to each other but to their own communities. They challenged every one of the assumptions described here, as well as specific aspects of Protestant and Catholic ideology. This was liable to bewilder a wide range of people with varying views of the 'other side'— people who were still locked inside tenacious beliefs from which it was difficult to break.

In our analysis of Protestant ideology, we may find reasons why some Protestants thought discrimination justified, or why they attacked civil rights marches. In looking at the assumptions above, we may find reasons why more Protestants thought of discrimination as inevitable, surely a part of any political system; or why they could only interpret civil rights marches through Protestant territory as deliberately aggressive acts, aimed at stirring up sectarian conflict and flouting unspoken rules of respect for difference.

2

Ulster Protestant Politics 1920-69: Social and Economic Issues

Under the Stormont regime, control of political, social and economic life was largely in the hands of certain upper and middle class Protestant groups. They strongly influenced social policy and sought to set the limits of social debate. Under this system, most working class people had little experience of independent action or leadership in political or social life, nor were they encouraged to gain it. This experience shaped their expectations both of their traditional leaders and themselves at times of political crisis. By 1972 it had become a cliché in Protestant working class areas of Belfast that 'you could have wrapped a donkey (or a pig, or a monkey) in a Union Jack in the old days, and people would have voted for it'. In fact, Unionist politicians tended to be drawn from narrow social groups: other humans, as well as animals, found it hard to break the pattern.

In his research Harbinson found that typical members of the Stormont House of Commons and Senate were male, middle aged, middle class, and almost invariably members of the Orange Order. Between 1921 and 1969 only 3.8 per cent of Stormont Unionist MPs were drawn from manual occupations, while thirty of them had sat for 15 years or more in the House.[20] His study of local Unionist associations showed that middle class people filled officer roles. This commonly happens in British parties too: but it does emphasise that despite the very large dues-paying membership (which he reckoned at 50,000) and the support for Unionism by all classes of Protestants, experience of political decision-making was still confined to middle class groups.

There is little research on local councils, but in a 1966 study Budge and O'Leary found only 7 per cent of serving Unionist councillors came from manual jobs, while 69 per cent were drawn from what the authors call 'semi professional' categories, including estate agents and small businessmen.[21] By and large, the policies of the Unionist Party reflected its class base. For example, the history of urban housing policy in Northern Ireland demonstrates the strong influence on private landlords.[22] Traditionally, too, the Unionist Party at Westminster accepted the Conservative whip. Harbinson concludes that anti-socialism was a major element in Unionist Party philosophy. For instance it was vital for the Unionist Labour Association (ULA), set up by party leaders in 1918 to woo Protestant workers from 'socialist and extreme organisations . . . where they are educated in views very different from those held by our body'. The ULA considered 'it is part of [our] duty... to expose the real aims of socialism and other anti-British movements'.[23]

The party's implementation of 'step by step' welfare legislation after 1945, which provoked some right-wing protest within Stormont, might seem to contradict its image. Though the new laws brought real economic benefits to poorer Protestants (and to Catholics) they did not really represent a change of heart, because the government had little option but to pass them. Also, they helped defuse social tensions in Protestant workers who might otherwise have turned to socialism. 'Step by step' may actually have obscured for workers the degree to which Unionism still represented, in social and economic terms, the interests of wealthier people.

What about relations between politicians and voters? Traditionally, a paternalistic relationship existed in some areas. For instance one landowner, a former MP from a country district, said he always encouraged local people to call round at his house if they had any problems. On the other hand he did not see why they would want an election (he had occupied an uncontested seat for decades) since they 'knew our family, trusted us to get on with the job and were satisfied with what we did for them'.

But in Belfast, with its more complex social structure, people rarely recalled such relationships. Rather they remembered (usually by name) a minority of MPs and councillors who were of the people and who worked tirelessly for everyone; and a majority who rarely appeared except at elections and paid little attention to constituents' needs. As these older Belfast people recalled:

'At local Unionist meetings you rarely got any of the old MPs to come and speak—it was always their agents.'

'Once something went wrong with the water supply and the councillor just told us we'd have to go without baths for a while.'

'About 10 years ago I went to a public meeting in Sandy Row addressed by the Lord Mayor. He said "in 10 years' time you can tell your children where Sandy Row was". We hadn't even been told it was going to be demolished. After a few minutes he looks at his watch and says "Excuse me, I've an important meeting to go to." That was how they treated us...'

It was the Northern Ireland Labour Party, rather than the Unionists, who set up advice centres for constituents, after they won four seats at the 1958 Stormont election.

One reason why people put up with cavalier treatment was that they would grudgingly support an unsatisfactory constituency man before they would split the vote on the overriding constitutional issue. Another reason was the attitude many of these public representatives had to working class voters, an attitude met by what is usually called deference. So the constituents who were told not to take baths 'just accepted what he said like lambs; we'd never have thought of asking, "why don't you do this or that".' The people at the Mayor's meeting 'never thought of questioning what he said' or standing up to ask 'what the hell do you mean?' Shankill people, explained one shop-keeper, 'used to call politicians and councillors "sir", and when the minister came into our primary school, we shot up and chorused "good morning, sir".'

To explain things by talking of deference merely begs the question: why were people deferential? One possibility is that they had been reared on an ideology that extolled traditional leaders. In his analysis of Orange ideology David Roberts[24] shows how since King William's victory at the Boyne, tyranny (which Protestants should resist) was associated with Catholicism, civil and religious liberty with a Protestant ascendancy that safeguarded 'the life and witness of the Protestant religion'. So Protestants were asked to support not just the Union, but the local political order that safeguarded it. Orange values also emphasised the solidarity of Protestant society, where the common bond of religion outweighed class differences. The Orange ethic proclaimed both the irrelevance and the danger of class conflict, for it undermined the common front against the enemy. Orangeism also provided a forum for defusing class tensions.

Rosemary Harris shows how some rural lodge meetings provided the only setting where, in a situation of temporary equality, poor Protestants felt able to criticise people like landowners. But in Belfast, Orangemen usually met members of their own class at Lodge meetings, which were generally occupation or area-based. They might have become foci for class discontent but rarely performed this role, which would have gone against the basic ethics and ideals accepted by working men in joining the Order. The lodges also provided a source of prestige to people of low status, for any dutiful member had a chance of becoming Master.

The Order also encouraged 'devotion to piety, concord and unity, and obedience to the laws'. Along with the churches it played a major part in organising social life, so that the activities of groups in which many people spent leisure time (like church social clubs or youth groups) were circumscribed by the values of the institutions which controlled them. This encouraged conformity to rigid puritannical values and limited innovation by communities themselves.

The importance placed on obedience to superiors (from husbands to political leaders) and on the virtue of imposed discipline; other militaristic values, including cultivation of group rather than individual identity; all were combined in activities in which many Protestants were reared, from Boys' Brigade events to Orange marches.

Several authors have commented on the traditional absence of a distinctive youth culture in Northern Ireland, and the involvement of young people in adult-dominated institutions controlled by religious or quasi-religious bodies. Sectarian views condoned by a whole culture and tradition were ritualised through adult-organised parades and festivities.[25]

On this perspective, modern paramilitary groups can be seen as products of traditional Northern Ireland society: not subverters of the old order, but extreme versions of it. Those who formed and joined them were used to uniforms, punitive discipline, parades, and a system where one gave or received orders. But they were unfamiliar with democratic organisations, and unused to taking their own decisions.

In any case, most leisure and welfare facilities were provided for people, either by religious/quasi-religious groups, or by central or local government. Housing groups were hardly established when O'Neill came to power, though a few tenants' organisations and groups concerned with rates or housing repairs existed in more prosperous city areas (like Finaghy).

Credit unions and co-operatives were confined to Catholic areas, where they found fertile soil in communities that had traditionally borne the brunt of unemployment, and which had a tradition of seeking alternatives to established institutions.

A further inducement to accepting control by others was the folk wisdom proclaimed by Unionist spokesmen, that the Unionist Party looked after Protestants, and took care of their interests. Misgivings about this were likely to be tempered by fatalism. In most people's lives, and the lives of their parents, Northern Ireland had always known great poverty and unemployment, and no government had been able to solve it. This was the way things had always been. The Unionists had excuses for their failures: were they not fighting for Ulster's very existence against enemies who sapped their resources? But none of this means that Protestant workers were widely contented with their lot. Sticks, as well as carrots, were used to keep resentments suppressed and maintain the status quo. There was usually a heavy price to be paid for criticising the established order, which Catholics did not have to face in the same way. Their community leaders in the RC church and the Nationalist party were hardly less conservative than the Unionists: but because they opposed the regime they were more tolerant of innovation that challenged the status quo.

In contrast the weight of established authority usually descended on Protestants who tried the same. Setting up alternatives, even a co-operative or housing campaign, was a radical step, a hint of rejection as well as discontent. It took courage and conviction, especially when Protestant independents actually challenged Unionists at elections and were branded as communists, vote-splitters or republican sympathisers. Local people were easily scared off giving support. So one disillusioned trade unionist on the Shankill summed up his experience: 'In 40 years here I've kept at it, going on about the conditions and leading strikes and the rest, and everyone agrees with me in private. They're unhappy and they know how things really are. But when you stand up you're alone, they're too frightened to follow you.'

This situation made it more likely that the only circumstances in which many Protestants would feel able to express real social griev-ances would be those where traditional leaders seemed to abandon their loyalist political principles. Opposition could not then be branded as un-Protestant or pro-republican. When leaders failed to fulfil their primary duty (protecting the traditional constitution) there would be safe grounds for protest, during which other (social) resent-ments could be brought into the open.

But even then it was likely that working class Protestants would suffer from a lack of confidence in their political effectiveness, and in their ability for independent action. Initially at least they would tend to search for an articulate and powerful leader figure to spearhead their protest, and speak for feelings they were unused to putting into words. They would search for someone to do things for them and put things right on their behalf, in a time of political crisis. Such expectations need to be borne in mind when we come to consider the appeal of men like Ian Paisley, not just to a small group of hardliners, but to substantial sections of the Protestant population.

The organisation of social protest

How were internal Protestant divisions, and undercurrents of resentment on social and economic issues, expressed through the ballot box or through other forms of organised action? The Unionist Party was more threatened by socialist movements and splinter groups than by dissidents within its own ranks. Small groups of Unionists did criticise Government achievements on socio-economic matters and called for greater welfare provision during the Depression and Second World War. But their protests were sporadic and they never became a coherent pressure group. Though three Unionist Labour Association candidates were returned in 1918 only Billy Grant was a vocal critic of Government, sometimes voting with Labour members. The ULA attracted few trade union activists and after its candidates were defeated by official Labour candidates in 1925, its influence and activity rapidly declined. The Progressive Unionists (q.v.) wanted the party to take more active steps to improve economic efficiency and tackle social problems. Mainly liberal-minded business people and professionals, their attitudes were untypical in a province of small businessmen and farmers.

At Stormont the most persistent lobby was populist. The difficulty in categorising them on a straight left–right dimension is shown by the position of Unionists like Major McCormick, who combined right wing suspicion of government extravagance with left wing demands for greater social welfare.[26]

The Independent Unionist tradition is more significant than internal party divisions. Under the Stormont regime, small groups of Independent Unionists were regularly returned to Stormont. Some, like Robert Nixon and Norman Porter, were basically ultraloyalist critics of government. But others, like Shankill MP Tommy Henderson, represented a more complex tradition in Protestant politics, which Ian Paisley's movements to some extent inherited.[27] They thought themselves loyal Protestants and tended towards puritanism on issues like Sabbath observance or temperance. But their concern about working class Protestants' living conditions sometimes led them into voting alliances with Nationalists and socialists.

Another important element was their opposition to the clique structure of local Unionist associations whom they accused of corruption, narrow class interest and lack of democratic accountability. Men like Henderson stood as Independents after being rejected as official party candidates for what they saw as class reasons. They called for measures that would curb personation in voting and, like other opposition groups, opposed property qualifications for local elections which disfranchised more working class Protestants than Catholics.

The Independent Unionist tradition is not really socialist because its adherents have not shared conventional socialist assumptions about class structure and class conflict. They sought 'not Labour minus Protestantism but a Protestant democracy that embraces Labour'. Unlike socialists they assumed there was nothing inevitable about class conflict, that the Unionist Party could represent the interests of all classes. This made them vulnerable to being bought off with an official candidature, and also to movement in a sectarian direction (where gains were sought at the expense of both middle class Protestants and Catholics). Nevertheless the Independent Unionist tradition sustained, and gave a focus for, Protestant working class hostility to traditional leaders and policies—especially in certain areas of Belfast, like the Shankill.

The Labour tradition

The image presented of Ulster Protestants, especially by left-wing analysts of Northern Ireland politics, can easily give the impression that labour politics was quite alien to an ascendancy population in the grip of Orange ideology. In fact, labour parties kept a precarious but continuing support among Protestant workers after 1920 (the Northern Ireland Labour Party achieved its peak representation of four Stormont seats in 1958). There was also substantial Protestant membership of trade unions, especially in engineering and shipbuilding. This meant there was a general knowledge, especially in Belfast, of the political arguments used by democratic socialists, and sporadic but repeated willingness to break with Unionism by actually voting for a party which asserted that social and economic struggles were more important than sectarian ones. Each generation also stored up its memories of strikes and industrial agitation, which again at least made them familiar with the methods and the arguments of militant protest, and fuelled their suppressed resentments against the view traditional leaders took of their deprivation. The outdoor relief agitation of the early 1930s is the best known: there was a major series of strikes in 1946 and 1947, including one at the Protestant stronghold of Short Brothers and Harland. In 1963, after 15,000 workers had been made redundant at Harland and Wolff, there were two mass lobbies of Stormont on the unemployment issue.

But labour movements faced enormous problems, as numerous studies have shown. They were in a catch 22: they could never win the lasting trust of Protestants when their candidates either avoided taking a constitutional stand, or differed about this among themselves (the typical situation in the Labour party till 1949). On the other hand, even taking a strong stand did not help them when constituional tensions were high: when the party (now officially named Northern Ireland Labour Party, NILP) unequivocally accepted partition in 1949, it lost its three Stormont seats and its vote crashed by two-thirds.[28] In the high tension surrounding constitutional changes in the South, Protestant voters simply defected to the Unionists and many anti-partitionists joined the breakaway Irish Labour Party. As Farrell writes: 'The whole saga of the break-up of the Labour Party over the partition issue had shown once again, as in 1920 and 1935 ... how easily a fragile working-class unity built up on social and economic issues, but ignoring, or ambiguous about, the constitutional question, could be fragmented when the basic issue of the existence of the state came to the fore.'[29]

If growth in Protestant support for labour movements needed low cross-Border tensions (as in the late 1950s or early 1960s) it also required a belief that Protestants would not lose out to Catholics: it needed belief that the cake could be made bigger all round, not redistributed in a way that left the majority with less. (This was not mere sectarian prejudice: where Protestants as well as Catholics were heavily disadvantaged compared with British workers, it was understandable that they hardly wanted their conditions to deteriorate even further).

After 1949, and until the mid-1960s, the NILP deferred (some would say pandered) to such fears in its strategy for winning Protestant support. Its leading figures avoided taking a sympathetic stance on Catholic grievances about special powers, the police and the B Specials, and declined to condemn discrimination against Catholics. Instead they concentrated on a gradualist policy of trying to win more benefits for all workers, with the implication that this could be achieved without legislative change to improve the Catholics' position. They encouraged Protestant workers to believe that socialist change could be won without confronting any awkward sectarian issues.

So a movement like civil rights was likely to throw them into turmoil by forcing them to take a stand on the very things they had avoided. It was also likely to lose them support among one section of the community whatever position they chose. In particular, the Protestants who backed them in the belief that this would mean more for everyone were likely to question their allegiance if the NILP supported policies that benefited Catholics at Protestant expense. An almost identical problem faced the trade unions: once they started saying that socialism was about civil liberties as well as wage rises, that the name of the game had been changed, they would find many Protestants as unprepared as they were unwilling to adapt to the new rules of socialism.

3

O'Neillism: The Challenge
to Traditional Politics

After Terence O'Neill became Prime Minister in 1963, a growing number of Catholics and Protestants began publicly expressing views that challenged many of the ideological and cultural assumptions we have discussed. Social changes also began which affected the Protestant social order and brought new tensions between different classes, which would influence future political developments.

O'Neill's conciliatory noises to both Ulster Catholics and the Irish government brought swift reaction from some loyalists who saw these as treasonous or foolish, since they did not believe Catholics could be so conciliated. For some who rallied round Ian Paisley's ample figure the main enemy was a scheming Catholic church bent on world domination; a church which, under Pope John, had (they believed) merely become a wolf in sheep's clothing. Others saw the new line as a sell-out to Irish republicanism, which they believed was planning another armed offensive. The Easter Rising celebrations of 1966 only confirmed this view. Dissent was expressed within and beyond the Unionist Party, and on many stages—in the streets, at Stormont, in constituency meetings: Paisleyites even used snowballs as a weapon when the Taoiseach, Jack Lynch, drove through Belfast in 1967.

These ultraloyalists have been widely discussed in the literature of Ulster's modern disorders,[30] but they were not the only people to be disturbed by the changes. The new politics challenged traditional assumptions in a far reaching way and nearly all the reassuring old certainties were turned upside down.

1. The civil rights movement proclaimed that democracy involved the rights of minorities, as well as majorities.

2. Constitutional issues were no longer supreme. Civil rights activists demanded reform of the regime rather than Irish unity. They called

not for Britain to be rejected as Ireland's enemy, but for the regime to conform more closely to British standards.

Material values were put above the non-material. O'Neill was suggesting Catholics could be reconciled by worldly benefits; that the value of North–South economic co-operation made old antagonisms undesirable; that the British link was to be treasured less for the spiritual values it protected than for the prosperity it guaranteed. Sectarianism gave a bad image of Northern Ireland to Britain and other countries whose investment O'Neill was trying to attract.

3. Parochialism and devotion to old values turned from virtue to vices. Traditionally people were obsessed with each other, and allowed to be: now liberalising Unionists told them their political world must encompass the British Isles and Europe, that their values were out of step with modern ways of thinking. The future, not the past, was now the god. Politics became a career for the go-ahead, the qualified, the ambitious who scorned parish pump politics.[31]

4. Compromise and tolerance changed from vices to virtues.

5. The zero sum game was declared obsolete. O'Neill implied that everyone could share the new prosperity, that Catholics could also work for the Unionist Party and not just for 'their own'. Civil rights leaders also demanded that Protestant leaders work in the other side's interests by putting through much-needed legal reforms.

6. The reassuring predictability of politics evaporated. Materialists and ecumenicals were both saying people's similarities were more important than their differences. Again, some Catholics were voting for O'Neill, others traditionally anti-British, called 'for full British rights— full British standards'. Civil rights people were hard to pigeonhole; they neither proclaimed allegiance nor opposition to the constitution; they were neutral. Those old hands who had been straight as a gun barrel were so much easier to work out.

It is simple to see how these changes piled on top of one another in an endless stream of alien, novel ideas. Thus large numbers of both Protestants and Catholics were likely to feel confused, and many would be hostile, because they were still locked inside traditional assumptions that could not be shed overnight.

The social order

It is changes in Protestant–Catholic relationships that have been most publicised about this era; yet social developments inside the Protestant community also sowed the seeds of future strife, of new organisations like the UDA and a range of self-help groups.

Support for O'Neill was not limited to one class, but he did speak particularly for a growing number of middle class Protestants who found themselves unable to identify with traditional views, and sought more political influence, at the expense of other middle class groups. They were galvanised into new interest and action. This lawyer sums up their feelings:

'In the old days a lot of professional and business people opted out of politics, usually with vague feelings of guilt. First there was the bigotry they didn't agree with and felt embarrassed about... then the sort of people who became politicians—all the dummies up at Stormont—you could laugh, but you despaired as well. Politics wasn't a desirable career, it was almost a bit shameful. With O'Neill an awful lot of people suddenly saw hope for change, a lot of enthusiasm, and politics also became more respectable.'

The Unionist Party structure was also being modernised. J. O. Baillie, who took over the running of Glengall Street HQ, was a trained Conservative agent. He appointed professional staff, tried to lay down rules on things like membership, and modernised publicity and propaganda. The party began attracting new activists who were often university graduates. But it was no part of O'Neillism to increase working class influence or party competitiveness. On the contrary he wanted to woo voters from opposition parties like the NILP. He was not questioning one-party rule, nor the view that Unionists were Ulster's natural leaders. Indeed, his policies and outlook were positively unattractive to working class Protestants.

Hardline ones disagreed with his conciliatory approach anyway, while liberal ones tended to be committed trade unionists or NILP voters. They were unlikely to agree with him that class divisions were outmoded, while his economic policies (especially the attraction of capital-intensive industries) were of a modernising conservative rather than a socialist kind. Also, his supporters were not particularly interested in recruiting working class members or paying more attention to the social and economic problems they suffered.

Indeed class tensions were in many ways heightened by 'O'Neillism'. It is true that Unionist leaders had traditionally been upper or middle class: it was rather the conspicuous nature of O'Neill's patrician manner and his Englishness that struck an offensive note. From a Shankill Road perspective, he seemed especially remote from, and insensitive to, things that were important to poorer people. His supporters could also give this impression, as a working class ex-party member recalled: 'Areas like Shankill or Clifton always had a lot of better-off people in the branch who tended to run things but often came from outside. But these "moderates" who began coming in, most were even snootier and even more removed from people like us. This caused resentment, even though most were too timid to speak out.' So some people felt there was even less internal democracy in the new party than there was in the old.

There were other developments that tended to increase social resentments, or dent traditional fatalism about living conditions. The welfare state and improved living standards raised the expectations of poor Protestants, as well as Catholics. In the materialistic society extolled by O'Neill discontent among all the underprivileged was likely to grow while resignation was replaced by impatience for the good things of life.[32] Research has shown that even Protestants of ultraloyalist views were increasingly prepared to vote NILP during high unemployment in the early 1960s.[33] When there was low sectarian tension other grievances could also foster resentment at traditional leaders and produce limited co-operation between Protestants and Catholics.

The mid-1960s saw the start of major urban redevelopment in Belfast and both religions found their traditional communities disrupted, sometimes brutally. New estates often lacked social amenities and brought new problems like high rents and vandalism. The idea that leaders looked after Protestants seemed less impressive. In the old areas property deteriorated and many facilities were closed down; the Shankill for instance lost public baths, a cinema, a roller skating rink and a snooker hall within a few years. There were also challenges to traditional hierarchies e.g. attempts to open licensed social clubs, which were strongly opposed by the Orange Order.

There were the beginnings of agitation on redevelopment, rents, transport etc, which sometimes crossed the religious divide and laid foundations for future community action groups.[34] But the new anger and the resentment at snooty O'Neillites was not the product of some emerging socialist analysis of Ulster politics. Co-operation across the divide was also new to most, and depended on a painful build-up of trust and understanding. Protestant social consciousness remained vulnerable to more traditional pressures with any resurgence of sectarian tensions. If these grew it was likely to move towards a form of Protestant populism that had deeper roots than socialism in working class areas.

This populism was likely to find fertile soil in a situation where public concern seemed to be turning exclusively to Catholics. In 1965 the NILP voted for repeal of the Special Powers Act (which poor Protestants did not see then as oppressive to themselves, though by 1972 they felt differently). In 1966 the NILP and the Northern Committee of the Irish Trades Union Congress called for 'one man one vote', an ombudsman and an end to discrimination in housing and unemployment: the NILP began attracting more Catholics, and more left wing socialists, including civil rights activists. O'Neill was also stressing the need to reconcile Catholics through material benefits, as well as tolerance. Nobody seemed to be talking about the hardships of poor Protestants.

Many Catholics felt O'Neill talked much and did little; or they found that new benefits, like high-rise flats, hardly improved their lives. But poor Protestants were unlikely to see things in this way. To the Shankill tenant, watching Divis Flats being built from his rat-infested house, it seemed traditional leaders were not even sharing their new-found wealth, but giving it all to the traditional enemy, the 'rebels'.

Thus one role of Paisley's movements was to articulate the social grievances of people left out of the new affluence, squeezed on one side by the middle class, on the other by Catholics. Thus, too, Protestant Unionist local election candidates appealed to the new concern about living conditions, redevelopment and high bus fares in their demands for justice for Protestants, no high-rise blocks for Protestants. Social and community awareness was vulnerable to being harnessed for sectarian political ends by those who sought to convince the poor that the rewards they had earned through loyalty to the regime were being snatched away by avaricious Malone Road snobs *and* pampered rebels.

4

Ultraloyalists before 1969:
Paisleyites and the UVF

Long before civil disorder broke out in the streets of Belfast and Derry in 1969, some Protestants were publicly protesting at O'Neill's new approach, and at the birth of the civil rights movement through statements, speeches and sometimes violent demonstrations. Loyalist groups which developed during the Troubles often had their roots in movements of this time. How were these movements launched, what sort of people were their members, and what did they believe?

One popular image of recruits to ultraloyalist groups during O'Neill's premiership is the backwoodsman—a somewhat unsophisticated and inarticulate person driven by anti-Catholic prejudice, and content merely to follow a messianic leader figure. In fact, people who conformed in some degree to this image were only one source of recruitment to new groups. They also attracted people who were more articulate and politically ambitious than their neighbours, more critical of the social system and the Unionist Party. They tended to emerge in times of crisis as community leaders to whom confused or frightened people would turn. They often provided the dynamic force in new groups, influencing policy, propagandising and recruiting new members. At the same time, just because the groups did draw in very different kinds of people, latent tensions existed which were only likely to sharpen in the future.

The Paisleyites: background

As leader of several political movements the Rev. Ian Paisley has consistently challenged official Unionism, as well as republicanism and moderate forces. Self-styled moderator of the Free Presbyterian Church of Ulster, which he formed in 1951, Paisley spoke most forcefully for those who opposed the growth of ecumenism in the Protestant churches, against those who would betray their faith to 'the forces of Popery and the scarlet whore drunk on the blood of the churches'. His first rift with the Unionists came over Lord Brookeborough's failure in 1959 to expel two MPs who suggested that Unionist Party membership be open to Catholics.

He thought of standing as an Independent Unionist in the general election of that year, sponsored by a body called Ulster Protestant Action, in which he played a major role. This was organised 'to keep Protestant and loyal workers in employment in times of depression, in preference to their Catholic fellow-workers'.[35] In the event, he waited till 1964 to field four 'Protestant Unionist' candidates in the Belfast Corporation elections.

Paisley first found fame as a street leader when he led thousands of followers in protest at the display of a tricolour by a Sinn Féin candidate in the 1964 Westminster election. Thirty people, including several policemen, were injured in the sectarian 'Divis Street riots'.

In May 1966 he published the first edition of the virulently anti-Catholic fortnightly paper, the *Protestant Telegraph*, which thundered against the forthcoming Easter Rising celebrations, and condemned O'Neill's 'appeasing' policies. But when the Ulster Volunteer Force decided to oppose what they saw as a republican upsurge by violent means, Paisley quickly dissociated himself from them. His intention to enter electoral politics in the 1966 Westminster election was not fulfilled, for he lacked a party organisation and finances. The organisation was built up via his own church congregations, via the Ulster Constitution Defence Committee and the Ulster Protestant Volunteers. This was a group of Protestant ultras, first organised by Noel Doherty, who attended Paisley's marches and rallies and drew substantially on his own church membership. Though their constitution allowed the expulsion of those involved with violent or subversive activities, some members were proved to have overlapping membership with the illegal UVF.

Paisley constantly stressed the link between religious and political change, organising protests against ecumenical churchmen and conciliatory politicians alike. While colourful incidents like the snowballing of the Irish Prime Minister's car brought public attention, the Protestant Unionists were working on more quietly and increased their representation on the Belfast City Council during 1967. They agitated on redevelopment issues and social conditions, as well as religious matters.

The first civil rights marches showed Paisley a master of the counter-demonstration technique, notably at Armagh in November 1968. An opinion poll showing that 200,000 Ulster people considered themselves potential Paisley supporters[36] demonstrated that by this stage, sympathy for his stand went much further than the immediate followers who turned up at each counter-demonstration.

Even in these early years, Paisley played a number of (sometimes overlapping) roles in Northern Ireland politics. On the one hand he spoke for traditional, recurring strands in Ulster politics, both in his ideology and his political style. He expressed the beliefs of Protestants who saw a vital link between religion and politics, who viewed Protestantism as under constant threat from a monolithic and aggrandising Catholic church. Thus ecumenism was as great a threat as the IRA, ultimately leading to Protestant absorption within the Church of Rome.[37]

When Paisleyites prevented the Anglican Archbishop of Ripon speaking in a Belfast cathedral in 1967 on the grounds that he was an ecumenist, they were demonstrating their belief that Protestant freedom depended on denial of free speech to opponents. When Paisley asserted his 'inalienable right to march' in face of a Government ban he was proclaiming the existence of some higher rights than those defined by the present regime. His purpose was never to cement Protestant unity, but to expose differences and force Protestants to ask: 'What does our religion really mean?' His followers have been concerned to enforce political Protestantism at all levels, seeing it as just as important to oppose an obscene or blasphemous film as to oppose a meeting with Dublin politicians. In his technique, Paisley stood in the tradition of street preachers like 'Roaring Hanna' or Henry Trew, who incited their followers against Rome's iniquities, and the appeasing policies of Unionist leaders. In his populist slant he drew on the independent Unionist tradition—as when he condemned living conditions in cottages on Terence O'Neill's estate.

Another traditional role lay in his legitimation of Protestant extra-legal violence: but this role was strictly limited. At the start, Paisley implicitly sanctioned protesters who put their point with fists or cudgels. But he quickly gave notice that he drew distinctions between blackthorn sticks and guns by disassociating himself from the Malvern Street murder or the Silent Valley bombings by the UVF. Those who wanted to take up arms against a rebel conspiracy soon doubted his willingness to lead them or express their viewpoint, and moved into other groups.

Paisley's caution partly reflected the fact that his support drew heavily on socially conservative people in rural areas. They saw themselves as law abiding and preferred to see tougher measures against Catholics by a legally-sanctioned force. Paisley was speaking for these people in his frequent calls for a 'third force' or 'people's militia' who would do the necessary—but in an official uniform, not as outlaws or criminals.

Apart from traditional functions, Paisleyite movements played another role as agents, in the jargon, of political socialisation. In the early years of civil rights, opponents of the new trends tended to flock to Paisley as to a beacon, whatever their individual differences. Many activists who later emerged in political, paramilitary, industrial or community groups had their first experience of politicking in a Paisleyite group, organising, canvassing and so on. This strenghtened the tendency in Ulster for the politically active stratum to be personally acquainted, but it also added to the fissiparous tendencies of Protestant politics after 1969.

For various reasons we shall go on to consider—including the strong personality of Paisley himself—his movements tended to develop into follower organisations, with strong pressures for conformity. This encouraged a lot of people, for ideological or personal motives, to leave his groups eventually—or be cast out like the Biblical demons. These antagonisms, mistrust and increasing political differences all contributed to the tensions apparent in post-1969 loyalist politics, especially at times when there was greatest pressure for a united front (for instance, after the imposition of direct rule in 1972).

The activists

What kinds of people were attracted to Paisley before he gained a wide following in Northern Ireland? Writers on extremist political movements have often suggested that they attract deviant personalities or those of especially authoritarian temperament. Boulton has also spoken of 'the weak and wanting minds every form of revivalist religion attracts'.[38]

Paisley certainly drew in a number of people with a strong emotive hostility towards Catholics, who felt he spoke for their feelings and who found satisfaction and purpose in working for him. Some, undoubtedly, would also have been an interesting study for psychologists. Mrs Y, of Shankill, showed a generalised hostility to Catholics, and had organised a public protest when her employers first took on Catholic workers. She believed strongly in 'keeping Ulster pure', and applied this to matters great and small. A mysterious, bubbling device in her living room 'kept the air pure', and when I sniffed, a box of handkerchiefs was thrust upon me. 'A few people round here' recalled another Shankill housewife, 'were very bitter and always going on: "There's no good in any of them [Catholics]". When Paisley came along he was a sort of god to them, they were all for him.'

It is also true that Paisley's movements attracted some people of low or marginal social status like the former vagrant and alcoholic who had been 'saved' by Paisley. Like some of the early UVF, they gained prestige and self-importance from bodyguard duties, message carrying, organisation of 'the boys' for a counter-demonstration, etc.

But it is dangerous and simplistic to over-emphasise this element in explanations of Paisleyism. A more significant part of his following were part of a religious and cultural tradition in Northern Ireland rather than individual deviants. In Belfast, the majority tended to come from a skilled working class or lower middle class background. Paisleyism attracted the 'politically certain', people already equipped with a coherent ideology which they used to interpret events. Many other Protestants at this time were much less certain about what was happening and how they should construe it: they either hoped 'things were getting better', or cautiously reserved judgment.

The politically certain tended to believe, with this Free Presbyterian schoolteacher, that 'the struggle in Ireland is essentially a religious struggle. All this houses and jobs thing, economic and social conditions is a lot of baloney.' They were fighting, not just against a scheming church of Rome, but for a certain kind of Protestantism. Hence it was not inconsistent for them to oppose, in the *Protestant Telegraph* and elsewhere, a whole range of anti-Protestant forces: secularisation, sexual licence, the pop culture, communism. Standing up to be counted was a duty and a necessity for people like this East Belfast shopkeeper, an Orange master: 'The O'Neillites were forsaking the past ... not just by letting Ulster's enemies take a hold on the country. It was the atmosphere all around, no pride and respect in the young people, all loose living and disobedience. I believed God's punishment would come down ... hasn't it happened since?'

International events were important to many Paisleyites: the conspiracy against religion was world-wide. When one enemy (Catholics) appeared to take on Communistic doctrines (as the IRA did after 1962) they merely appeared doubly dangerous and indeed, doubly authoritarian and doubly anti-Christ.[39]

Paisley also attracted people who held most strongly the historic Protestant conviction that Catholic 'rebels' were treacherous and devious people, with an undiminished desire to destroy Protestants physically. The belief that the leopard never changes its spots only led to more suspicion when Catholics started making conciliatory noises. The first reaction was to look more intently for ingenious plots and subterfuges. So the possession of inside information was very important and was used to win over the doubting at Orange lodges, workplaces, churches or Unionist Party branches. People like the schoolteacher could spread the word: 'I had been forewarned long before it happened ... by certain sources ... that an attempt would be made to take Northern Ireland over—the first stage was the discrediting of the police force and the Government ... I saw it in terms of a great conspiracy.'

What made many people of these beliefs content to be followers? First, a leader was just what most fundamentalists lacked at this time: they felt rudderless, no longer represented by their elected leaders. Secondly, a messianic figure who was himself in the religious profession was a likely candidate for leadership. If potential followers believed a saved man or man of God had special moral qualities he would also enjoy a freedom not shared by other political leaders. For instance, if a saved man cannot lie, the blame for dishonesty or deception in any political dispute will pass to opponents! Members who want to challenge their leader's decisions will also face problems in winning support from other members.

Thirdly, Paisley's church won many adherents by conversion. People made a dramatic commitment which involved total trust, not just in God's truth, but in Paisley's version of it. These two men, the East Belfast Orangeman and a clerk, were looking for a leader to follow before they found Paisley: 'We ought to follow Dr Paisley and make sure his words were heard. I felt he was a man of God, not a deceiver, who would lead the people of Ulster back on the right path. Who listened then? Yet his words have all come true.'

'Ulster needs a dynamic leader who keeps his promises. My final decision to join Dr Paisley came after he was sent to prison ... I thought, what sort of man goes to jail for his beliefs? I was converted to Christ soon after, a decision that made the greatest impact on my life.'

But Paisley's movements also attracted people who were less content to be followers than their neighbours, and more critical of the political and social system. Usually they were already members of parties or trade unions, and were often the children of Labour voters, who had bettered themselves socially. Outright socialism frightened them, but they sought a movement that would improve Protestant working class living conditions, provide more political advancement for themselves and more internal democracy than the Unionist Party had done. This plumber, who later became a Democratic Unionist candidate (Paisley's own party), recalled:

'I had been on trade union committees and though I never joined a party, I was always interested in politics. I served in the army abroad and when I came back I saw things with different eyes... that the Unionists had never done anything for the people, especially about unemployment. I felt Dr Paisley would be strong on the Constitution, yet determined to do something for the ordinary people.'

This woman has grown very frustrated as a member of Shankill Unionist party:

'I was always interested in politics but got very disillusioned. Most MPs didn't consult their branches much and the members themselves were often better-off people. But... people round here lack confidence; they need a democratic party that does something for their problems and encourages them to put their point of view.' One veteran Independent Unionist saw Paisley as his spiritual descendant, who would fight the the IUs against 'the filthy corruption of the Unionist Party'.

As Paisley attracted the Unionist left, he also appealed to the NILP right at a time of NILP trends that alarmed people like this elderly trade unionist. 'I couldn't support what the civil rights people were saying, that discrimination was all against the Catholics. Having been right through the strikes in the 1930s I felt we got it as hard as them. I am a socialist but not a communist, and there was a known republican element getting in [the NILP]. I always wanted to work for the people here, but not that way.' Other NILP voters felt it was 'being taken over by commies and republicans'. They felt Paisley could lead a movement 'with a social conscience' if they pushed it in this direction.

Not all the fundamentalists were happy to be 'organ grinders' monkeys; men like the schoolteacher clearly ambitious politically. Nor were all the socially discontented ambitious and independent minded; like the Independent Unionists, some had their radicalism bought off by a post in the movement that turned them into obedient followers.

But nonetheless, latent tensions existed in early Paisleyism, just because it attracted very different sorts of people. Serious questions arose for the future: given that Paisley attracted people who were actively seeking a democratic party structure, how far could a movement with inbuilt pressures for a prophet–disciples structure meet their needs? Secondly, how far could it meet hopes for social change in Ulster? The socially discontented were but one element, largely confined to Belfast. Other elements were strongly conservative and extolled a more traditional social order.

Paisley's ability to hold the socially critical would depend not just on the kind of social policies he developed, but also on the extent of commitment to real social change among his supporters who claimed an interest in this. His ability to become a mass political leader, rather than the messiah of a minority, would depend on much wider political developments in Ulster which might make his solutions suddenly look appealing to large numbers of confused people.

Ultraloyalists: The Ulster Volunteer Force

In March 1966 Belfast newspapers reported that the Government was inquiring into rumours that the UVF was being re-formed to oppose Republican plans for Easter parades. Questions were asked at Stormont about 'members of an illegal armed organisation of Unionist extremists' who were said to be 'actively drilling'. The Royal Ulster Constabulary (RUC) looked into a spate of petrol bomb attacks on Catholic homes in Belfast. On 21 May 1966, the UVF announced itself in a letter to Belfast newspapers, in which it declared war 'on the IRA and its splinter groups', concluding: 'We are heavily armed Protestants dedicated to this cause.'

The conviction of Gusty Spence and three other UVF members for the murder of a Catholic barman in June 1966 resulted in the group's proscription by O'Neill, who called it 'a very dangerous conspiracy' and compared it with the IRA. At this time the UVF's main support came from a small group of shipyard workers and others in the Shankill area who had tenuous but proven links with John McKeague—future editor of the fiercely anti-Catholic *Loyalist News*—and with Paisley's Ulster Protestant Volunteers (UPV). Its leader, Gusty Spence (a shipyard stager and ex-soldier) had worked for the Unionist Party while his brother was a Unionist election agent. The UVF was condemned by all major parties in Northern Ireland and Paisley strenuously disassociated himself from it.

Little was heard of the group till a series of explosions in April 1969 brought a new crisis for O'Neill's credibility, and led directly to his resignation. The death of a man while planting a bomb in October of that year led to inquiries which confirmed UVF responsibility for earlier bombings. The organisation was greatly weakened by its leader's imprisonment and by extensive Special Branch investigations, and it appears to have retained only a skeletal structure in Belfast and some country areas until 1971.

The role of the UVF in O'Neill's time was to represent the extreme of resistance to any change in power relationships between Protestants and Catholics. It was a potent reminder that some Protestants would fight to the last any change in traditional Protestant concepts of the constitution. It also gave literal expression to the traditional Protestant notion of the public band—where groups of men banded together to protect themselves against the 'rebels', and considered that as citizens they had both a right and a duty to do so.

Relating the UVF to historical movements, Boulton comments: 'When the UVF began to kill Catholics in 1966 . . . they were acting out the traditional role of the Ascendancy's bully boys.' But in fact, it would be truer to say the UVF was the militant section of those who opposed the new reformism of the Ascendancy class who, far from sanctioning them, called them fascists and compared them with the IRA. Even O'Neill's loyalist opponents (like Paisley) denied them legitimacy. Thus the UVF's own claim that they were heirs to a heroic Protestant tradition (embodied by the original UVF) was not accepted by most of their compatriots. To hardliners they were a double-edged weapon: in 1966 they discredited Paisley, in 1969 they hastened the downfall of O'Neill. That double-edged role was to continue throughout the conflict.

The popular stereotype of the early UVF activist often resembles the Paisleyite one, in more extreme form: a prejudiced backwoodsman with a pathological hostility to Catholics and a naturally violent personality. Certainly these people existed, as one UVF member himself recalled: 'Boys you knew who felt very strongly against RCs, or hated them . . . there again some would have killed their own grannies for a quid.' That this stereotype was inadequate would be confirmed by the speaker himself. Like a number of his colleagues he had extensive contact with Catholics before the Troubles (he belonged to a mainly Catholic boxing club for many years).

The UVF had other attractions besides sheer anti-Catholicism; like Paisley's movements it both drew on wider cultural traditions, and appealed to people for a range of reasons. In many outsiders' eyes, the early UVF appeared squalid or incompetent, or both. For people (especially young men) in families or areas where heroic, martial aspects of loyalist ideology were extolled[40] the ideal—even the reality—could look quite different. As one UVF prisoner recalled: 'The Shankill was called the jewel of Ulster, heart of the Empire etc. You were raised on this as a kid, rushing out to see the banners and the marching men... especially if you came from a strong loyalist family... So when the republican demonstrations started again [in 1966] you thought ah, the IRA's getting ready to attack again. We were Ulster's first defenders and would lead the fight.'

The belief that Protestant heroes were defending (as in Derry, or at the Somme) was as important as the belief that rebels were constantly planning to attack and destroy Protestants. This rationalised violence which many others would see as pre-emptive, indeed, as part of a loyalist tradition of pre-emptive attacks. In order to justify violence by law abiding Protestants they needed to prove, both to themselves and others, that their actions were provoked; hence the importance of having proof. A founder-member of the UVF, a factory worker, claimed to have discovered it: 'The IRA had secret training camps here and in the Free State. We found out where one of them was and saw it with our own eyes. They had explosives and weapons stored there.'

Like a number of other members he was an ex-soldier. His training and experience reinforced his belief in the IRA's militant plans and encouraged him to a militant response: he also expected the IRA to think and act as he did. The world in which they operated was comprehensible to him. Workplaces, Orange lodges and public houses became important centres for passing on 'proof' of insurrection, and for recruiting. Shipyard stagers had a particularly strong loyalist tradition and one senior UVF member described how, as a shop steward, he had used their workplace to encourage UVF recruitment and 'tell them what the IRA were doing'.

Orange lodges were a forum where men from the same area and class could meet and transmit rumour. 'The informed' could sound impressive to listeners like this UVF prisoner: 'After the Shankill meetings you'd get together and talk politics and discuss plans. I was very young then but I met a lot of UVF men and listened to them, they were my heroes in a way.'

Public houses were particularly conducive to misinformation and the exaggeration of rumour, as Boulton has shown. The fact that most Catholic victims of the UVF were unconnected with the IRA does not mean no UVF supporters made mental distinctions between 'good' and 'bad' Catholics. Given the quality of information possessed it is not surprising that the attacks were random, or bungled, or both. Ferreting out and passing information, sharing clandestine excitement, being in the know and gaining status by this, also appealed to those of low social status or low intelligence and unemployed men with little to do but sit around in pubs. It was always likely that people like this would gravitate to the UVF. As a former Unionist Party agent in South Belfast recalled: 'It used to be a great game before elections for some characters to put on things like Pioneer badges[41] and sit around in Catholic pubs getting information. The Unionist Party used odd-job boys like this... but some got mixed up with the UVF.'[42]

In Belfast the B Special constabulary never had the prestige or political importance it gained in rural areas and was not a key source of recruitment. But it helped to influence the attitude to law enforcement of this UVF man, an ex-B Special: 'In our area we did more or less what we liked... knew all the RCs and kept close watch on them. Sometimes some of the lads gave them a roughing up—I'm not saying this went on a lot, but the politicians never complained then.' The UVF men, whether ex-Bs or not, were expressing similar views by their actions, that the public band had a right to take independent action against resurgent rebels and deserved praise not condemnation from politicians for doing so. Hence Gusty Spence's reported disillusionment on his arrest: 'So this is what you get for being a Protestant'!

Though the UVF took initiatives they were essentially followers rather than leaders, in that they believed they were doing something for someone else: for Paisley or the 'real' patriots in the Unionist Party. Most took little interest in politics, but were content to be the instruments through which other loyalists would assert control in government. Nor were the UVF seeking to remedy working class social grievances, despite their overwhelmingly working class composition.

Yet one contradiction about the UVF was that—in Belfast at least—it also attracted some people who were discontented with the social order (just as Paisley's movements did). By 1974 a number of longstanding UVF members claimed that they opposed O'Neill 'on class grounds' in the 1960s. Clearly there were strong elements of retrospective justification here, and they were also saying what they thought interviewers wanted to hear. On the other hand, they were people who had accepted fairly readily a leftward turn within influential elements of the UVF after 1971. Other comments they made probably captured a more complex truth more accurately, as when one leading member explained: 'I despised [O'Neillites] and those like them like our MP; what did they know about us—they couldn't care less.' Another 'officer', a skilled manual worker who was in the Unionist Party in the mid 1960s, recalled: 'The branch members in South Befast were worlds apart from me. I'd had a pretty tough life ... they didn't care about the people I knew, and were so condescending. I got more and more angry and frustrated. I'd wanted to do something for the people—that's why I joined the party.' Reliable sources also suggest that the early UVF attracted some Labour Party members.

These were people with social grievances, sometimes latent or badly thought-out, who were more discontented than their neighbours and more interested in politics. They wanted to express protest against the traditional system without appearing 'disloyal' or weakening Protestant defences against a republican threat they still believed to be real. The O'Neillites only heightened their anger and resentment. The UVF was a way of hitting back at them, as well as the 'IRA threat'. Others whose social resentments and suspicions of republicanism were confusedly linked in their opposition to O'Neill, but who came from different backgrounds and environments, chose different avenues of protest, like the Protestant Unionist Party.

The ex-soldiers and others discussed here, with their martial view of the loyalist tradition, made choices that seemed more familiar and natural to them. But for some there were contradictions that just waited to be spotted. First, the leaders the UVF were trying to please did not congratulate them after all: why? Secondly the UVF was really just another follower organisation, doing favours for the powerful. Was this the kind of group the socially discontented wanted to belong to—or escape from?

One individual, like Gusty Spence, had a special impetus to confront these questions: a 20 year prison sentence. Others with latent political awareness were only potentially likely to question their role and activities. But in their vulnerability to this process lay the seeds of future instability and dissension in the UVF.

The early years of the group also gave a hint of future dissension among different loyalist organisations. It is beyond question that some religious-minded Paisleyites were also involved in physical-force activities at this time. Nor has there ever been a shortage, in Ulster, of 'men of God' prepared to hold up a gun as well as a Bible.

Nonetheless, most UVF sympathisers did not hold the coherent religio–political analysis of the typical Free Presbyterian. They were more interested in what the IRA man up in the Clonard might be plotting than in a gathering of ecumenical clergymen, and few were fighting to close the floodgates of sin. Indeed, some lived just the kind of lives that devout, teetotal Orangemen condemned. Loyalist political figures more often used UVF sympathisers as bodyguards than as philosophers. Mutual suspicion and resentment was easily aroused between militants and devout Paisleyites: this included class friction. The comments of this factory worker prominent in the UVF and the later Ulster Defence Association (UDA) and this Free Presbyterian businessman, speak for tensions which were only to grow during the Troubles.

'As a rule each knew who the other lot were; but we felt the Paisleyites let us down. They went on about fighting but wouldn't put their money where their mouths were, and they didn't want to get their hands dirty. Or if they did, they wouldn't admit it afterwards; we know what some of them were involved in and they know we know. That's why relations are so bad today [1975]. Anyway, the militants felt more and more that they'd be better off without these people.'

'You take X [a high ranking UVF man and Free Presbyterian]. Now, most of the congregation knew what he was, but to tell the truth a lot didn't like it. They were good living law abiding people and there was a lot of worry about getting mixed up with corner boy elements, frankly, and people who preferred a drink to going to church on Sundays.'

On the one hand, then, settings like Free Presbyterian churches provided a forum where activists got acquainted, swapped information and planned protest. On the other, mutual suspicions made it likely that those who wielded blackthorn sticks and those who dreamed of guns would at best keep an uneasy relationship if the situation escalated into community conflict. At worst, they would go their separate ways in distinctive organisations, into which a sense of bitterness and betrayal was deeply implanted.

5

Making Sense of 'Civil Rights' and 'Discrimination'

It is not hard to see why the ultraloyalists we have discussed would be hostile to the civil rights movement in Northern Ireland. What is less clear is why so many other Protestants, including MPs who would later become staunch moderates, were opposed to it and refused to accept its allegations.[43] We have also to explain why opponents of reform like Paisley suddenly drew a wide following. As these housewives in Protestant working-class areas of Belfast recalled: 'In 1969 Paisley was God round here, you couldn't say a word against him... he was suddenly the greatest, he'd been proved right all along.'

After all, the O'Neill era was a time of great hope and optimism for many people: most Protestants were feeling more, not less, conciliatory towards Catholics. The old entrenched attitudes seemed to be weakening on both sides and tolerance was visible: nuns could even be seen shopping in the most sacred pastures of loyalism, like the Shankill! In such a climate, the civil rights activists might have expected a widespread willingness to consider and adapt to the demands they made. Instead attitudes rapidly hardened and eventually sparked conflict in the streets.

One way of understanding the reaction is to look at how different Protestants made sense of political realities when the civil rights movement emerged. Their reading of the situation gave them the tools for interpreting the movement's demands. We have already discussed some traditional beliefs about the zero sum game, but it is useful to look more broadly at what people meant by 'things are getting better in Northern Ireland'. For most Catholics, and some of O'Neill's Protestant supporters, this meant more than a willingness to chat to the other side over the fence, or to avoid inflammatory statements. It involved openness to the possibility that all had not been right with the way Ulster was governed: that lasting reconciliation would need concrete political reforms which must be initiated by the majority community.

The outlook of Mr M,[44] a Unionist Party member who spent his life in the youth service and favoured ecumenism, suggests that Protestants who really accepted this need were in a small minority at the time. Mr M, who had friends of both religions, was just the sort of Protestant the civil rights movement probably hoped to attract; yet his reaction to them was a mixture of anger and hurt bewilderment. For him, 'getting better' meant that Catholic leaders were taking part in public life and accepting the regime's legitimacy, while Unionist leaders were guiding the party away from traditional bigotry. He felt there was nothing inherently wrong with Ulster's institutions: bigotry was a boil on their surfaces, kept alive by fundamentalists and uneducated people, who were finally being replaced in government. People would gradually be coached out of intolerance, and abuses would slowly disappear.

He also felt Catholic clergy and politicians had been mainly responsible for Catholic disadvantages in the social, economic and political fields, so his first reaction to claims that these were the fault of Unionists was: 'This is an unfair version of the truth.' One reason why he viewed Unionism so optimistically was precisely that he was not intolerant of Catholics, and assumed his circle of Unionist friends would be the same. Conservative in outlook, he trusted his party as many mainland people trusted Conservatism—as a patriotic party of order and fair government. Confronted by evidence of injustice, his defensive reaction was to search all the harder for other causes. Almost obsessively, he would go over allegations of discrimination point by point, trying to convince himself and others that there had been nothing wrong with the world he had been part of.

For people like Mr M, perceptions of reality were shaped not just by ideology but by simple limitations of experience. He had not been in Ballymurphy or the shipyard, the district he lived in had harmonious community relations, and the caring values of his profession opposed intolerance. Like many other Protestants with Catholic acquaintances, he simultaneously knew and did not know the other side.

Secondly, the civil rights movement hit hardest at the integrity of Unionist politicians and public servants. These were prominent middle-class people whom men like Mr M., in the small world of Ulster, both mixed with and respected. This hit Unionist self-esteem as well as Unionist rights to power: it implied that they were neither competent nor trustworthy to run their own affairs. It is hard to understand why so many sections of Unionism—from a Stratton Mills to a William

Craig—opposed civil rights if their views on Catholics are the main criterion; easier to understand if their shared characteristic as a threatened elite is considered.

Once they had got over their shock and indignation, many people who were basically moderates accepted the reforms and became, in their own eyes, the true British loyalists. So Mr M later became a supporter of power sharing, because he was basically trustful of Catholics and respected the British government. People like him might have blamed Catholics for most of their disadvantages, but they could still see there had been faults on both sides, and understood why inflammatory statements and acts offended Catholics. But others who sincerely believed things were getting better under O'Neill did not acknowledge that Protestants had appreciably contributed to community divisions.

People[45] were saying things were improving because Catholics were accepting the status quo, so proving there was nothing wrong with it; because Ulster was prospering as never before and because people were living and working together without any 'trouble'. So, they felt, why on earth should people want to make trouble now, when there was least reason for it?

Catholic leaders were not just taking part in state functions but Catholic were accepting cheerfully traditional Protestant expressions of feeling. So one group of East Belfast Orangemen recalled: 'One Catholic farmer used to look after his Protestant neighbour's cows on the 12 July, and everyone knew most ice cream sellers at the Field were Catholics.' As for the 11th and 12th celebrations, they were just 'social occasions' where Catholics took their kids to watch the bonfires or parades. Economically Ulster was becoming 'the greatest wee country'. A Unionist factory worker voiced one popular point: 'The RCs were getting their grants and coming through university. Look at Bernadette [Devlin] or Austin Currie. Started with nothing and got it all free.'

As for community relations, an engineer recalled: 'We had RCs, working here, there was no trouble ... we played cards ... everything more relaxed than before.' An old shipyard worker put it thus: 'Once there were very few RCs in the yard, and always trouble breaking out. Now there was far more of them and everyone got on OK ...'.

We can crudely summarise what people are saying. The Catholics were contented because they showed us. The Catholics should have been contented because things were better than anyone could have expected; and certainly better than 'rebels' might deserve.

The O'Neillite atmosphere almost encouraged Protestants to believe

'the Catholics are contented', just because it was superficial communication that got better—all the more so because in friendly times,
people were especially keen not to give offence by raising contentious
political matters. A few people were confronting painful differences,
but the whole tenor of the era was rather that past divisions could be
forgotten without analysis—and everything would be fine, with a bit
of prosperity and goodwill all round. But in such a divided and segregated society, it was not just the hostile or the prejudiced who were
likely to misinterpret feelings across the divide. People would have
needed a great deal of sympathetic imagination to avoid doing this.

Clearly there could be other reasons than acceptance—like a keen
commercial sense or resigned wish to make the best of the inevitable—
behind Catholic participation in Orange celebrations. (That these
could approach being social events at all was entirely dependent on
Catholic behaviour. When Catholics challenged the political status
quo, Orange parades tended to regain their defiant political significance.) A genuine breakthrough in mutual understanding would have
involved the optimistic Protestants we quoted gaining a sense of the
real feelings their demonstrations provoked in most Catholics.

The idea that Catholics should surely have been contented was
stronger among poorer Protestants. They discovered a better quality
of life than they had ever known: this dented the resignation felt by an
older Protestant generation. It was almost as if the new prosperity was
a stroke of luck, more than anyone could hope for, which ought to
have filled Catholics with the same (almost grateful) feelings.

Again, many such people's expectations of normal religious relationships were shaped by generations of harsh experience. 'Trouble' at the
yard, violent demonstrations, street conflict and intimidation were
recurring facts of life. Segregated housing, mutual suspicion, an
uneasy truce, were what one called 'peace'. What more could one ever
hope for than partial integration and actual friendliness? So time and
again, people would say of the 1960s with relief, even pride: 'There was
no *trouble*.' By implication they were asking: 'Surely the Catholics too
must have been satisfied with that, how could they expect anything
more?'

In addition, while many people associated discrimination with expulsions from the shipyard, they did not necessarily even connect it
with certain practices in private employment. So an aggrieved group of
Shankill housewives put it: 'We knew we couldn't get a job in X [a
Catholic-owned] bakery but we didn't complain, we just accepted it.

Then they suddenly started complaining about "discrimination"!'

'Looking after your own' was for many people a natural if regrettable part of Ulster life, which would only wither away after a long build-up of mutual trust and reconciliation. Likewise many people expected, with little animosity, politicians of the other side to prefer their own people to Protestants. So Gerry Fitt was often complimented by working class Protestants: 'I'll say this, he's worked his heart out for his own. Pity we don't have someone like that on our side.' Now it seemed that Catholics, who had also played the game, were turning round and declaring it was immoral.

Parading through your own district also seemed not only natural to many people, but also tactful and respectful to the other side. So civil rights marchers who breached unspoken rules on territory in the name of nonsectarianism seemed deliberately aggressive.[46] People would even appeal to 'outsiders' like myself for explanations: 'Look, say going through Antrim or some of those Protestant villages. They knew the political views of people there so surely, it must have been just to stir them up? What other point could there have been (could you tell me?)' Thus the marchers were in an impossible dilemma: they were liable to be seen as sectarian whether or not they remained within Catholic areas.

The notion that Catholics were doing 'as well as they deserved' suggests some people saw discrimination as not just natural, but justified.

The Calvinist view of the relationship between religion and politics justifies denial of free speech and actions which threaten Protestant liberty. But interestingly enough few Protestants, even hardliners, were prepared to openly justify discrimination by appeals to their ideology. One Vanguard supporter did insist on reading the whole of the 1707 Act of Union between Scotland and England to prove his contention that Britain had betrayed Protestant principles in abandoning certain forms of discrimination against Catholics. But most people saw their religious and political beliefs as a reason why they should not give Catholics fewer rights than Protestants. Protestants had always fought for freedom, they said and invoked a catch-phrase that was often to figure in the loyalist press: 'Protestantism means equal rights for all, special privileges for none.'

What they did instead was to blame the malign influence of traditional RC leaders for Catholic disadvantage: the Church for encouraging large families; the Church and politicians for discouraging Catholic involvement in politics, or in the security forces. So they were saying

Catholics were not inherently lazy, dirty or different from themselves in any racial sense. They had been made different artificially.

In addition, the idea that Catholics were hostile to them was far more significant than any folk belief about Catholics being less industrious, etc. Asked what they had been told about the other side as children, most people recalled stories of atrocities or killings. Catholics and Protestants were, first and foremost, people who fought each other. Thus, many people felt, you could not expect Protestant employers to trust RCs, with their history of treachery and sabotage, till Catholics proved their loyalty positively. (Just *how* they were supposed to do this was a more difficult question, as a minority of liberal Protestants were able to see!)[47]

Protestants in poorer areas of Belfast also expressed an exasperated gut feeling that if Catholics had a rough time, they must have asked for it, somehow. Protestants had a hard life too, but they didn't grumble, they 'went and looked for work'. If Catholics couldn't find work it must be because they didn't really want it. As this loyalist song expressed it:

And when their babies learn to talk
They shout 'discrimination'
Their dad just lies in bed all day
And lives upon the nation.[48]

All these arguments exempted the majority from blame, and put the onus for change on the minority.

So we can see that when the civil rights movement emerged, a few Protestants were prepared to make a leap of trust and accept that Protestants must change both their attitudes and their policies. A larger group felt Catholics could never be trusted, that their demands must be fought to the end. The rest were to varying degrees unwilling to accept that Protestants had any major responsibility for Catholic inequality, for past bitterness or future reconciliation. Civil rights offered them no proofs of Catholic loyalty, and challenged their definitions at every point by putting the blame squarely on the majority. The movement also said: 'You are not the sort of people you claim to be, fair and freedom loving: you are frauds or hypocrites.' People's definitions of themselves were fundamentally challenged.

In this situation people were likely to try and maintain their self image and integrity for as long as possible, and search all the harder for alternative explanations, especially as their own ideology did not give them the let-out of a proud admission: 'Yes, we discriminated and it was *right*'. Conspiracy theories gained wide circulation because they met the needs of many people at a particular time and reassured them that surely nice, contented Mrs Murphy down the road had nothing to do with this business:

'I've always thought there must be foreigners behind it all.'

'Things were going so well here that the Free State got worried support for the republicans would finally melt away. So they saw it as a last chance to stir up trouble and win the RCs back to the old cause.'

'The revolution is worldwide... Commies saying they were out for the people but really in it for themselves.' etc.

When political reforms did not bring peace but a devastating IRA campaign started after 1971, many Protestants felt their fears at this time had been vindicated, and that civil rights was indeed just an IRA front.[49]

Answering back: inadequacy and its results

Hostility to the civil rights movement was not just a consequence of people's (often confused or ambivalent) political beliefs. It was also linked to the way the campaign developed on a world stage.

Ulster gained world attention very rapidly and publicised incidents like the Burntollet ambush painted a very unflattering picture of Protestants. World ignorance of the situation increased the tendency of outsiders to see Protestants simplistically as 'baddies' and Catholics as 'goodies'. The idea that Catholics had contributed to the situation in any way was just not discussed at, for instance, the enthusiastic civil rights meetings held in British universities during 1969. It was assumed that Protestants had subjected Catholics to all sorts of oppression for no comprehensible reason.

These reactions could frustrate and anger even moderate Protestants, supporters of reform who found themselves tarred with the same brush as hardliners. People who travelled to Britain and abroad, or met visitors from outside Ulster, said they were told that RCs were completely disfranchised, that RCs were kept in concentration camps or starved; etc. They felt that no points they made were treated seriously.

The sense of grievance among poor Protestants was sharper still. A trade unionist from Woodvale, Belfast, recalled the situation. 'Most of our people wouldn't talk to journalists, they were so angry, but I tried. When I took them round the area their eyes would be popping... they seemed to think us Prods lived in castles and suchlike, like O'Neill. But most of them never got further than the Europa hotel, and all we would hear was how well off we were.' A group of Shankill housewives told me with great agitation: 'It was all the Catholics this, the Catholics that, living in poverty and us lording it over them. People looked around and said what, are they talking about us? With the damp running down the walls and the houses not fit to live in.'

This made many Protestants feel it was just not worth talking to the media, who must have a conspiracy against them. Their silence merely helped to ensure that reporting was indeed one sided; this further angered them, while incidents like the smashing of TV cameras painted them even blacker on a world stage.

Secondly, belief in a conspiracy by intellectuals and the media disadvantaged Protestant groups for many years, cutting them off from resources they could use for their own benefit (e.g. from civil liberty groups who could have advised prisoners' families, community groups etc). World reaction simply reduced further any willingness dispassionately to consider real Catholic grievances. It also produced a vicious circle. Protestants appeared just the aggressive, intolerant people they vehemently denied themselves to be. Finding themselves inarticulate was also painful and humiliating; this increased hostility towards those who had damaged their self esteem: 'We were the dummies, the eejits', said a UVF man bitterly.

Many Protestants also became openly discontented with the failure of traditional leaders to express their case. The politicians were short of practice: in contrast Catholics had long learned to use words, as well as guns, in their political struggle. As we have also discussed, the old Stormont did not tend to attract the most sophisticated and intellectual Unionist representatives. The O'Neillites were more so; but they no longer spoke for most working class Protestants.

Unionist ineptitude at this time galvanised some hardline and moderate Unionist party members into more active political involvement, and sharpened their discontent with existing structures. A minority of the less involved or experienced also gained a new determination to improve the situation by their own efforts. This clerical worker, then a Unionist, recalls: 'I first decided to go into politics when I saw a TV programme in 1969. A camera crew went up the Falls and talked to a man at a barricade ... he gave this great long speech and suddenly I realised from his accent "hang on, he's not local at all" ... we had no one like that, we just felt so helpless ... I went on a TV programme because that seemed a better way [than smashing TV cameras] but everyone thought I was a heroine.'

A group of housewives in this woman's house clearly regarded her public speaking with awe, and felt they would never have the courage or ability to do what she did. Like most other working class Protestants they lacked self-confidence and found any notion of independent political action novel. They expected traditional leaders to fight their corner and felt betrayed and bewildered when they did not. In this situation the appeal of someone like Paisley was likely to increase: he could appear as a saviour figure who would somehow put across the inexpressible feelings of whole populations.

It is often said that working class Protestants in Northern Ireland consider themselves superior to Catholics. But in many ways this prelude to civil conflict sharpened an already existing sense of inferiority. Even a community worker from Woodvale who was himself an articulate man could say with conviction; 'You know, I'm sure Catholics are schooled in the chapels in public speaking and that.' This group of UDA men from the same area put some fairly typical feelings; their conclusions suggest that any process of building up confident, independent political and social action in such areas would be slow and painful and always vulnerable to setbacks.

Officer 1: 'Once it was the RCs who were all in disorder, and us united. With the civil rights it was the other way round. They seemed to educate themselves and had good people to speak for them like Bernadette and we had nobody.'

Officer 2: 'Yes there was no one to give leadership or speak for the Protestant people. You expected them to... we were made to look stupid somehow.'

Officer 3: 'We should have been educating ourselves though, the ordinary people. Could you imagine someone like Paddy Devlin on our side? You could not.'

Officer 1: 'We left it too late. But people round here aren't used to speaking and that. That's why we need a strong leader, someone educated, that sort of person... like, say Bill Craig...'

Officer 3: 'No, he might make a strong leader, but he'd also make a good dictator, I'm afraid.'

Officer 1: 'But we've got nobody else to rely on, have we?'

PART TWO

COMMUNAL STREET VIOLENCE:
AUGUST 1969

Outbreaks of violence at marches and demonstrations became more common after the civil rights movement stepped up its campaign in 1968. The RUC's conduct in baton-charging the Derry march of October 1968 was seen on TV screens across the world: so was the loyalist 'Burntollet ambush' four months later. Such events not only set the Northern Ireland drama onto a world stage: they also revived or hardened political animosities among sections of both religious communities. But it was the August 1969 riots in Belfast and Londonderry which brought personal experience of physical violence to large numbers of people. In some areas, everyone suddenly became 'the involved', and had to cope with an insecurity that was emotional and political, as well as physical.

Paradoxically, the turmoil brought a certain kind of reassurance in traditional loyalist areas. The political world became familiar and comprehensible again after several years of uncertainty about what was happening to old divisions and old values. Falls was fighting Shankill; people were fleeing their homes; riotous crowds gathered in the streets. Old people re-lived the 1920s; young ones found that the stories told them by relatives had all come true. But the reassurance was a depressing and fatalistic one: that after all, nothing had changed nor could do. The world was still 'them against us'; old fears and suspicions were resurrected, and the tentative conciliatory steps made in recent years were suddenly nullified. As one very old Shankill woman, gazing from her front room into the street, eloquently expressed it: 'I seen it, before ever Ireland was divided, and in the twenties, and each time after that; and Ireland will never be at peace or us and them stop fighting, till the end of the world.'

So, for many people, traditional slogans and warnings struck a strong responsive chord, just because traditional events were repeating themselves. Hardline politicians had suddenly been proved right all along: their appeal widened dramatically, as this Donegall Road housewife, an O'Neill supporter, recalled. 'People round here were never that good at thinking about politics, we weren't brought up to it. Things were changing ... but when this trouble started, it was back to square one. It seemed to me people were looking for a way out from thinking. Paisley had been proved right all along and he was going to save them. They didn't want to think things through or look to the future at all ... if I dared to question him, my neighbours called me all the names in the book.'

So the disorders strengthened the position of some established hard-line politicians. But they also paved the way for new individuals, and new groups, to emerge through vigilantism, for instance, or emergency welfare work. Not everyone was happy about the growth of new power bases, and the tensions that resulted foreshadowed later and more serious conflicts about control. These were often linked to class differences.

Events also forced Protestants to confront some uncomfortable political issues. The conduct of the RUC and B Specials brought sharp criticism within and beyond Northern Ireland, which called for some response. How should law and order forces behave, and just whom did they represent? Loyalist violence—like the Burntollet ambush, or the burning of the Catholic Bombay Street, in Belfast—called in question the Protestant's image as law-abiding people. How did they square their self-perceptions with their actions? The intervention of Westminster and the mobilisation of British troops on the streets raised constitutional issues. Did the British have a right to intervene, or were they just meddling in Ulster's internal affairs? Whose side were the British on now, and what did this imply for the future of the Union? People may, as the housewife remarked, have been 'looking for a way out from thinking', but the new civil disturbances merely forced more and more awkward questions in front of their eyes.

6

The Impact on Organisations

The 1969 riots made an impact on traditional and established groups. They also acted as a catalyst for new groups. Civil disorders gave hardliners in Protestant political parties a stronger sense of purpose, and a feeling that their suspicions had been vindicated. Civil rights was a front and Unionist liberalism had been dangerous appeasement; now the enemy had emerged in its true colours to wage open rebellion against the regime. The issue seemed quite simple: the status quo ante must be restored by crushing the rebellion. The prophets who had been laughed at for warning of conspiracy must now have their solutions adopted quickly.

The Unionist Party did not break up at this stage because hardliners were optimistic that they could assert themselves from within, and turn the party on a strong course under the leadership of someone like William Craig. Activity did intensify, though, in Unionist party branches, especially where liberals had been influential. Internal struggles in branches that had traditionally been dormant gave both moderates and hardliners new experience of politicking and forced them to think about how the party was organised. The more articulate and ambitious learned political skills that some were later to take into new parties, like Vanguard or Alliance.

The intervention of Westminster also goaded a minority in the party into rethinking about the whole constitutional relationship between Westminster and Stormont. As we shall discuss later, they represented a strand of 'Ulster Sinn Feinism' within the party who began canvassing strongly for support among other members for their views on the meaning of the Union. Many were later to join the breakaway Ulster Vanguard.

Paisleyites (who did not believe Unionism could be reformed from within) felt that their views had been vindicated by the riots, and that they now deserved to be treated as respectable political activists. For both reasons, the waters of constitutional politics in which they had hesitantly dabbled looked more inviting now. In the 1969 Stormont election the Protestant Unionists fielded six candidates and five finished as runners-up, Paisley almost inflicting a humiliating defeat on Terence O'Neill in Bannside. The Protestant Unionists also stepped up their involvement in nascent community organisations, like the Shankill Redevelopment Association (SRA). As we have discussed, these groups were vulnerable to sectarian manipulation. This Protestant Unionist teacher, who was active in the SRA, had no doubt of the political implications of housing issues, nor of the wholesale nature of republican conspiracy. 'One of our planks was opposition to integrated housing. The RCs had been taking over new districts, like the bottom of the Shankill. What they do is, they get enough votes to elect a nationalist councillor, then eventually an MP... then gradually they will take over the whole of Northern Ireland.'

Paisleyites also continued to move in and out of the extra-legal, extra-constitutional orbit. Those of Paisley's supporters who were shop-keepers, teachers, small businessmen and so on were well known, often respected, in their areas. They were people others might turn to for help in times of crisis and disorder. But this help could involve more than the setting up of first aid posts. For instance, the teacher above became an 'officer' in John McKeague's Shankill Defence Association, a group which figured prominently in the riots and attacked Catholic homes in the area.[2]

Vigilantism has a long history in Belfast, and each generation has its memories of bad times when the clubs or hurley sticks were dusted and taken out of the cupboard. The vigilantism of summer and autumn 1969 was one of the foundation stones of the Ulster Defence Association, which became the largest paramilitary group in Northern Ireland. The activity accustomed large numbers of people to the business of street organising and local defence. But it also provided some future recruits for the UDA's vigilante work, assassinations, and welfare campaigning.

The 1969 vigilantes consisted, like so many groups, of several different kinds of people. They might be articuate, politically minded figures in the area; teenage youths with no thoughts of politics; or 'head cases' spoiling for a fight. For instance, three UDA interviewees had all been vigilantes in 1969. The experience sparked off their interest in playing an active role during the Troubles. One, who joined a killer squad, was spoken of with some fear in the UDA, and was seen as a man personally attracted to violence. Another had been a regular soldier as a teenager in the 1960s while a third, who became very active in community politics after 1972, was already seen as a community leader in 1969.

> I was always fascinated by psychology and saw myself as a bit of an amateur Freud. People often came and talked to me about their marriage problems and suchlike! I was also interested in community work, but it was an undeveloped thing with me then. When the violence began, people in my street approached me and asked me to organise local vigilantes. My interest in community work dropped into the background; there seemed more pressing things to attend to. I went through a phase of being a 'hard man'.

Vigilantes operated in the home environment but this period also saw a renewal of workplace organisation among loyalists. The key to the ability of loyalist workplace groups to attract members and carry out actions lies in Protestant dominance of the skilled manual sector in Ulster.[3] Only in Derry and in some small West Belfast factories have Catholics sometimes been able to mount collective political action (e.g. strikes against internment). In contrast the workforce at Harland and Wolff, Short and Harlands, Gallahers, Sirocco and so on is overwhelmingly Protestant (not forgetting, of course, Ulster's power stations!) Strikes by workers in these key areas have been able to undermine, even cripple, daily life in Northern Ireland.

Loyalist workplace groups are usually associated with anti-Catholic activity—people think of expulsions from the shipyards, or protests at the employment of Catholic workers. But though skilled Protestants were among those most likely to feel threatened by the dismantling of discriminatory practices, workplace movements have not been merely rearguard action groups of the labour aristocracy. Nor have they necessarily opposed, or usurped, traditional trade union activities (like wage bargaining). They have reflected general anxieties and beliefs of Protestant workers at times of political tension. On these occasions groups with support in the home environment have usually found parallels in the workplace, and there has been much overlapping membership.

They have often gained strength when grassroots trade unionists have felt particularly alienated from the political utterances of their own trade union leaders (especially on constitutional questions). These leaders have always been drawn disproportionately from socialist parties, including those (like the Communist Party) who supported

Irish unity. An uneasy coexistence was possible so long as constitutional issues were submerged. But in the late 1960s, most Ulster trade union leaders supported (enthusiastically or cautiously) the main goals of the civil rights movement, and some demanded positive intervention by Westminster. But many Protestant workers did not just see civil rights as a possible threat to their jobs: they also believed it was a front for republicanism, and aimed for Irish unity. Those who were NILP members often became increasingly alarmed at the recruitment of left wing Catholics. A group from this right wing of Labour politics was one element in the new Workers Committee for the Defence of the Constitution (WCDC formed in autumn 1969).

Another faction had rather different origins. They were trade union members of the Unionist Party who felt Unionism should pay more attention to working class grievances, and who were dissatisfied with the inertia and deference of the Unionist Labour Association.[4] They had formed a 'ginger group' called the Unionist Trade Union Alliance, to press Unionist leaders on issues like unemployment. They represented, as it were, the left wing of Unionist politics.

The first meeting of the WCDC included future stalwarts of the Loyalist Association of Workers like Hugh Petrie and Billy Hull, and drew mainly on shop stewards in large Belfast factories. But at this stage, their aims were not properly thought out: they only shared two general beliefs. First, that the Unionists were preparing to betray the Protestant population by failing to stand up to the 'republican' civil rights movement; secondly, that Unionism had done little to better the lot of loyalist workers. These two pre-occupations came through clearly in the WCDC's articulate and radical-sounding news-sheet, the *People's Press*, which ran for about a year. But despite the paper's independent tone, and a WCDC decision not to affiliate to any party, the Unionists still maintained links with the WCDC (possibly in an attempt to buy off elements whose political naivety was sometimes obvious). For instance a former Unionist MP was involved in the financing and production of the *People's Press*. The importance of this relatively ineffective group was that it sowed the idea of harnessing industrial muscle to a political movement, brought activists together, and provided future leaders for groups like Loyalist Association of Workers (LAW) (Billy Hull was elected chairman of the WCDC).

What effects did the riots have on community groups? The small number of activists who had begun co-operating with Catholics on issues like redevelopment found their achievements badly undermined.

Not only were their organisations infiltrated by those with sectarian intentions, but co-operation across the divide was abruptly halted. The Protestant public would no longer tolerate them mixing with the enemy. Some activists also felt somehow betrayed by their Catholic acquaintances. As one female trade unionist on the Shankill put it:

> The things we were fighting for weren't sectarian. We were just beginning to get people thinking—about the closure of public baths, the new high rise flats you wouldn't keep self-respecting rats in ... but the redevelopment association was taken over by people more interested in defence than houses, and there were different ideas about what defence meant! A lot of people were disgusted and dropped out of the organisation for several years. Also, to tell the truth I felt a bit bitter myself ... it was as if the people I'd worked with on the other side as friends had stabbed us in the back.

It also became harder to pursue community issues within the Protestant community, let alone across the divide. First, such topics had dropped dramatically on the public's scale of priorities. Those faced by physical danger look for defenders, not housing campaigners. Thus, for instance, John McKeague (despite local bad feeling at his being an outsider) rapidly managed to achieve a power base on the Shankill, because he seemed to meet the needs of a particular time.

Secondly, community issues became identified with republicans and 'commies'. It was groups like People's Democracy who now appeared on television talking about unemployment, bad housing and '50 years of Unionist misrule'. The people who were making these noises happened to be those whom working-class Protestants found it hardest of all to trust. Any Protestant who began talking in the same way was immediately suspect.

Despite these setbacks for fledgling community groups, the 1969 disorders did provide 'awakening experiences' for some people who later became active in community groups. This woman, who with her husband was a shopkeeper in West Belfast, was a member of St John's Ambulance Brigade in 1969, and was asked to help with emergency services in the area. 'This was a pretty shattering experience and opened my eyes for the first time to all the problems here, like the state of the houses and conditions for children. I realised people like us must do something for ourselves.' She also voiced the fears of people in the district who felt more and more anxious about local organisation passing into the hands of men with guns.

'You saw new faces emerging here very quickly when the trouble started ... people felt very uneasy, even strong loyalists felt unhappy about being under the control of people like this ... or working with them when you don't know where you stand and what you mustn't say. Better not to get mixed up with them but run something yourself, instead.'

Her anxieties were more than shared by one major traditional organisation—the Orange Order. For some of its members, the challenge to established authority by upstarts brought fears of social chaos. No activity alarmed them more than political violence by unauthorised guardians of 'law and order'.

7

Law, Order and Political Violence

Law and order was a key issue in the civil rights campaign and in the riots of August 1969. The Northern Ireland Civil Rights Association (NICRA) claimed bias and discrimination against Catholics in the Royal Ulster Constabulary and B Special force. NICRA marches also revealed that Protestant civilians and off-duty B Specials would take the law into their own hands and attack demonstrators. In August 1969, law and order broke down so far that Westminster felt bound to send its army on to the streets of Northern Ireland.

How did different groups of Protestants view law, order and political violence? Interview evidence suggests a complex picture. Many Protestants were ambivalent about the role of the security forces, but most felt it important to see themselves as law abiding, in contrast to the 'rebellious' Catholics. They found it hard to accept that they would initiate violence and only a minority would speak proudly of violent incidents. Most were disturbed and made strong efforts to rationalise these as defensive stands, or unfortunate lapses. Community myths were important in helping people repair their self-images. These were supposed facts that were seized upon by large numbers of people, and kept re-appearing in the loyalist street press.

First, what did Protestants think the role of their security forces should be? We can start by considering two extremes. A minority of liberal Unionists and Labour voters were deeply shaken by what they saw, on TV or during student demonstrations, of security force behaviour in 1968 and 1969. This experience galvanised them into thinking about what kind of regime they had been supporting as citizens, and impressed on them the need for reform. They had a notion of impartiality that was probably similar to the ideals many liberal Western Europeans hold about their security forces.

So a social worker who later joined the Alliance Party recalled: 'I'd always thought of the RUC as a bit like the British police I suppose. I was very shocked at RUC conduct in Derry... I didn't realise what sort of country we'd been living in... things had to be changed.'

Likewise an East Belfast teacher admitted: 'Well, you always thought it was IRA propaganda about the police being sectarian. But when I saw the way they behaved in the civil rights marches I was a bit shattered... the police have to be above politics, or there is no law and order.' People like this could not see any circumstances where those who were not in the security forces had the right to use force against their fellow citizens. Respectable, middle of the road Unionists like Mr M (page 68) shared many of these assumptions and rejected overtly political roles for the police. One difference was that they found it harder to believe that their security forces behaved unfairly and made stronger efforts to maintain their benign beliefs in the face of disquieting evidence. But in this, they were simply behaving like many conservative, middle class people in other countries who have a strong faith in the integrity and importance of 'authority'.

At the other extreme we can consider the public band tradition, which encouraged the belief that legitimate public order derived from the collective activity of Protestants in maintaining it. The UVF man (page 64) seemed to be proclaiming this view. Law and order was about keeping a close watch on Catholics, for the protection of Protestants. He did not understand why Unionist leaders sanctioned what he did as a B Special, and condemned his UVF activity. What gave his deeds legitimacy was not an official uniform, but his intentions as a loyal Protestant. What is surprising, perhaps, given this tradition and the boastful, aggressive nature of some loyalist songs, is that relatively few people felt comfortable expressing these views openly or without qualification. Most Protestants fell somewhere between the two extremes we described, and were sometimes visibly confused about the issues. On the one hand, they instinctively saw local security forces as 'theirs', and found it hard to imagine security forces who did not play a political role. Like most Ulster Catholics, they thought of the police and B Specials as people who not only arrested shoplifters or football hooligans, but also took action against political insurgents. So, unlike the shaken liberals, they saw nothing incongruous or unnatural in the spectacle of RUC men squaring up to civil rights marchers. So too, at a gut level, they felt threatened at any reforms which might weaken Protestant defences against potentially dangerous nationalists. On the other hand, they did not like to think their forces were sectarian or undisciplined, and they felt uncomfortable about law abiding people taking action without legal backing.

So an Orange master I was interviewing in East Belfast was most put out when his teenage son volunteered engagingly: 'Everyone knew the police and B Specials were for us. You know, the Protestants, against the Catholics; we were on the same side.' Respectable Orangemen and many grassroots Unionists had two ways of getting round the sectarian problem. First, they blamed Catholics for making the forces unrepresentative by refusing to join. Secondly, they claimed (and in fairness, this often seemed a genuine belief) that their security forces would be able to distinguish between 'good' and 'bad' Catholics. It was this ability which legitimised the security forces' political role. They would not, it was felt, harrass innocent Catholics, but only keep an eye on known troublemakers. To say 'the police/the B's were for us' implied that all Catholics were bad, and this seemed wrong. Some people were very upset and disturbed at public allegations: 'People felt the stories against the Bs were terribly untrue, the opposite from how it was. They did not terrorise the RCs but kept the peace for everyone and stopped the violence in this country' (group of housewives, Shankill).

'The B Specials' discipline was renowned. Going on the rampage was against their whole tradition. It was the IRA they were against, not the ordinary decent Catholic' (senior Orange official).

Both before and during the civil disorders, the great majority of Protestants—even members of 'extremist' groups—maintained a belief in the existence of 'good Catholics'. But many people were uncertain exactly which Catholics fitted into the categories of good and bad, especially at times of high tension. One way of reducing uncertainty was to say the security forces would know. Any evidence that shook this conviction was very disturbing, not just because it increased the uncertainty, but also because it challenged basic moral beliefs about how authority figures had behaved in their name over a long time.[5] It was more tempting to try and find ways of discrediting the evidence.

Cherished beliefs about the Protestants' role as fair, efficient and disciplined guardians of public order also affected the way respectable figures like Orange leaders viewed new leaders who emerged during the street disorders. These traditionalists accepted that the security forces took a political role by putting down rebel insurgents: most of them even felt that, if properly organised and disciplined, Protestant civilians should be allowed to assist the security forces on limited, 'home guard' duties, but only if traditional leaders, with values like their own, were in control! One senior official at Orange Order HQ voiced typical fears about the threat to Protestants' image and values.

> We could understand that because the Government were not taking action many people would be tempted to form vigilantes . . . but it worried us. The lawlessness could escalate . . . the criminal aspect greatly increased, especially with this change of values in Ulster now. We were a force for peace in those troubled times, touring the streets and keeping people calm, maintaining respect for law. The security forces had to take command in the province—not just to stop republican disorder, but to stop this slide into anarchy on the Protestant side.

Some of the Paisleyites were also starting to cast anxious eyes at rivals within their own community. But they often took a more liberal view than the Orangeman of the extent to which Protestants could help out uniformed forces. The teacher who joined McKeague's SDA combined a willingness to take part in physical force actions with a wish to refute charges of lawlessness or illegality. He denied that the SDA had launched a pogrom or deliberately intimidated Catholic families, explaining this as the work of freelance hooligan elements. Yet he also believed that 'the SDA could have finished this rebellion in a week if the army hadn't come in. Maybe 100 would have been killed, but there's 800 dead now.'

But this apparent willingness to break the law has to be seen in the context of how he and other Paisleyites anticipated political developments. They felt that had O'Neill been a 'true' Protestant, he would already have formed them into a legal militia. They expected that after a short and successful war, a Paisleyite government would retrospectively justify their actions and give them official sanction, so they would be law-abiding citizens in both name and spirit. People like this man—who were dissatisfied with the regime and wanted change, including limited social change—wanted to be prominent in the new order. They also wanted to control the security forces' 'helpers' during the emergency. So within groups like the SDA, power struggles were already starting between those we might call the old new leaders (like the teacher, below) and the new new leaders (like McKeague): 'It was vital the people be given proper leadership now. We spoke for the ordinary people in a way the Unionists never did. But there was a danger in hooligan elements getting in, and some of the types you get in the UDA now [1973], who have no respect for us either and are, in my opinion, dangerously left wing.'

This man's claim that the trouble could have been finished off in a few days was a popular view in loyalist areas throughout the civil conflict. It gives an image of a community ready and willing to justify widespread extra-legal violence—as sections of the Catholic community have been prepared to do in a different cause. But boasting is easy if your bluff has not been called. Did John McKeague speak for the majority of Protestants, even the loyalist wing, in the unashamed, almost gloating attitudes to violence expressed in his evidence to the Scarman inquiry? The kind of community myths that circulated about August 1969 suggested, instead, that most Protestants had considerable difficulty coming to terms with instances of their own extra-legal violence.

For instance there was a widespread belief, even among people who were remote from the violence, that the riots were part of a coordinated attack by Catholics on Protestants. This belief also helped people to justify strong-arm tactics by the police against the minority. The rioters were clearly 'bad Catholics', and so, it now seemed, had been the civil rights marchers. So there was no pre-emptive aggression, merely a desperate defensive action. Stories relating to weaponry suggested that the Catholics, far from being defenceless, were actually bristling with guns. Some people claimed to have seen them, other's related friends' accounts, which became more exaggerated in the telling. The saga of the broom handles, for example, had numerous variations. It was said that Catholic leaders, like Gerry Fitt, claimed their people had only broom handles for protection, but these were actually rifles. Some people, like this UDA man, had seen them 'and I know a rifle from a broom handle any day'. Others merely knew people who had seen them and had been assured that the offending handles were, indisputably, lethal weapons.

In the Shankill area there was another community myth that the Catholic Bombay Street had been burned down by its own inhabitants. Some people who were interviewed clearly found the whole subject upsetting: some had made themselves believe the myth, others knew it was untrue even while they were repeating it. So this Shankill Orangeman pleaded anxiously, several minutes after stating the myth: 'Anyway, there was none of them touched, no one was hurt, and when you think of what the IRA has done to Protestants since...'

Clashes between the British Army and Protestants (who were meant to support 'their' army) also clearly upset people in loyalist areas. Instead of justifying the violence people sought explanations which kept their self-image intact as loyal and law abiding people. The 'it was all a mistake' theory implied that neither soldiers nor respectable Protestants were to blame for these regrettable confrontations. Instead, the Labour government had given the army wrong, unjust instructions. So this shopkeeper explained: 'The poor soldiers didn't understand anything about Ulster... the politicians told them to go for the Protestant people and unfortunately some of the lads round here went too far in their protests.' An East Belfast housewife felt 'the Army had orders to hit the Prods hard. But these wee soldiers didn't know how things were. I don't blame them, but there again you get hotheads over-reacting, because people were so taken aback.'

Another explanation was that particular units of the army were biased and untypical. So a Welsh regiment on the Shankill in 1969 became the subject of another community myth. It was said to be notorious that they were all Catholics and taunted the locals at every opportunity. So this housewife, whose son had been charged with riotous behaviour against the army, could convince herself it was all the fault of particular soldiers, and nothing to do with Protestant disloyalty or lawlessness. 'We wanted to make them welcome. But these Welsh boys, I don't know what it was, they were determined to make the people upset. I heard them myself singing rebel songs and Mrs X's son was told down at Unity Flats to wait, for they were going to get Orange scum like him.' Community myths, which usually (though not always) contained a grain of truth, began as bits of inside information held by a few. They quickly became common knowledge because they confirmed what people feared or wanted to believe at a particular time, and helped them do a repair job on threatened self-images.

Violent as they were, the 1969 disorders did not basically change the views of most Protestants about physical force. The riots did not make them more willing to justify prolonged extra-legal violence, but nor did they make most Protestants confront contradictions in their behaviour and attitudes which seemed so glaring from a Catholic perspective. By and large, people patched up the uncomfortable cracks and hoped the world they knew would soon re-emerge after, at the most, some minor reforms in the system.

Widespread Protestant discomfort at extra-legal violence was unlikely to impress Catholics, or their supporters on a world stage. They felt that actions spoke louder than excuses or reservations. But it would be simplistic to see the reservations as insignificant. They suggested that despite the bravado of some loyalist songs and verses, despite even the history of the public band, any Protestant tradition that legitimised or glorified sub-state violence was weak in comparison to the Catholic tradition. This was especially true when it clashed with other traditional values, like respect for authority and the social order. Most people might swallow their misgivings for a while if, as in 1912, their very existence seemed threatened and their protest was sanctioned by those at the pinnacle of social and political life. But when the upper classes were divided, and when so-called hooligan elements wanted to lead the fight against the enemies of Protestantism, the majority of Protestants were much more reluctant to tolerate extra-legal violence. These reservations in 1969 hinted that if paramilitary groups developed in the future, they might face even more problems than the IRA in winning legitimacy, attracting support and maintaining any prolonged military role in Northern Ireland.

8

Loyalty and the Union

In 1969 (and, indeed, for some years afterwards)[6] it appeared that many mainland British people were not even aware that Northern Ireland was part of the United Kingdom. It is unlikely that any Ulster people shared their ignorance of this basic fact: it is more likely, however, that many Protestants at least no longer recalled the detail of a vital clause in the Government of Ireland Act, 1920. For the British government convention of non-intervention in Ulster's internal affairs had been so long established that, to modern generations, it appeared to be the natural order of things.

The clause read: 'Notwithstanding the establishment of the Parliament of Northern Ireland... the supreme authority of the Parliament of the United Kingdom shall remain unaffected and undiminished over all persons, matters and things [in Northern Ireland].'[7]

In August 1969, at the height of bloody civil disturbances in Belfast and Derry, the British Labour government finally acted on this clause. After prolonged and unsuccessful pressure from Westminster MPs like Gerry Fitt, it intervened in Ulster's internal affairs. First, troops were sent in to restore order on the streets. Then the British government committed itself to backing a series of reforms in the Downing Street Declaration, signed and agreed by Ulster's new premier, James Chichester-Clark. The first steps were taken towards depriving Ulster Protestants of their own private army: the B Specials were placed under British army control and phased away from riot areas. Unionist leaders' freedom of action over both politics and physical force was now curtailed by the mother of parliaments.

The storm of protest these moves provoked from many Unionist and loyalist politicians seemed to suggest that strong elements in the Ulster Protestant community did not accept the authority of Westminster—or were only loyal to the Crown so long as the Crown was loyal to Protestants. A leading Unionist politician, William Craig, had already voiced publicly an Ulster Sinn Féin position. Within O'Neill's Cabinet, he had suggested that Harold Wilson's threat to intervene should be met with a counter-threat of independence. In his famous 'Crossroads' speech in December 1968, O'Neill retaliated with some harsh views on Protestants like Craig. They were, he said, 'not loyalists but disloyalists: disloyal to Britain, disloyal to the Constitution, disloyal to the Crown, disloyal to . . . the solemn oath they have sworn to Her Majesty the Queen'. Next day, Craig told a Unionist meeting he would resist any British government efforts to use their reserve powers over Stormont, calling British moves 'blackmail'. He was immediately dismissed as Home Affairs Minister by O'Neill.

But despite the publicity and the protests, were the views of people like Craig typical of any substantial Protestant grouping at the time? Craig's views certainly struck a sympathetic chord among a number of activists in Unionist constituency parties. The people who came to his support were often educated, articulate and ambitious party members and officials, rather than the stereotyped backwoodsmen. They were people who had thought about what Ulster Unionism meant, who were able to express their position in words, and who had the confidence to contribute to a debate which had been made highly public by O'Neill and Craig. This debate, and the subsequent intervention of Westminster, galvanised them into attempts to organise, and win wider support for their views—which included the belief that Ulster Protestants were distinct, not just from Ulster Catholics, but also from mainland Britons. In contrast, O'Neill was telling his compatriots that they must be more like modern British people. Three Unionists who later joined Ulster Vanguard put their position:

'Unionism was always a form of Ulster nationalism. Protestants are a separate and independent community. There has been a wish to remain part of the wider unit, the UK, but also a wish for some self determination' (university lecturer).

'The need to reassess the link had been coming for a long time. The reality was that Britain had lost her sense of identification with the province and favoured an Irish republic. 1969 brought the issue to a head again. From then on Unionists had to be galvanised into thinking about a different relationship—a federation was my choice' (senior civil servant).

'I joined the party from a love of Ulster, its customs, character and heritage. Unionism to me always meant "Ulster first": this I felt was the true Unionism, in the tradition of Carson and Craig. Our leaders were weak, allowing Britain to interfere when it was clear they had lost any loyalty to Ulster . . . so I think for some of us the priority was to get Bill [Craig] at the head of the party and stand up to British attempts at appeasement' (party branch secretary and local councillor).

These people were speaking for one historic element in Ulster Unionism—people who believed the Union had always been a tactical device for protecting their own identity, rather than the symbol of a strong emotional bond. A strong Northern Ireland parliament was an essential expression of that Protestant identity. Indeed, however shaky was their reading of history or their studies of Carson, they virtually thought of Northern Ireland as an independent state. If they acknowledged loyalty it was as something reciprocal. To propose independence was not disloyal if Britain had already shown disloyalty to Ulster Protestants.

At this stage these people were only beginning to think seriously about the exact meaning of Ulster nationalism, or Ulster identity, and only starting to tax their minds about alternative constitutional arrangements. Their heyday was to come after Westminster imposed direct rule in 1972: but 1969 gave them the vital impetus for thinking, planning and organising.

However, the reactions of other Unionists and Protestants at this time were much less straightforward. Despite the impression often given by writers on Ulster politics, there is little evidence that even the extremists who clashed with British troops rejected British authority once the British failed to support their cause. Nor did most people find themselves any more prepared to contemplate changes in the relationship between Northern Ireland and Britain. Instead, they made every attempt to continue thinking of themselves as loyal. They also went on hoping that the uninterested, even hostile British people would understand and sympathise with their community. They did not, unlike some of Craig's coldly practical followers, decide the time had come to face facts and give up on the uncaring British.

It might seem surprising that most Paisleyites appeared to reject talk of rebellion or independence. After all, few people can have been more sharply aware than they of the unProtestant, secular, permissive aspects of modern British life. They had even more cause than Craig's followers to see a lack of identification between themselves and mainland Britons. But strong emotional currents also pulled against rebellion. Even though loyalty was conditional (on the monarch being Protestant) it was still a very strong strand in the fundamentalist tradition, hardened by repeated displays and demonstrations. So, too, was obedience to authority.

For most Paisleyites, Unionists and the uninvolved, the Westminster intervention resurrected a historic mistrust of Britain, but not thoughts of open disloyalty. They disputed the nature of British response, not their right to intervene. They also felt shocked and confused, and were absorbed in trying to make some sense of events, not in elaborating a new constitutional theory.

The notion that a simple republican rebellion was happening was strongest among Paisleyites, and among the politically unsophisticated. So they were most dismayed by deployment of troops against Protestants, and Westminster pressure for reforms. They were first and foremost bewildered that the British did not know who their real friends were; that the British could not see a plot against their way of life was in progress. People like this shipyard worker had also assumed the British would be grateful for his loyalty and help him out in troubled times. 'We were always very loyal and supported them through thick and thin, it was a way of life. We expected they would know what sort of people we were. We wanted no trouble with them, on the contrary. People found it hard to understand.'

So the natural tendency was to define events in a way that left intact existing beliefs about their own loyalty and British goodwill. It must be a mistake, or the British did not understand properly yet, or some definable villain in Government had led the British on the wrong course. We have already given examples of how people did this in relation to the presence of British troops. Another solution to the problem was to blame the Labour government. The Conservative Party, of real, ordinary British people, would behave differently or put things right. It was only a temporary lapse.

So a Unionist party agent expressed it: 'There was a tremendous suspicion here, you know, about the Labour Party (and the Liberals, from previous Troubles) and 1969 brought it all out again. There's this large element in the Labour party who want a united Ireland or want to appease their Irish voters, like Harold Wilson; and with the noise Jack Lynch[8] had been making, people thought it wasn't just going to be civil rights but a united Ireland shortly.'

People also frequently remarked that at the time they believed a Tory government would have understood, been more sympathetic, or restored order. Insofar as many Unionists trusted the Conservatives as friends, their sense of betrayal would be the greater if Conservatives took drastic action against their institutions—as Edward Heath did in imposing direct rule in 1972.

Another reason for hostile reaction and rebellious talk—at least among Unionist politicians and leading constituency activists—was simple pique. As we mentioned earlier, the intervention implied that Unionist politicians and party organisers were neither competent nor trustworthy to run their own province's affairs. This was a heavy blow, not just to people's egos, but to the way they regarded what might be a lifetime in the public service. Those who had worked for change, or even wished sincerely for reform without doing much about it, felt the British were branding them in just the same way as the ultra-loyalists. But it is simplistic to see their unsurprising indignation as some evidence that loyalty was a highly conditional thing throughout the Unionist party. The future political direction of these politicians (and some who made the loudest protests later became political moderates) it is more reliable guide, both to their genuine feelings about the British link, and to the limits Protestant politicians would set on identifying with rebellion when the political survival of themselves and their community was at stake.

So 1969 did not, by and large, goad Protestants into any serious rethinking about the future of the Union or the meaning of loyalty. Most people just did a repair job on their longstanding beliefs. But the very fact that they made such efforts to do this, that so few would contemplate open rebellion or sustain hostilities against Crown forces for any length of time, sounded a note of warning to the minority of Protestant rebels. There was little evidence of deep-rooted support for an anti-British stand, and the bases of support were not nearly as obvious as the 'Ulster Sinn Feiners' or foreign observers might assume. It was a topsy turvy world where respectable professional people dreamed in their drawing rooms of the new 1912; where the men they hoped would fight the battle, who might even have thrown stones at troops during the riots, sang maudlin songs about the Somme, Korea and British loyalty in their drinking clubs. Nobody could quite count on anyone else to lead Protestant rebels into battle against the Brits, as Ulster Vanguard were to find out three years later.

PART THREE

THE IMPACT OF DIRECT RULE

In this part of the book, the scene switches to what was probably the most turbulent time for Protestant politics in recent years: the aftermath of direct rule in March 1972. We look at some developments between that major constitutional move and another: the Northern Ireland Assembly elections of June 1973. With direct rule. Westminster suspended the fifty year old Stormont parliament and assumed full government powers in Ulster. In the Assembly elections, Northern Irish people were asked to vote on proposals that would bring Cabinet office to Catholic politicians, and establish formal links with another state, the Irish Republic.

This time saw the birth or the dramatic growth of several new groups. Ulster Vanguard was an attempt to re-create the anti-Home Rule alliance of politicians, physical force militants and industrial workers in a three-wing movement against various enemies of true loyalism (including the British!). The experience of Vanguard also led directly to the founding of a political party, the Vanguard Unionist Party, in March 1973. Secondly, a new paramilitary group, the Ulster Defence Association, became the largest and most influential Protestant organisation of its kind in Northern Ireland. Thirdly, many community action groups in loyalist areas of Belfast can trace their origins to 1972–3.

There were also plenty of dramatic political developments, like the massive Vanguard rallies, clashes between the British Army and Protestant militants, and the campaign of sectarian killings by assassination squads. In addition there was a change in the relationship between Protestant communities and their traditional leaders. Class tensions and disagreements grew, both within organised groups and among the wider populations, and were a major source of tension in the Vanguard umbrella. Paramilitants and community activists became far more prepared to carry out political or military action independently.

To recap on some developments between 1969 and 1972: in general, this time much increased polarisation between the religious communities. Catholics came to feel that all the paper reforms had brought little change in their conditions. Right wing Protestant pressure seemed to have brought down successive governments and installed a premier, Brian Faulkner, who was much distrusted by Catholics. The army that was first looked upon as their protectors had now come to appear, under a Conservative Westminster government, as the armed wing of the Stormont regime, searching their houses and lifting their menfolk. Internment and 'Bloody Sunday' were the most dramatic and alienating examples of the change. Catholic confidence in a just settlement was at a low ebb indeed in March 1972.

But many Protestants interpreted the situation very differently. They felt the Catholics had had every reform they wished, yet were still not satisfied. The Provisional IRA campaign confirmed fears that civil rights had been a mere front for a new onslaught against the regime. The withdrawal of the SDLP from Stormont and the united anger of Catholics against internment further alienated sections of the majority. It seemed harder to distinguish between rebels and 'ordinary decent Catholics' and confirmed in some the time-worn suspicion that every Catholic was a Fenian.

But Protestants were still able to feel they had made some gains. As conflict hardened between Catholics and the Army, Protestants could again take on the role of injured party rather than villian. The strong military policies pursued by Stormont and Westminster gave loyalists hope that governments were seeing the light, making them more prepared to sit back and wait for results, for the restoration of the status quo. This situation changed again after August 1971. Internment was the last card: yet it did not stop the violence, which escalated dramatically. Governments were unable, after all, to protect loyal citizens from violence and bombings. More drastic measures, like the involvement of civilians in the fight, now seemed both necessary and attractive to hardliners.

But the British were having other ideas. They increasingly doubted the value of propping up a regime that was producing anarchy and alienation, rather than order and reconciliation. 'Bloody Sunday' brought the situation to a head: some new alternative had to be tried. So it was almost inevitable that a turn-about in policy would bring them into headlong conflict with a number of loyalist groups in the Protestant population.

What state were loyalist groups in for the battles ahead? On the political front, Paisley and his party had been going through some strange gyrations after an impeccably hardline spell of pressure on the Unionist government. With his victory in a Westminster by-election in April 1970 which followed his election to Stormont Paisley had achieved success, not just as a street leader, but at every level of constitutional politics. He strongly pressured the Ulster premier, James Chichester-Clark, on security, demanding harsher measures against the IRA and the ending of republican no go areas. Though he had cut links with militants like John McKeague, he continued to demand that a loyalist people's militia or third force be set up, to fight the rebels with official blessing.

The first shock to his supporters came when he opposed internment in August 1971, along with his close adviser, the political maverick lawyer Desmond Boal, on the grounds that the government would intern as many Protestants as Catholics. After the massive disorders that followed internment, there was an attempt to form a Unionist Alliance between Unionist Party hardliners, leading Orangemen and supporters of Paisley. But it lasted barely a week, and instead in Sept, 1971, Paisley announced a change of name for his party, to the Democratic Unionist Party (DUP). The title emphasised its populist appeal, and Boal said the DUP would be 'to the left on social policies'. At Stormont the three DUP MPs took up the role of official opposition. For loyalists, it was bad enough that all this populism was attracting favourable comment from Southern press and politicians: but when the republican leader David O'Connell described republicans and DUP as 'allies in the cause of a new Ireland', they nearly had apoplexy.[1]

More shocks were to come when Paisley not only prophesied direct rule but said it should be welcomed, as it would cement the ties between Ulster and Britain.[2] When direct rule was imposed, the DUP was promoting a policy of direct integration with Britain.

Unionist hardliners had been aided in their quest for the soul of the party by the departure of many O'Neillite moderates. In April 1970 some (though by no means all) of these had joined with Catholic liberals, former NILP members and previously nonpolitical people to form the Alliance Party—a nonsectarian, mainly middle class grouping who took a pro-union position but strove to build a strong electoral middle ground.

But though there was now a stronger element in the Unionist Party who sought harsher measures against Catholic insurgents, even hardliners were by no means united in their attitudes to Britain. Many felt far more cautious about taking on the mother country than they did about backing drastic measures like internment. So, given that there was also an Ulster Sinn Féin lobby in the party who supported Craig, internal conflict was likely as soon as Faulkner faced any difficult decisions about his government's relationship with Westminster. Unlike Paisley, Craig had been maintaining an impeccably hardline stance. With four other Unionist MPs, he had resigned from the parliamentary party in 1970 over the government's handling of security: he led opposition to the Hunt Report and the disbanding of the B Special constabulary.

During the post-internment civil disorders there were growing rumours in Ulster that Westminster might suspend Stormont. The abortive Unionist alliance was an attempt to form a united hardline front that might either overthrow Faulkner, or force him into taking an uncompromising position with Westminster. Its failure hinted not only at continuing tensions among loyalist personalities, but more important at a basic unhappiness and reluctance among politicians and respectable Orangemen to dabble in such dangerously disloyal waters. By January 1972 Craig was convinced that direct rule was imminent. While he could count on some party members, he felt forced to look beyond parliamentary circles for a concerted opposition force to direct rule. He had already had discussions with the fledgling UDA and workers' groups, and in February 1972 he formally launched Ulster Vanguard.

He called it an umbrella movement for traditional loyalist groupings. It was backed by some Orange leaders, by many Unionist local branches, by the new Loyalist Association of Workers and the UDA, who announced a series of mass rallies. At the first one, Craig announced after inspecting the massed ranks: 'We are determined . . . to preserve our British traditions and way of life, and God help those who get in our way.'[3] It soon became clear that this threat was aimed against both the Catholic minority and the Westminster government. At a 60,000 strong rally on 18 March, he talked of 'liquidating the enemy' and threatened to form a provisional government if Westminster tried to impose a constitution against the wishes of the Ulster majority. It was in this climate of tension and threat that Edward Heath, the British prime minister, suspended Stormont a week later.

Craig's new movement was a direct challenge to the Unionist Party, as well as Westminster and the Ulster minority. It put a continuing dilemma before leading party members. Tolerate its extreme words and actions, and have the party branded as sectarian, violent and disloyal; expel Vanguard members from the party and split that party, causing an angry outcry among numerous grassroots members and activists, as well as pro-Vanguard politicians. There was another dilemma for party members: would Vanguard cause Britain to abandon the Protestants in disgust, or could it be used as a piece of bluff to make Westminster back down from its policies for Ulster?

Of the physical-force militants the Ulster Defence Association was the largest Protestant paramilitary organisation to arise in Northern Ireland after 1969. At its peak in 1972 it had about 25,000 dues-paying members. Several different pressures contributed to its formation and it met a number of needs: hence it was always likely to develop into a multifunctional group whose leaders would face problems in imposing internal discipline and a clear political line.

The main catalyst for its official launching in September 1971, as an amalgamation of Protestant vigilante groups in Belfast, was the post-internment violence. Amid large scale disorder, house burnings and population movement, ad hoc defence groups sprang up who sought some means of co-ordination. Though the situation was new, the UDA was taking on here a traditional role as area defenders.

Another traditional role was that of Protestantism on the march. The UDA enabled large groups of Protestants to express discontent at the political situation, and pressurise political leaders, through marches and demonstrations. Many Protestants felt an urgent need to do this because of the escalating campaign of bombings by the Provisional IRA, uncertainty about Ulster's constitutional future, persistent loyalist criticism about security policy and the existence of republican no-go areas. More generally, the UDA met emotional needs: many young working class men were impatient to play some role in the war, as their counterparts in the army and IRA were doing. They wanted a sense of participation, glamour and status. The new uniforms and masks restored pride and proclaimed to TV cameras 'anything our enemies can do, we can do too'. In Protestant areas, it was common to see small boys of 4 or 5 strutting proudly behind their elders, dressed in make-shift uniform.

But the new UDA also attracted people who wanted to do more than march about and demonstrate. It drew in those who believed in the old Protestant dictum that the best form of defence was attack: who wanted to take the war directly to the enemy with bombs and guns. At the time, there was dissatisfaction in many areas at the apparent quiescence of the UVF. This group was still recovering from the security force attentions of the late 1960s, and it was also showing, in loyalist eyes, alarming signs of going soft. Gusty Spence, its imprisoned leader, had been doing some rethinking in jail: his public statements increasingly spoke of developing the UVF as a left of centre working class group. He was also known to have had contacts with the Official IRA. So it was likely that a number of militants would soon seek to use the UDA as 'cover' for some kind of military campaign against Catholics.

Finally, the new UDA was a product of social, as well as political upheaval. So it was likely to develop social roles in local communities.

Leisure, welfare and housing services were destroyed or in a state of upheaval in some areas, and communities were being forced to rely more on themselves. Any powerful, organised group had the opportunity to step in and take over some activities, from the running of drinking clubs to the allocation of empty houses.

Because of its size and its grassroots base, the UDA was likely to reflect any confusion and ambivalence the Protestant working class felt towards military, class and constitutional issues of this time. In its structure and rank system the UDA borrowed from the British Army: it copied some of the uniform and the methods of both the Army and the IRA. While it was always strongest in the Belfast area, well-supported units developed in suburban housing estates and in parts of County Down. Smaller units in Derry and mid-Ulster had more autonomy from the centre and made greater use of cell structures. In country areas, as always, there was more blurring of lines among loyalist groups, and between these groups and security forces or reservists.

Meanwhile, Protestant workers had been turning their thoughts to workplace demonstrations as a means of showing disapproval of political events. In March 1971 Billy Hull (who had been elected chairman of the Workers' Committee for the Defence of the Constitution) led 8,000 shipyard workers in a march through Belfast to demand the internment of IRA men after three young Scots soldiers were killed in the city. Soon afterwards Ian Paisley held a commemoration service for the soldiers, to which loyalist workers marched from different parts of Belfast. Meanwhile another WCDC leader, Hugh Petrie, had been touring factories in the province and holding meetings to discuss the formation of a new workers' movement. At one such meeting in autumn 1971, a group of shop stewards from major factories decided to call this organisation the Loyalist Association of Workers (LAW). They first came to public attention when a sizeable contingent of the new group attended Craig's first Vanguard rallies shortly before Stormont was prorogued. There was a clear hint that some sort of organised industrial protest, like strikes, could and would now be used to oppose unacceptable British policies. But at this stage there was little thought within LAW about aims, structures or policies: it was swept along on an initial wave of enthusiasm.

Community groups

As we discussed, the 1969 disorders had been a big setback for Protestant community activists. The hostile climate continued while local people who were preoccupied with security, greatly distrusted civil rights talk about social conditions. Prospects for religious co-operation had their heaviest blow when internment was introduced: polarisation and segregation were almost complete, and the last remaining mixed working class communities (like Roden Street) were broken up. But at the same time new community needs were developing and old ones became more pressing. The disorders were disrupting social facilities; violence and vandalism by teenagers heightened the youth problem. Alarm and resentment about redevelopment and housing grew steadily in several areas of Belfast.

So the foundations were there: what was needed was a change in attitudes. People had to be willing to carry out the two key aspects of community action: self-help, and challenge to established authority. This part of the book examines how the needs and resentments built up, and how the trauma of direct rule freed people from the loyalty which had restricted community protest in loyalist areas.

The new anger (and enthusiasm) gave birth to several kinds of community activity after 1972. There were community groups which aimed to meet the needs of people in a geographical area (e.g. Glencairn Community Association). There were those which organised around issues (e.g. Sandy Row Development Association). In practice the distinctions tended to become blurred. There were the beginnings of umbrella groups which tried to embrace several organisations (like the Greater West Belfast Housing Association).

Many small scale self-help groups sprang up, like playgroups or pensioners' clubs. Paramilitary linked groups, like the Orange Cross, emerged to campaign for specific people like prisoners and their families. Then there was a burgeoning of advice agencies, which both provided a service and increased the know-how needed for independent self-help. A great variety of people were involved in these: for instance the Legal Advice Centre, Education Workshop and community bookshop on the Shankill used at different times people from statutory bodies, local residents, and outside volunteers (like law students).

— conclusion ?

9

Ethnic Identities: Britishness, Irishness and the Vanguard Challenge

The 1969 disorders brought Ulster Protestants and Catholics into direct conflict with each other. Despite the intervention of Westminster, most Protestants were chiefly concerned about the intentions, and the nature, of their Catholic compatriots. But when Edward Heath suspended their parliament on 24 March 1972, the emphasis shifted dramatically towards external relationships—with Britain and with their neighbours in the Irish Republic. British policies and plans for their future forced them to think seriously about their ethnic identity: What does it mean to be British, or Irish, or Ulster, and are the answers acceptable to us?

The suspension of Stormont was followed, that September, by a constitutional conference to which only the Official Unionists, NILP and Alliance Parties accepted invitations from the British Government. In a Green Paper the following month, Westminster suggested that any settlement should be acceptable to the Irish Republic, and should recognise Ulster's position within Ireland as a whole. The White Paper of March 1973 proposed a single chamber Assembly for Northern Ireland, elected by proportional representation, and an executive that must not draw support from one side of the community alone. All security powers would remain with Westminster. There would also be a Council of Ireland, involving politicians from both North and South.

So Protestants had to confront the unpalatable fact that their autonomy was to be much diluted and that they were expected to tolerate some involvement in their affairs by their traditional enemies in Dublin. They were to be at once a bit more British, and a bit more Irish.

How did different groups of loyalists react to these shocks and pressures? And what does this suggest about their feelings of national identity? Vanguard can be seen as the extreme of Protestant opposition to British policy at this time. The new umbrella movement made the strongest statements condemning direct rule, issued direct or veiled threats against Westminster, and was chiefly associated with alternative constitutional plans for Ulster (like independence, or a federated British Isles). Yet even this extreme seemed either unable or unwilling to take much action when its bluff was called. For instance, the promised provisional government, after suspension, turned into a two-day protest strike and rally. There was a pattern of bluffing and backtracking. Craig could take part in a rally one day where the effigy of William Whitelaw was burned, and another day urge his followers not to vent their anger against Crown forces. Likewise the UDA, supposedly Vanguard's paramilitary wing, would engage in furious battles with the army one day and declare themselves staunch supporters of the army the next.[4] Even the huge rallies had contradictory elements. They were a focus for anti-British resentment, but also provided a safety valve where this bitterness could be marched and shouted away.

One reason for the backtracking was that even Vanguard's political wing was not united about taking on the British or going independent; nor did they all have a clear picture of that Ulster identity that would underpin independence. While they all deeply resented direct rule, some members wanted to use Vanguard in a delicate game of bluff with Britain, to frighten her into giving them back a parliament. They did not visualise actually having to use violence or set up a breakaway government. Another reason for the backtracking was more practical: the hardliners could not persuade the other wings, or the Protestant population generally, into prolonged disloyalty. Some of their beliefs actually provoked internal conflict in Vanguard. For instance their very notion of an ideal Ulsterman was likely to make working class loyalists feel uneasy!

People in Vanguard's political wing were usually present or former members of the Unionist Party. They belonged to that strand of the party who saw Stormont as an essential expression of Ulster Protestant identity, as well as a bulwark against a republican threat. Edward Carson, even though Vanguard members invoked his name, did not see an Ulster parliament in this way: neither did Ian Paisley, who told Protestants that direct rule should be welcomed. It was rather the viewpoint of a modern generation who had been brought up under a regime they had come to view as a state, not a subordinate administration. It also appealed to those Protestants who felt most strongly the historical distinctiveness of Protestant Ulster from the Irish Republic and from modern Britain.

Vanguard pamphleteers argued that direct rule was unjustifiable because Westminster had ridden roughshod over a fundamental right the English had themselves established: freedom from arbitrary power.[5] They also claimed that Britain had forfeited the right to loyalty because Union was no longer the guardian of Ulster's British tradition—first because Westminster was now prepared to consider Irish unity: secondly, because she could no longer safeguard her subjects' physical security; thirdly, because she had lost her old values. 'Both in terms of permissiveness and attitudes to religion, urbanised society in Great Britain is far out of step with Ulster...'[6]

So, it seemed, plenty of moral reasons could be found for making the break. Resentment and a sense of betrayal encouraged people to stop suppressing their feelings of difference, to search harder for historical proofs of this difference, and to plan for a new future. In early 1973, for instance, historical roots formed a very popular discussion topic among activists up at Vanguard headquarters, and provoked animated debate and respectful attention. One enthusiastic branch secretary even claimed he had traced Protestant ancestry from some remote European tribe, who were renowned for their industrious temperament.

Activists were much more sure of their separateness from the British and the southern Irish than they were of their difference from their Catholic fellow citizens, though some had strong and colourful views on that subject. One clergyman said: 'There's a difference between Protestants and Catholics in terms of honesty, industry and thrift. For example, the docks in Londonderry went downhill after the RCs took control. But that might have been because they were trade unionists as well.'

Here are some examples of the thoughts one might hear bandied about among a group of Vanguard's political adherents.

'Ireland has never been one nation, I support the two-nations theory. Ulster Protestants are more hardworking and somehow more ... dignified' (businessman).

'What's needed is a return to basic Christian standards ... law and order, rooting out terrorism, the dignity of the family, more incentive to those who work' (senior Orangeman).

'The things that's happening in England have crept in over here. I think Cromwell had the right idea, a strong government. I'm against all this ... too much freedom of speech and welfare benefits. Government should be more puritannical ... a country that works hard is unbeatable. Look at the Israelis[7] now, and the Germans, we'd be like that.

Of course you'd have to have a dole but say it was only for 3 months and then the unemployed could be put to building roads . . . this would also bring down road taxes' (clerk, former factory worker).

Thus people often conceived of an Ulster that was not just Protestant but idealised Protestant. Indeed their views, or fantasies about Protestant characteristics were important elements in their willingness to go it alone through UDI if necessary:

'We'd have to tighten our belts initially but I think the loyalist worker would be prepared to make the sacrifice. The Protestant has dignity, and would rather eat grass than be humiliated' (businessman).

The problem about views like these, of course, was that such notions of ethnicity were liable to provoke distrust and conflict among the different wings of Vanguard. A certain unease tended to be felt among the workers who would be eating grass and mending the roads, and who had not been consulted about their glamorous future. Members of the political wing tended to think of themselves as the controlling force, the intelligent head on the brawny body, who would co-ordinate resistance as the new Carsons and Craigavons. By and large, they did not imagine themselves doing the fighting or the starving. It was the workers who would have to pay the price for being ideal Protestants. But while many workers undoubtedly clung to folk beliefs that they worked harder than Catholics (and indeed, harder than strike-prone British workers), this did not mean they were prepared to suffer for their virtue even more than they had done already!

Another problem about these images was that they were so exclusive. They did not just proclaim Ulster Protestant separateness from Britons and from Southern Irish people, but also from Ulster Catholics. But accommodation with the minority was one practical way in which Vanguard Unionists might have been able to achieve at least some of the goals dear to their hearts—like a strong local parliament and some independence from Britain. Any sort of negotiated independence or federation, for instance, that won a measure of Catholic trust would greatly reduce internal security problems, and might even persuade Britain to reach a financial accommodation.

The idea of Vanguard Unionists making a deal with Ulster Catholics—so long as no links with the South were involved—was not so outlandish as it might seem to many outside observers. In Belfast at least, most members who had been recruited from Unionist not Paisleyite ranks did not hold the strongly fundamentalist religious beliefs that were a permanent stumbling block to any identification with Catholics.

Many were visibly more hostile to the British than to their Catholic neighbours, who had taken second place in their outraged thoughts after Westminster suspended Stormont.

In February 1973 William Craig put some novel proposals to Vanguard's first anniversary rally. Claiming that the divisive factor in Ulster was 'not how you worship God, but different national loyalties' he asked: 'Could we not all owe allegiance to Ulster... a dominion of Ulster must not be... something for the Protestants as such to control... perhaps we should be considering checks and restraints.'[8] Such ideas, which resurfaced some years later among proponents of agreed independence, led to short-lived talks between Vanguard and the SDLP. *(SDLP's 'natural' solution is devolution.)*

A heated discussion in Vanguard headquarters soon afterwards revealed several different reactions. Some people were simply hostile to any deal with republicanism while others, like the clerk who wanted his freedom taken away, believed 'Mr Craig's got more in his head than I have, he must know what's right'. A third group felt quite hopeful and interested, as this teacher put it: 'Yes you could have a common loyalty to Ulster. The British link has always been an irritant to republicans and it would be gone, so the terrorist threat might be a small one after that.'

The problem was to decide just what did they share as a basis for this identity? Good will alone could not resolve this question. One side's victories were the other's defeats, and the idealised Protestant image they had themselves proclaimed was supposedly the antithesis of the Catholic character. As their pamphlets on a federated British Isles and other ideas showed,[9] Vanguard members were certainly more willing than other Protestants to contemplate new constitutional forms and relationships but none of the pamphlets really offered any basis for a shared Ulster identity. The only common thread was a strongly right wing outlook on social and economic matters, which was unlikely to appeal to the interests of disadvantaged people on either side of the divide.

The reactions of the other wings of Vanguard, and of DUP members, illuminate their own feelings of national identity. They also show how complex issues like this can be. For instance, people most antagonistic to co-operation with Catholics were not necessarily the most prepared to rebel against Britain when she seemed to be giving in to the 'Fenians' (or the Antichrist!) Again, people who took part in physical violence against Catholics were not necessarily the most prepared to fight the British.

There was an initial honeymoon period among the different wings of Vanguard. Each met the others' needs, long frustrated, and gave the other kudos. But the idea of partnership was still important to the UDA and LAW. Where other political parties had ignored or spurned the grassroots, Craig seemed to be saying Vanguard would back them to the hilt and give ordinary people a major role in the conflict. Vanguard also gave UDA and LAW leaders new importance: they were somebody for the first time, on television and in the papers, and they didn't want to lose their new influence. So the workers' wings were much more reluctant to accept the politicos as divine leaders. They would not necessarily accept orders or suggestions about how they should behave to the British or any other group. But this did not mean their own ideas were clearly thought out. The workers' wings often reflected the uncertainties of the Protestant working class at a time of great anxiety and confusion. This was especially true about their feelings of national identity.

There was least confusion about the Irish Republic. Like other loyalists, most people in the workers' wings saw that a society as alien and hostile. Few could think of anything they had in common with southerners, and were convinced these would only use any proposed Council of Ireland as a base for extending their political power over the North. A favourite slogan of the time, 'Six into twenty-six won't go', was very revealing of the general outlook among loyalists. Outsiders (including for this purpose southern Irish people) often assume Northern Protestants have such skills, experience and confidence that they would automatically exert a strong influence in any unitary state. Few Ulster Protestants seem to believe this: they cannot visualise unity that does not involve annexation or suppression, and seem to feel great foreboding about their own weakness and ineffectiveness. Six goes into twenty six: it does not make thirty-two.

So the power aspect was more important than supposed differences in cleanliness or work habits. A group of Woodvale Defence Association 'officers' who discussed the South believed the Church controlled most spheres of life and lived off the people 'with the priests running greyhounds and suchlike'. Far from seeing themselves as clerical-dominated or oppressive they believed they were fighting for freedom (a theme to which we shall return). Most important was their belief that the South was implacably anti-British and anti-Protestant. It insulted all the symbols they respected and the things which were familiar. 'What could we ever agree about?' asked one officer, with a hopeless shrug.

But they were much less clear about what they thought of the British. On the other hand, recent events had fuelled rebellious feelings. Many in the UDA and LAW suspected that suspension of Stormont was a prelude to splitting the link and pushing Ulster into an all-Ireland republic. Their belief that the army should not be neutral and had no place imprisoning Protestants, plus their frustration that at a time of unprecedented IRA militancy the army prevented them attacking republican no go areas, easily lit the fuse of confrontation.

On the other hand few seemed to have a sense of a distinct Ulster nationhood, nor had they spent much time thinking about the alternatives that so absorbed the political activists. The WDA group, for instance, seemed unfamiliar with Vanguard arguments about UDI, dominion status or a federal British Isles, and had not even heard of John Taylor's well-publicised scheme for negotiated independence. They felt they were no less British than Scots, Geordies or Yorkshiremen; many had served in the army; they were, they said, even more loyal than most Britons, because they accepted far lower wages than mainlanders!

The main impression gained from UDA/LAW activists at this time was that they felt puzzled and aggrieved that a country to whom they were loyal was behaving so inexplicably. The British would surely correct their errors when they saw the strength of loyalist resolution to stay within the UK... resolution shown through things like marches and rallies, which were somehow going to restore their parliament, though most people had not worked out how. As one UDA leader put it, they understood the marches and UDI threats would be 'a sort of shock thing' that would make the British give them back their parliament—'we didn't think what we would do if this failed'. Actually going to war with the British seemed emotionally impossible to most because it conflicted with persisting sentiments of loyalty and common identity. On a practical level it also seemed 'like suicide', especially to the many ex-servicemen in these wings. As one teenage UDA 'officer' in west Belfast put it: 'When we started mixing it with the army our ideas about them changed. They've made my life murder and I wouldn't have a good word to say about them now. But there's no way we could beat them in a fight. Besides, an all-out war seems daft to me, we're supposed to be fighting to stay British.'

Feeling as they did, the workers' wings could not do other than dabble in the waters of rebellion when something set their frustration alight, then retreat. Against the British, at least, the Vanguard politicos were bound to find the workers' organisations in Boulton's words, 'an impotent Gargantua'.

What about the DUP activists? They found themselves arguing positions like support for direct integration with Britain and opposition to Vanguard militancy that were unpopular among loyalists at the time. Indeed Paisley was visibly losing support at all levels among the uninvolved grassroots as well as among the politically active. In areas like Shankill, insulting graffiti were plastered over his name on gable walls. Local people began talking of Craig as the loyalist hero who had never changed and had always been right. Yet surprisingly, DUP activists showed a strong commitment to Paisley's policies at this time: even the less articulate would argue their case with conviction. One reason for this might be unquestioning loyalty to Paisley; he always attracted some followers who would probably support him if he suggested emigration to Mars. So one branch chairman in Belfast, who had been converted to religion by Paisley, explained: 'To tell the truth, there were an awful lot of discussions about direct integration in the branch. Some people were very unhappy about it. But most decided Dr Paisley must have looked into it before he said it and must know what's best for the country in the long run.'

But this is inadequate as a general explanation. Paisley's arguments had appeal for many Protestants because they were far-sighted and accurate. There were huge political and economic risks attached to UDI, and threats of this, or attacks on the army, did weaken British commitment to maintaining the Union. Paisley was saying things many Protestants would have liked to echo, had they not been unfashionable at the time. But his supporters could shelter from the blasts of criticism under his ample skirts, and appeal to his arguments for justification.

Thus, in a sense, Vanguard and the DUP played general political roles at this time. Vanguard expressed the anger, betrayal, frustration and confusion of Protestants against the British, with whom they had always had an uneasy and distrustful relationship. The DUP which had always been broadly integrationist with loyalty to the crown a central theme, expressed their reservations, especially Protestant disquiet about fighting the army or taking the law into their own hands. It also spoke for the extent to which they did feel British and could not find a separate identity. This quote, from a plumber who stood as a local election DUP candidate, also suggests how the demands made on idealised Protestants by Vanguard actually made many feel un-Protestant, like the rebels, in fact!

All right, we're not the same [as the British] but we're only as different as a Geordie is from a Londoner. We're still British. These Vanguard just seem anti-British ... the things they say are more like the republicans sometimes. Now British morals aren't what they were, but we should be setting an example to them. Also, I think Vanguard want us to start behaving like the RCs do ... rattling bin lids, going on rent and rates strike ... which is against our inclinations as Protestants.

Paisley's line also appealed to supporters who thought themselves educated, intelligent people, who planned ahead and saw a way out of relying on unruly, unpredictable animals (like the paramilitaries!) to achieve one's ends. So this young graduate member from North Belfast commented:

People think the DUP hasn't an idea in its head ... to me it's the only party that's thought things through at all. It's the English who are different from the rest of Britain through their own arrogance. I've been to Scotland and Wales and feel they're more like us. We are safer in the UK in the long run. They're planning assemblies for Scotland and Wales, so we could have the same thing. We can make power sharing unworkable in the Assembly and the British will have to back down—there's no need for violence.

10

The Sectarian Killings: A Religious War?

One way of exploring Protestant attitudes to Catholics during this period of constitutional and physical upheaval is to look at the campaign of sectarian killings. During 1972 and 1973, it is estimated that more than two hundred civilians were assassinated in Ulster, the majority victims of Protestant killer squads. Why did the killings happen, and what did they signify?

The most commonly-heard explanations have been simple and sweeping ones. They were the work of deranged psychopaths; they showed the depth of sectarian prejudice and anti-Catholicism among the Protestant working class as a whole;[10] they were an inevitable, understandable response by patriotic people to Government policies and plans, and to a devastating IRA campaign, which threatened the very future of the Protestant population in Ulster.[11]

But there are major problems about these theories. If all these psychopaths or virulent anti-Catholics existed, why did they not kill or torture at the same levels throughout the conflict? Why, for instance, would their retaliation practices decline so much in the late 1970s even after atrocities like the La Mon restaurant bombing in 1978, when 12 Protestants died in horrific circumstances? Alternatively, if they were all simply normal patriots, would they really torture some of their victims for hours on end or stab them over 100 times?

Again, if we affix characteristics to a certain group—if for instance the UVF were all psychopaths, sectarians or patriots—why did they behave differently at different times? Why does it appear they were only marginally involved in the campaign of 1972 and 1973, yet went on an orgy of killings in 1975? It is clear, then, that any explanation will be multi-faceted and linked to the influences of a particular time. It will have to account for political events in 1972 and 1973, including the words and actions of politicians; the state and development of para-

117

military groups; and the attitudes of the wider Protestant population to the killers. It will also have to deal with the problem that members of killer groups could be, and were, very different kinds of people.

The sadistic actions of some suggested deviant personalities with an abnormal hatred of Catholics or enjoyment in inflicting pain. These propensities were likely to be reflected in other areas of their lives, including work and personal relationships. Though recent research[12] confirms that most brutal or ritualistic killings were carried out by very small numbers of people. In Belfast, they were largely the work of two squads only, one in East and one in North Belfast. The terror and distaste they created was quite understandably widespread: but their numbers must be borne in mind when any generalisations are made about Protestant attitudes and behaviour.

But other evidence particularly from loyalist prisoners, who provide a captive sample shows that, like the IRA, most loyalist militants at this time were broadly representative of their age group and community. They were mainly young working class men between 17 and 22, who differed little from others in their area in terms of education, employment and police records.[13] For example, the trial of Ronald McCullough, William Smith and Thomas Reid for attempted murder in July 1973 gave one insight into the type of young men who were taking up the gun against Catholics. They all came from respectable working class homes, took GCEs at school and held skilled manual jobs. They had no criminal record, and they had mixed with Catholics before the Troubles.[14]

This gives us two important questions to answer when we consider the sectarian killings.

1. Abnormal, insane or psychopathic people exist in any community, but usually their behaviour is neither encouraged nor tolerated. What made politicians, paramilitary groups and Protestant communities prepared to allow, justify or ignore their particular talents for a certain time? Did their actions work to the advantage of certain interest groups?

2. What made normal members of certain Protestant communities prepared to kill Catholic civilians? And what made people in those communities willing to look the other way, shelter or even defend the militants?

We can first consider the impact of the political situation at this time. There were several components to this. The first was, ironically, not directly connected with Catholic actions, but involved fear and anger at what the British were doing. Most obviously, several constitutional landmarks caused more than resentment and frustration among many Protestants: they actually created fear that domination by their historic enemy and Irish unification would result. Thus the suspension of Stormont was followed by establishment of a power sharing executive and finally, at the end of 1973, by the Sunningdale talks on a Council of Ireland. But in between there were plenty of incidents that angered and alarmed whole sections of the Protestant community.

The secretary of state, William Whitelaw, continued his policy of releasing internees even while the no go areas existed and after the Provisional truce broke down: by October 1972 the Provos has killed 132 soldiers. It emerged that Whitelaw had talks with Provisional leaders during the July 1972 truce. Sporadic gunbattles and confrontations soured relations between the UDA and 'their' army: in September 1972 paratroopers killed civilians on the Shankill while in February 1973 the British actually interned 'loyal' subjects. *how many? 3 ?*

Yet as anger increased, it became ever more clear that no mass force would or could emerge to fight the British with guns or with civil disobedience. It also grew obvious that most Protestants were deeply unhappy at the prospect and withdrew support from anti-British militants. So the blasts of fury and alarm had nowhere to go ... except along a diversionary course. And as Desmond Boal of the DUP well perceived, this was likely to be towards their traditional enemy. After some militant speechmongering by William Craig in March 1972 he warned (as sectarian killers fired the first shots of their campaign): 'People who were fearful or frustrated ... if not given specific targets ... would find their own ... that would mean innocent Roman Catholics would suffer.'[15] The campaign revealed a perennial truth of Northern Irish life: when political alienation and frustration were high among Protestants, that whoever was responsible for their grievances, the first and the major victims would be Catholics.

IRA actions were in any case increasing bitterness against that historic enemy: more important, many Protestants were finding it harder than before to distinguish between the IRA and 'innocent Catholics'. The IRA bombing campaign was at its height: daily life in Belfast, with regular city centre bombings, often took place in an atmosphere of tension and fear. There were many harrowing civilian casualties which produced reactions of shock and disgust, leading some Protestants to feel the perpetrators were despicable, inhuman people who would only understand a taste of their own medicine.

Whether or not the gunman who traced his involvement in sectarian killings to the day he watched the Bloody Friday carnage in colour on television was being quite honest,[16] such events often proved the last straw for potential militants. More importantly, they could provoke normal people, rather than psychopaths or anti-Catholic fanatics, into thoughts of violence. Meanwhile the statements of some Catholic politicians increased Protestant animosity and fear and helped convince many that all Catholics were behind the IRA. For instance the statement of the SDLP's Austin Currie at an anti-internment rally of 2 January 1972 was well publicised: 'Within the next six or seven months, Faulkner and his rotten Unionist system will have been smashed ... we are winning.'

There was also a large pool of potential recruits for violent action. In 1972 both the army and the IRA were engaged in regular armed activity, yet Protestant youth had not found a role to play in the war: they had to watch while others performed the heroics that young men from areas of a martial tradition found appealing. Even when they joined the new UDA they often found they were simply playing soldiers, strutting through the streets, manning barricades or simply standing around. This also frustrated older members of the UDA, many of whom were ex-servicemen, and who wanted real action. So both the manpower and the impetus existed for large scale aggression.

Nor is it surprising that this took the form of one-for-one, random killings. The army literally stood in the way of invasions of Catholic areas. Security and restraints on movement made people who had strayed into the wrong places at the wrong time the most vulnerable targets. Even if some militants did distinguish between the IRA and innocent Catholics (as some court evidence suggests)[17] communal segregation had now so increased that accurate intelligence about the IRA was at best difficult for Protestant militants to obtain.

In fact, it appears there was no single attitude to their deeds and their victims among the assassins. Some, like Bernard Moane's killers, apparently thought he was definitely in the IRA. Some didn't make such distinctions; as one young Red Hand member wrote: 'At the time I thought more or less that all Taigs were bad and all Prods good.' Some felt that lack of retaliation against the IRA reflected on their own community, suggesting it was weak and without the will to survive. Insofar as members of sadistic killer squads have justified or explained themselves at all (or insofar as it is possible to understand them anyway) they have tended to say: 'We just couldn't go on taking this; it was a way of hitting back at them.'

But there is also evidence of tactical thinking in some of the killer squads. These people, one a Red Hand member and the other a high ranking UDA man, saw political logic in apparently random strikes against uninvolved civilians:

> In the 1972 troubles the Prods did get the story across to the other side that the IRA were not their protectors, but the men responsible for bringing the war to the RC community. I believe we succeeded in making the IRA turn its campaign away from bombing ordinary Prods... and in lessening support from their own people,.because of our retaliatory campaign.

> The RCs had to be shown that they would pay a price if the IRA went on like this. Doing nothing, tolerating the IRA, wasn't enough.

The possibility that the campaign might make ordinary Catholics feel even greater need of their armed defenders for protection was not considered by many Protestant militants I talked to. They also tended to believe Catholics in ghetto areas could reject the IRA quite easily if they really wanted to. A recurring theme (or naive hope) was that the Official IRA could get rid of the Provos if they were really sincere. Catholics also expressed the same opinion to me about ordinary Protestants rejecting the UDA and UVF: the complexities of relationship between militants and population were accepted in their own areas, but not in their opponents'. *N3*

What about the role of the wider Protestant population? Despite their secretive organisation, the killers still needed silence or tolerance from their own communities in order to continue operating. Conversations will have been overheard, cars will have been seen speeding back through Protestant areas, and families must have had their suspicions. One much-quoted letter to a UDA bulletin from a Protestant woman suggests that perhaps the loyalist population generally had their dislike and distrust of Catholics so inflamed by the IRA campaign and the political situation that they welcomed any sort of retaliation:

> 'I have reached the stage where I no longer have any compassion for any nationalist man, woman or child. After years of murder, destruction, intimidation... why have we [the Protestants] not started to hit back in the only way these nationalist bastards understand? That is ruthless, indiscriminate killing...'[18]

But this was not the impression given to anyone who worked in a loyalist area at the time. People reacted on several levels. In districts like Shankill and Sandy Row, they usually knew the people who were arrested on terrorist charges. Like the Ardoyne Catholics in Burton's book, they judged them on who they were, almost more than on what they had done. Thus while A might be 'no good, a drunken sot', X and Y had always been 'good boys', hard working and respected in the area, who were generally supported in their claim to be soldiers and prisoners of war.

This is not quite the same as saying that local people made excuses for or justified terrorism. Most felt you had to hit back at the IRA and wanted to believe their side would know who the IRA were. After killings of uninvolved civilians, community myths would often circulate which gave 'inside information' that the victim really was in the IRA. Many people, who felt the security forces were doing little or nothing, were not prepared to condemn illegal action against Catholic terrorists.

So they wished to believe the best about their own militants. The kind of people who were arrested, or whom they knew to be active, shaped their perceptions of the campaign, and their attitudes to it. They knew, saw and accepted—as counter-insurgency theorists, many politicians and outside observers did not—that many militants were not psychopaths or sectarian fanatics. If good boys (or their own boys) were involved, they must have behaved honourably in a just cause. Thus many people were not prepared to condemn or inform on them, even if militant groups also contained men they distrusted or disliked.

On the other hand, people would speak with distaste or condemnation about sadistic killings, sometimes openly, in conversations on the street, or privately in areas like Glencairn where hooded bodies were found with some frequency. But even in the areas where militants came from, many people simply would not believe Protestants had done the killings at all. Outside these areas, disbelief was still more common. Of course, parties to wars everywhere are reluctant to believe their own side's atrocities: what was striking was the length of time the belief persisted. It is interesting that while few paramilitants denied that the substance (if not the detail) of Dillon and Lehane's book was accurate, many Protestant civilians and politicians seemed unable to accept its conclusions several years later.

As in 1969 this was linked to Protestant self-images about their morality and respect for law. One prevalent theme in the loyalist street press of the time was Republican cowardice and brutality. They shot people in the back at night, blew up babies etc. It was not at all congenial to confront the fact that Protestant militants behaved as brutally as the IRA, and against innocent people.

Refusal to believe gave leeway to the killers: so did denial that innocent people, rather than the IRA, were being attacked. Ironically, these mechanisms were almost as effective as outright support for the killers in permitting the campaign to continue. Most of the Protestant population was not ghoulish or vindictive cheerleaders in the assassinations. But if there were lessons about their own community's behaviour to be learned from the campaign, they were largely unwilling or unable to confront them.

What about the role of the Protestant politicians? As simplistic generalisations have been made about the sectarian assassins, so black and white views have been expressed about loyalist politicians' role in the killings. On the one hand the theory that men of violence on both sides were generally to blame for the Ulster conflict plays down the contribution both politicians and population have made in allowing, or encouraging, particular events to happen. This notion (which leads to the view that if gunmen were removed or locked up violence would cease) has usually contained an unspoken class bias. The working classes, who carry the guns, are the most extreme and prejudiced; if the middle classes (including most politicians) had been in control of them (for instance in 1972 and 1973), they would never have tolerated such vicious acts.

On the other hand some observers, especially left wing groups, have tended to see Vanguard as a tightly knit, united right wing force whose political leaders approved, or even orchestrated, the sectarian killings. Some of William Craig's public statements seem to support this view: for instance his much-publicised quotes about 'liquidating the enemy' and being prepared to 'shoot and kill'.[19] In December 1972 he appeared to condone the murder campaign with the words: 'I am not happy about this sort of thing, but if it is impossible to win our democratic rights without these happening, then I am prepared to tolerate it.'[20]

But reality was more complex than either of these views suggest. The campaign was not the result of joint planning between politicians and gunmen. But politicians' statements did affect the killers' views, and members of the political wing often had a highly equivocal attitude to the killings. To some extent the campaign served their interests: in other ways, it damaged them.

Any researcher who talked to loyalist prisoners, their families and friends, certainly gained the impression that these people thought men like Craig were sanctioning militancy against Catholics. It was precisely this belief that made them feel so bitter and so betrayed when loyalist politicians declined to support the prisoners' cause, or even condemned them. One young loyalist prisoner expressed his feelings thus:

'If it had not been for some politicians and their speeches of fighting the IRA and Protestant backlashes, a good many men would not have ended in places like Long Kesh. I know when some young bloke from the Shankill listens to the rantings of celebrity loyalist politicians who are respected in the area, he feels "if they think it's all right to take up arms, it must be"' (personal communication).

Members of the political wing denied that they, or their leader, had sanctioned the killings. But their equivocations hinted at their dilemma. On the one hand Vanguard had been made to look a bit silly when all its anti-British threats came to nothing. It seemed the much-vaunted Protestant backlash was not even going to materialise against the traditional Catholic enemy. So any action that showed this backlash was not empty bluff boosted their credibility: 'See, we warned you what would happen if you didn't give us back our parliament.'

However, as some members admitted, the killings shocked some of their adherents (especially very religious people), lost them support and increased the image of Vanguard among Protestants as 'definitely not respectable ... a bit untouchable'. Those Unionists who would admit the campaign was going on tended to condemn it (as did the DUP, partly from genuine feeling and partly because they wanted another stick with which to beat Vanguard at the time). So anyone prepared to justify the campaign put themselves out on a limb with the law abiding.

Some members comforted themselves rather unhappily with the excuse that the law had already been set aside by the unconstitutional suspension of Stormont: British security forces had abandoned their responsibility to protect citizens so it was not surprising if some hotheads took the law into their own hands. With their own government restored, this sort of thing would never happen. But others were obviously prepared to tolerate the killings, both on grounds of morality and political expediency, so long as they could find phrases which enabled them to avoid admitting any direct contribution to the events. The quotes below from two senior Vanguard officers—one with impeccable religious credentials—are familiar to researchers who have talked about violence to middle class people who have never themselves lifted a gun.

'One must condemn these things of course. But one wouldn't like to say there weren't those who weren't satisfied, deep down, that the other side was learning the fear brought on by indiscriminate attack.'

'I'm not saying there weren't people in Vanguard prepared to accept the killings. I was appalled at the nastier murders, but that was the work of undesirable elements ... in their heart of hearts, many people felt Protestant action (or reaction) was, if not to be welcomed, at least not to be frowned upon.'

People like this were undoubtedly concerned that they were not in control of the killers. To some extent this was because they disliked some of the murders, but it was more to do with general anxiety and annoyance that groups of people were acting independently from themselves, instead of falling in behind their natural leaders. So, without further evidence, it would be rash to conclude that disciplined forces, led by educated people or politicians would have behaved less militantly towards Catholics. They might have used armoured vehicles rather than switch-knives or pitchforks, but the casualty rate could have been the same or even higher.

To be fair to the politicians, one should also point out that the campaign could probably have continued even if they had all condemned it. But the willingness of some to make excuses for it contributed to the general lack of urgency about stopping the killings, while violent public statements helped young militants lay any doubts aside. Ironically, this was not because the workers had lost respect for their 'betters', but because they still looked to them automatically for guidance and for moral justification.

Like the Vanguard politicians, UDA leaders found certain advantages in allowing the assassinations to go, even if some found the methods distasteful. At the least, this was an easier option than clamping down on the killers. Like Vanguard, they had lost face when all the marches and strong words led to little that an army could be proud of. The UDA leaders did claim credit for the ending of Republican no go areas in July '72 (though their actual role is less clearcut). But they could not bask in this for ever: many members of an organisation which boasted 50,000 supporters at the time (with an estimated 500 activists in Shankill/Woodvale/Springmartin alone) were champing at the bit for action. Mass invasions of Catholic areas were impossible, while bombings or openly-acknowledged killings invited proscription or strong army action (Catholic politicians constantly pressed for proscription). Allowing small groups to operate under other names (like the Ulster Freedom Fighters) took the heat off them, avoided conflict between UDA leaders and ultra-hardliners, and partially saved face by showing that the Protestant backlash was real.

In any case, it is doubtful if high-ranking UDA men could have stopped the killings, even were they determined to do so though, as Tommy Herron showed in early 1973, they could put on pressure to halt them for a few weeks when this seemed politically necessary. The internal feuding in the UDA at this time was symptomatic of an organisation which no one strong man had brought under control.[21] What some leaders and factions wished to do (e.g. racketeering) could not be stopped but only partially ordered and controlled, or given limited outlets.

The chaos and conflict in the UDA reflected not just the wider political upheaval among Protestants, but also the social upheaval. In some areas people were disoriented after flight from other districts and/or bombing and disruption of normal facilities. With new social problems, like homelessness, it was no cliche to say the normal fabric of society had broken down. In that situation not only did new groups (like the UDA) fill the vacuum, but more lawless, bullying or extreme elements often pushed their way into strong positions in the UDA in certain districts even if many did not survive in the long term. So even if less violent or sectarian UDA commanders existed, they had to face formidable opponents in any power struggle.

That this was more related to the times than to some naturally large percentage of virulent anti-Catholics is suggested by the fact that all kinds of nastiness were also unleashed by Protestants on Protestants during the same period (via, for instance, the UDA's notorious punishment centres, or 'romper rooms'). Disoriented and demoralised communities were ill-equipped to put restraints on the paramilitaries as they were able to do on the UVF in 1975 (see Chapter 14). People in loyalist areas would recall how the 'romperings', the fights, the hooded bodies in alleys made them feel paralysed, fearful and quite without power to control the situation. Even the sons they had cheered when they first strutted about in UDA uniforms often turned into confused spectators and increasingly reluctant members.

Again, disruption of normal law and order, plus souring of relations with army and police as conflict grew between loyalists and the state, gave violent men a simple, practical advantage: leeway for their actions. Such practical considerations, some commentators have suggested, gave sadistic killers the luxury of being able to torture their victims all night in lock-up garages, etc. After security forces stepped up their presence, and their searches (for instance, when the Military Police moved into East Belfast) such freedom of movement and action was much reduced.

The UDA then, did not provide a coherent and organised leadership of the campaign: nor did everyone who joined have the motivation and intention to kill Catholics. But the UDA did give useful cover (and guns, and assistance) to the minority who wanted to assassinate 'Fenians'. And leading figures who were not directly involved in the killings were either powerless to stop them, or they found it politically expedient to let them continue.

The UVF's position was slightly different, as we shall see in the detailed case study in Chapter 14. That the UVF was not involved in a concerted way in the killings was linked to the influence of 'doves' who were putting pressure on the leadership at this time. But even in the UVF the picture was confused. Groups like Red Hand Commandos and the Young Citizens Volunteers, who both had links with the UVF, were certainly involved in assassinations. So were individuals associated with the UVF, as the sensational revelations after the killing of Lennie Murphy in 1982 suggested.[22]

Such a complex, even messy, picture of how the killings happened, and what groups felt about them, is unsatisfactory to those who seek to see blame, responsibility or control located in a single group. But it more accurately reflects a time when political events, and the feelings of different sectors of the Protestant population, interacted to allow a unique unleashing of anti-Catholic violence during the modern Ulster conflict.

11

Class Identities: The Explosion of Resentment

One of the major and most visible effects of direct rule was that it stirred a new class consciousness, both among members of Protestant paramilitary and workers' groups, and among residents of loyalist working class areas. This caused new tensions between these groups and loyalist politicians which had particularly disruptive effects on the Vanguard umbrella.

Six months before direct rule, anyone who whispered certain phrases was liable to be branded socialistic or republican by their neighbours. After Stormont was suspended, the same phrases became clichés, and any UDA or LAW man who was worth his salt felt he had to sprinkle them liberally through his conversation. They included 'fifty years of misrule', 'fur coat brigade', 'we'll never be conned by the Unionists again', 'from now on working people will have a say' and 'they never did anything about our bad houses and unemployment'. This new bluntness went along with a willingness to take independent paramilitary and community action.

Why the change? It seemed direct rule acted as a kind of mental trigger. Unionist capitulation was the ultimate political betrayal: far from defeating the IRA and restoring the status quo, they had not even preserved the Protestants' own parliament. Unionist claims that they looked after Protestant interests were ultimately exploded and they had finally forfeited the right to loyalty and forbearance. It was now possible to confront the possibility that if Unionists had not looked after Protestants in one way, it had not looked after them in other ways either—so suppressed social and economic resentments were able to spill over. What the civil rights movement had tried and failed to bring home by cajoling was conveyed by a single traumatic event. People began to shift the blame for their social ills from traditional scapegoats (like the Catholics) to those who bore the main responsibility.

This new self-consciousness and awareness of longstanding grievance made working class political or paramilitary groups much more sensitive to high-handed treatment by politicians, or to any hint that they were intended for cannon fodder (or for road-mending squads!) This meant that a movement like the Vanguard alliance was doomed to experience edgy, tense relationships, with plenty of mutual mistrust. Middle class politicians and traditional leaders were also likely to feel threatened by the workers' new assertiveness.

Indeed, the feeling of threat was heightened just because Vanguard's political wing tended to attract middle class or lower middle class Unionists who were particularly suspicious of Protestant workers. So the people who had to make alliances with the UDA and LAW were often those who found this necessity the least congenial!

We have already seen that some Vanguard members held strongly right wing views on social and economic issues, and expected 'good' Protestant workers to accept economic hardship under any Vanguard controlled regime. This meant they also had strong views on 'bad' workers who went in for communism and confrontation and they tended to identify the new organisations with this kind of socialist menace. Observers who labelled the UDA and LAW as at worst, fascists or at best, no sort of socialists, often failed to appreciate just how seriously traditional groups took the workers' behaviour and their confused 'socialist' noises. These quotes illustrate the depth of suspicion that existed, and the genuine belief in intersectarian conspiracies:

'One of our problems is, how can we keep the masses away from Communism? In Sandy Row ... they're not talking like they used to, they're influenced by people who want disruption and uniting the working classes! Rumour has it LAW may be out-and-out Communists' (teacher, Vanguard organiser).

'Strange things were happening in 1972 and 1973. Some Orange halls were burned down for instance, and not by republicans—why? It was well known that there was collusion between elements on both sides and there were some people in LAW or the UDA whose policies were clearly communistic ...' (high-ranking Orangeman).

These political fears were often mingled with more general snobbery about characters who didn't speak the Queens English, who flagged them down and demanded identification on country roads, who kept marching up to their headquarters. For instance, when I visited Vanguard headquarters during 1973 there was visible distaste among the regulars for the LAW chairman Billy Hull, who was standing as an

Assembly candidate and who kept plying them with both his leaflets and his presence.

Even those who lacked prejudice or strongly right-wing views believed, as people from a political background, that their wing should be in the political driving seat. They felt frustrated that members of the other wings would not go through the proper channels but expected as of right Vanguard nominations for local elections or Assembly seats. So there were strong pressures to try and exclude the other wings from power and influence in the long term. The situation in Derry gave ominous hints of the dangers of a *laissez-faire* policy. Glen Barr, who said openly he was a socialist and who became a bugbear to many right wing traditionalists, controlled the Vanguard machine at this time and seemed to be directing it along more radical lines. He drew on the local LAW and on workers loyal to himself for support, rather than on Unionist party branches.

On social and economic issues, it was likely that Vanguard would either reflect its right wing strain or would say as little as possible on these issues for fear of antagonising any one element in its support. When Vanguard formed a political party in March 1973 it clearly had to hop about all over the place. Officially it had a pragmatic and un-doctrinaire approach to economics; but as Bill Craig himself admitted, there was a strongly anti-socialist attitude in the new party. Again, it originally called itself the Vanguard Unionist Progressive Party as an apparent sop to more radical members.

But the Progressive label was quietly dropped after a few months, and in neither the local nor the Assembly elections did the new party stress social or economic policies. Instead it concentrated on constitutional issues, calling for a 'democratic parliament according to British standards of democracy' (i.e. no PR or power sharing), preferably within a federal UK framework. The candidate selection process had caused acrimony among all the wings, but the workers had tended to lose out and become disillusioned with using the party as a vehicle for their interests. Hull's derisory vote also strengthened the hand of those who argued that the electorate would not vote for paramilitary-linked people. In general, a party was easier to control than a loose movement, and those with political experience and acumen could shape it according to their own wishes. Its formation also opened the way to links with other constitutional parties, at the cost of paramilitary links.

So Vanguard, despite its formal consultative processes, never really got off the ground as a structure that might unite people politically on class issues. As time went on that hope receded still further, some workers understood and accepted this more readily than others who went on alternately hoping for support from Vanguard politicians, and indulging in periodic outbursts of angry resentment at the politicos.

Mutual mistrust was fuelled by other factors. Growing numbers of Protestants were interned or imprisoned for political offences after 1972, while in areas like Shankill more and more people felt the impact of rough army searches and screenings. But most of Vanguard, along with DUP and Unionist politicians and Orange leaders, failed to support indignant local protest or show interest in the prisoners' fate. Finding themselves in an awkward situation, they either said as little as possible or backed the law and security forces. This caused great bitterness, as we see in this comment from a group of prisoners' wives and girlfriends.

'That Bill Craig and the rest of them said "You must fight and pick up the gun and liquidate the enemy." When our men did it, what happened? They're in jail and the politicians condemn them for it. Two-faced liars, that's what they are. Some people round here like to forget it—we never will.'

Class based conflicts of interest within Vanguard showed through in incidents like the two day strike against internment of Protestants in February 1973, organised by the UDA and LAW. They claimed that a joint Vanguard decision making group, the Ulster Loyalist Council, had called the action, and billed it as a Vanguard strike. Much violence accompanied the strike and it was widely condemned by the Protestant population. Vanguard politicians, who felt they had lost much public support, angrily denied that they had been consulted. The political wing's largely middle class membership were generally enthusiastic supporters of internment, and were in any case unlikely to suffer internment themselves. But feelings ran high in the UDA and LAW, whose own working class supporters were being 'lifted'.

But bitterness against politicians, and socialist sounding rhetoric, did not necessarily add up to a clear understanding of class issues, nor to well-thought out ideas for future policy. Least of all did it mean paramilitary and workers' groups were ready to take over the country in some kind of political coup, though right wing traditionalists, and some outside observers, seemed to believe this.

Consider for instance the views of this Woodvale Defence Association (WDA) officers' group. They trotted out the clichés, stressed the Labour tradition of Woodvale, and were most upset at accusations that the UDA were fascists. But several confessed they had little interest in politics; after all, that was why they had rejected politics for a para-military form of action. While they were uneasy about Bill Craig, who 'might make a good dictator', they still felt you needed educated men to run the country, not people like them. Though they insisted 'we'll have more voice in the next government, the working class people will have a say' they could not think how, when pressed for detail. They lacked a basic confidence in people like themselves as political leaders; nor could they see how Ulster's housing and employment problems could be solved except by 'RCs working for the country which they don't do now, because they want to bring it down'.

These men were sincere in their wish for change. But as Frank Burton's interviews with some of the young Provisional IRA volunteers also suggested, sincerity does not guarantee that people know where they are going, or what they are talking about!

It also becomes clearer why people of low confidence or political awareness sometimes behaved militantly at political meetings. Van-guard politicians were often irritated or unnerved when UDA or LAW delegates to joint meetings shouted them down, obliquely threatened violence or failed to go through normal procedures. This increased the fear of some that the hard men had the will and capacity to take over the country. But in fact their behaviour often reflected feelings of in-articulateness, inferiority or confusion. Their only status lay in their uniform, their only strength in the armed force behind them. As one former member of the UDA inner council recalled: 'You felt they looked on you as eejits and could make you look stupid with words. We stood for all the ordinary people, but they thought they could run over us. We had thousands behind us and told them so—one day they'll find out. The only time you could put one over on them and have a right laugh with them about wetting themselves was when you patted your jacket or put on the masks... .'

Two LAW officials (trade unionists) typified a more politically aware element than the WDA officers. They did not believe LAW should be-come a political party, but thought it could and should press Vanguard into passing policies beneficial to the Protestant working class. This faith sprang partly from their incomplete understanding of the interests different groups stood for. In their minds the fur coat brigade were those snooty Unionists who now backed Alliance or Brian Faulkner: these Vanguard people would surely be different?

They had some ideas about how working class people would gain a greater say in government, e.g. through better representation via PR elections in the Assembly and future parliaments. They also had some political ambition themselves. This opened them to disillusionment with Vanguard as time passed or, more often (given their limited class awareness) to being bought off with some minor office in Vanguard.

A factory shop steward and member of LAW's governing council described the confused situation all these uncertainties and half-baked ideas could produce in a single organisation.

> After direct rule LAW grew too quickly and it was hard for us to gauge feelings, and who we spoke for. Some [members] felt we should be a working class political party—the political wing of the UDA. But most weren't interested in politics and were disillusioned with politicians. Another lot said we should be talking about trade union issues; others that we should be backing up the UDA in an attack on the no go areas. There were even disagreements about whether we should work with RCs in the factories.

This reflected only some of LAW's problems. Like the UDA it had undertaken a mass recruitment drive with little thought about future aims or policy among either the leaders or the dues paying members. When the euphoria generated by the strikes and rallies died down, what were they to do? They put on an efficient front, printing for some months an articulate weekly newspaper, while officials claimed to hold weekly delegate meetings and to plan an annual conference. But under the surface there was confusion and conflict. Some members suspected the NILP background of the LAW leader, Billy Hull, while others resented what they felt to be his dictatorial, self-glorifying leadership. The lack of strong organisation and consensus about basic aims helped to create conditions for personal bickering and self-gain activities.

Thus for instance LAW fell into disrepute financially. Money collected from members was sent to a central fund which kept inadequate records and from which cash was siphoned off by individuals. This reduced credibility with other groups and with loyalist factory workers. The oneday strike against internment of loyalists in February 1973 and the public opprobrium this brought was the final blow. Hugh Petrie resigned and by mid-1973 LAW had virtually collapsed; while in the Assembly elections of June 1973, Billy Hull polled a derisory vote in his own West Belfast territory.

But Petrie, chairman of LAW's largest branch in Short and Harland, had learned lessons from the debacle. He remained convinced that the idea of using strikes against unacceptable political plans was viable if the organisation was right and could eliminate LAW's weaknesses. A tightly knit organisation of key workers whose withdrawal of labour would bring maximum disruption to the economy was his strategy. It should also be independent enough to take action with or without the blessing of politicians. He kept exploring the idea with selected individuals in key factories. In November 1973 Petrie and others held a meeting at Vanguard HQ, which was attended by men like Harry Murray and Bob Pagels. All were to play a major role in the Ulster Workers' Council (UWC) strike of May 1974. Murray was appointed chairman of the group, which called itself the Loyalist Workers and which met regularly thereafter.

During 1972 and 1973 a minority of working class activists merged, not just in LAW, but also in the UDA, UVF and in Vanguard's political wing, who had both political ambition and a growing understanding of class issues. For instance they could think through the implications of UDI for the working class, and reject it as a solution. They also understood that opponents of workers' interests could be found in loyalist parties too, not just among the traditional 'fur coat brigade'. The difference between them and other loyalists was that instead of complaining loudly against politicians and then hoping things would improve or deciding you still needed educated people to run the country, they became convinced by their disillusioning experiences of the need for independent political action, such as a separate workers' party. This UVF member, whose family traditionally voted Labour, explains how his hopes as a Vanguard member were dashed.

> [We hoped] Vanguard would be the nucleus for a new working class party. Glen Barr's branch in Derry was a very hopeful development and in East Belfast there were quite a few people who felt like me ... we thought the workers wings would gradually impose themselves [on Vanguard] but it didn't work out ... their members didn't have much of a political sense. Also it got clearer in the business over choosing candidates for the Assembly that the politicians were completely right wing, and trying to cut the workers out of all influence.

This man later helped to form the UVF's Volunteer Party (see next chapter), an unsuccessful attempt to form an independent political movement.

Apart from realisation that the Unionists had done little for Protestant workers' social conditions in the past, and that few present politicians saw these as a priority nor wished to bow to working class influence in future, there was a third factor causing disquiet among these people. They began to doubt some of the beliefs and myths that maintained rigid sectarian divisions. Experience forced them to ask: Suppose some of the things that Catholics say are true? And suppose we have some interests in common, where does that leave our political ideology? The people below describe their various awakening experiences.

'I was on the Shankill the night the Paras went mad[23] and couldn't believe what I saw. I thought: suppose they [Catholics] were right about Bloody Sunday? This put awful doubts in my mind... and everything I had believed in looked different then (engineer, LAW official).

'Being interned was a great shock to me, but a bigger shock was that Dr Paisley, who I'd worked so hard for, never visited me or lifted a finger to help. I couldn't trust him any more, and realised we were on our own... also, I met Catholics [internees] in there I believed were innocent... (UVF officer, DUP member with longstanding involvement in Paisley's movements).

'I started to think for the first time. The politicians didn't give a damn what was happening here, or when people were lifted... I saw the area differently too. We used to think we did better than the RCs. I realised the civil rights people had been right about us being conned for so long. That's how I got interested in the redevelopment and I believed from now on we'd have to do things for ourselves... I realised some of the Catholic councillors had things in common with us...'

This working class councillor, another longstanding associate of Paisley's, was now faced with the contradictions of staying in a traditional party, but especially in Paisley's. 'I never like being under a dictator going "yes sir, no sir", and now it seemed ridiculous: the whole party looked ridiculous to me.'

It seems incongruous that often those most amenable to radical shifts in thinking were formerly the strongest loyalists who had fallen foul of the security services and been 'lifted', interned or imprisoned. But it is not really so surprising, because such experiences were particularly likely to shock loyalist minds into a drastic re-appraisal of their beliefs. Army hostility, ill treatment by security forces and abrogations of civil liberties or 'normal' law merely confirmed the existing beliefs of Catholics who suffered these experiences. In contrast, they challenged basic loyalist notions—that the British would see them as allies, that loyal action against the rebels would be rewarded not punished, that their politicians would defend them, that internment was only used against the guilty, etc. etc.

For a minority of loyalist workers, then, direct rule and its aftermath brought an irrevocable split with traditional loyalism. But it did not bring a clear solution, nor was it obvious with whom they could form alliances, on either the Protestant or the Catholic side. It is all very well to realise that you share interests with Catholics on social issues and against emergency legislation, but when you also reject Irish unity and are faced with a continuing Provisional IRA campaign how do you reach out the hand, and to whom? It is fine to dream of an independent workers' party, yet the majority of members in the UDA and LAW, and the majority of the working class population, felt unwilling or unable to try putting one together, There was, of course, the NILP, but the Troubles had shrunk its size, strength and credibility to a new low, and it was regarded with great suspicion by most Protestant workers.

In the next few years, the influence of the 'radical' nucleus—who wanted change, disliked overt sectarianism and sought to involve Protestant workers in an independent movement was visible in community groups, in paramilitary organisations (especially the UVF leadership) and in loyalist workers groups (especially after the UWC strike). But they faced an uphill battle, constantly risking rejection by their own community and distrust from Catholics and liberals. They also tended to be further split by diversion in two directions. No workers' party existed that drew significant numbers from both religious communities. There seemed to be no one vehicle for furthering their new goals of fighting for working class interests, and working with the other side. Community action work could meet the two needs but if they wanted to move into political party campaigning, they would probably have to choose between one priority and the other. For instance the Alliance Party—strongly anti-sectarian but largely middle class in its social and economic interests, and distinctly unenthusiastic about the class struggle—never stopped trying to recruit in loyalist areas, and picked up a few well known loyalist workers over the years. Peace movements of various sorts, which again tend to put class struggle low on the agenda, have also diverted (or used to best effect, according to your viewpoint) Protestant trade unionists and other workers who have broken from traditional loyalism.

We have mentioned two activists who chose to sever themselves from Paisley in the aftermath of direct rule. Did the turmoil of this time further radicalise his party, which seemed to be turning in more populist directions during 1971, exciting reckless enthusiasm among some Republicans and nationalists? Despite the wishful thinking of some people, the answer would seem to be no. Rather, its coming of age as a constitutional party saw established social conservatism asserted over working class radicalism.

Desmond Boal was said to have pushed the party into giving higher priority to social issues. But a senior member of usually sound political judgment claimed realities had been ignored: 'The bulk of the party, especially in the country, remained quite unaffected by Boal's views. He took some in Belfast along with him. Most of it was so much rhetoric and those who pushed it had little power in the party, but it caused disproportionate excitement in the media and some Left organisations.'

Certainly, the party said little about social and economic issues at an official level. The post-White Paper strategy it agreed with other loyalist groups concentrated on security at the expense of these issues. The DUP even declined to stand in the May 1973 local elections, spurning grassroots topics altogether, till pressurised to do so by more populist members. Even then, candidates stressed security and opposition to the White Paper, not social or housing issues. The same was true when the DUP fought the Assembly elections in June under the banner of the Loyalist Coalition.

Why might even the 'Boalites' accept that constitutional issues had to be resolved before social issues could be raised, which was the argument they usually trotted out? Partly because, as we discussed earlier in the book, Paisley's movements attracted a number of people who came from a Labour or Independent Unionist background, but who had risen above their working class neighbours like shopkeepers, teachers, city councillors. They wanted some limited social change, but were nervous about the people below them too. Equally important, they wanted more political power and influence than they had under the old regime. If the old order was splitting up, they wanted to be running the new show not watching new faces take over as they did in such numbers after direct rule. While they were content that less affluent Protestants should get a fairer economic deal, they either had not worked out or were not prepared to accept socialism with atheistic or inter-sectarian overtones, and the growth of independent working class movements.

If they first increased their political power at top levels by helping to bring down the Assembly and being part of a future government, they could dictate both the pace and direction of social change.

'Boalism' also attracted less articulate or more confused people from a Labour background, like one skilled manual worker whose youthful experiences of harsh living conditions had turned him against Unionism. But he also believed Catholics were heavily to blame for the country's state: they didn't want to work, and their morals were lax; you needed a strong Protestant leader who, like Paisley, would 'never forget the poorer people and improve social conditions'.

He expressed one version of 'you need learned leaders, not people like us, to run things'. Like councillors and local party organisers etc. of this ilk he also had a stake in the party, which had put him forward successfully as a council candidate. He gained his rewards from staying in a party which, since the days of blackthorn sticks and counter demonstrations, had increasingly become an establishment, if an alternative one. Like the more articulate and ambitious, their circle of contacts tended more and more to be other activists in constitutional politics who, whatever their differences, shared an interest in maintaining the supremacy of conventional parties.

But the more it became an establishment, the less the DUP was likely to attract working class people affected by deep disillusionment with conventional politics and politicians, nor those for whom social, community and civil liberties issues had suddenly become disturbing and exciting. In the late 1960s Paisley's movements could mop up some of these disaffected people; now they were more likely to turn to alternative movements. In this sense the party had reached a kind of watershed. Its ability to absorb new working class leaders who were emerging, or win control of new movements, was cast into serious doubt. So, more fundamentally, was its ability even to understand the changes which political events of 1972–3 were bringing about in the thinking of Protestant working class communities.

On the other hand, despite the visible distrust between DUP and Vanguard members, the DUP's changing character made political alliances with other hardline Unionists more possible and more palatable. When Vanguard became an orthodox political party in March 1973 it rid itself of some features the DUP disliked like its belligerent anti-British warmongering and its formal links with paramilitants. There seemed clear tactical advantages in forming working coalitions that had a chance of overthrowing British plans by constitutional means, without the need for violence. People like the Woodvale teacher (who always went about in a fur coat) had no difficulty rationalising coalitions with such right wing elements. 'Ah you see, that's the clever thing. You can't have social reforms till the constitution's safe. So the sooner we achieve that by working with Vanguard in the assembly, the sooner we'll have the social reforms... I'm confident we'll get the better of the fur coat brigade, win control and force through more socialist-type policies.'

Whether or not social and economic differences between the DUP and Vanguard were really significant, there were genuine tensions between the parties. Differences of emphasis about religious or constitutional issues were sharpened by memories of past conflicts, and the DUP in particular jealously guarded its independence. They did not intend to be swallowed up in any coalition.

Nonetheless, the common interest that constitutional parties had in overthrowing the Assembly and the plans for a Council of Ireland pushed them towards more joint action, realising that unity is strength. In November 1973 delegates from the VUP, the DUP, the Orange Order and the anti-power sharing wing of Official Unionism met to form a new United Ulster Unionist Council. This would fight elections on a united anti-power sharing platform. The merits of a strategy that sought to defeat constitutional proposals by constitutional means was clearly shown when the UUUC won eleven out of twelve seats in the February 1974 Westminster election.

But these moves also sent clear messages to the Protestant workers to whom the events of 1972 and 1973 had brought new turmoil and discontent. Members of the coalition might (and did) squabble fiercely about power and influence in the future; but they squabbled about how the political cake was to be divided amongst themselves. And if they argued about social and economic policies for the province, these arguments reflected their own concerns and interests. As far as most of them were concerned, the recent social upheavals and conflicts either had not happened, or could not be acknowledged by any change in political and social structures, and social policies. Traditional politicians were again in the driving seat and they aimed to determine the future of all groups in the province, including Protestant workers.

But some of the people who had been sent back to the sidelines were not content to stay there and keep their mouths shut. In a few months, they were to assert the power of loyalist workers to effect political change in a dramatic and historic way: by a two-week general strike which toppled a government.

12

Community Identity: The Growth of the Community Action Movement

In September 1971, there were four known community groups[24] in the South Belfast area. A year later, there were six in Sandy Row alone. This dramatic growth was also visible in other Protestant working class areas of the city.

These groups did two things that were traditionally alien to Protestant workers. They made demands on politicians and civil servants to remedy housing, welfare and environmental grievances. They also took independent action to tackle the problems of their daily lives.[25]

In part, this activity was a response to new needs and problems caused by the Troubles. But it also reflected changes in attitudes towards powerful groups in society, and towards themselves. They were no longer prepared to tolerate grievances which they had reluctantly swallowed until their parliament was swept away.

A look at the growth in Protestant-based community groups cautions us against glib generalisations about its form and impact. People were not affected in a uniform way, except in terms of heightened self-esteem and confidence. Some people's involvement barely dented their political and social beliefs. Others found it shook them into re-thinking about all sorts of things: the class structure, traditional Protestant dogmas, Catholic grievances and civil liberties. Involvement had a snowball effect, it became a learning process which propelled them into thought and action on broader issues than narrow community ones.

Again, factions had no single role or impact. For instance paramilitary groups' involvement could vary among different areas of town. In some places their members played a positive, enthusiastic role while in others they had a sectarian or disruptive influence on community action. From 1972 onwards disagreements among community activists on the meaning of their work also became more visible. Conflicts between traditionalists and radicals reflected similar tensions in Catholic areas (and in Government circles!).

The foundations

Events between 1969 and 1972 sharpened some existing community grievances (e.g. on redevelopment). The Troubles caused disillusionment with politicians' caring record (e.g. if they failed to assist an area after a bombing) and forced communities to mobilise (e.g. to tackle homelessness or disruption of leisure facilities).

Concern about redevelopment plans grew steadily in areas most affected by the Belfast Urban Motorway scheme. The aims of planners and local people often seemed at odds on every point, as on the Shankill where most residents wanted rehabilitation, not redevelopment, houses not flats and shops along the road. In addition, problems and misery caused by redevelopment blight, repair, vesting and compensation were literally overwhelming many people as Ron Wiener describes in his admirably detailed book on the Shankill.[26]

Feeling was strong enough to produce organised protest even at times inauspicious to Protestant community action. The Sandy Row redevelopment association (founded in 1970) was one of the first Protestant-based groups to open an advice centre.[27] Pressure from the Shankill redevelopment association contributed to the abandonment (in 1971) of plans to build fifteen storey blocks in the area. On new estates people had to face not just rent rises, poor amenities, vandalism, and high transport costs but structural problems were becoming brutally obvious with time. In areas like Springmartin, dampness in the new houses caused growing anger and frustration.

Redevelopment also strained old class alliances, even among local people themselves. Wiener shows how small businessmen (well represented among councillors and the Unionist/Paisleyite party machines) began veering in all sorts of directions over the motorway plans. Some, for instance, decided to cut their losses and try to make it in the new shopping centre, which most locals did not want.

Even good old fashioned sectarianism could conflict with local wishes. The numbers game demanded that as many Protestant voters as possible be packed into high density housing on the new Shankill. The DUP activist (Page 82) put the point in an indirect way: local community activists, including people who thought themselves good loyalists, claimed DUP and Unionist councillors/activists argued this quite openly. This caused increasing friction, because the popular wish was for low density housing! Politicians' lack of reaction to the physical devastation of neighbourhoods could also shake traditional myths like 'the Unionist party looks after Protestants'. One group of Sandy

Row residents who were talking about redevelopment recalled: 'When we started to get bombs and riots and all, the MPs and councillors like X were usually nowhere to be seen and if you wrote, they still weren't interested. This caused a lot of bad feeling and, to be honest, a lot of people started thinking for the first time "just what have they ever done for us really?"'

At the least, Unionist governments were supposed to give loyalists physical protection. As the IRA bombing campaign got under way this claim looked increasingly shallow: even internment only escalated, rather than halted the violence; 174 people died in 1971, compared with 25 in 1970. The government seemed unable to fulfil even its primary function.

We have already touched on some of the reasons why festering grievances did not produce open or large scale protest. The whole language of community action was firmly identified with 'those civil rights agitators' as were the direct action methods people were later to use about housing or rents or development plans. The increase in violence only confirmed loyalist fears that these slogans and methods had been a mere front for republican plotting. Bitterness against intellectuals, academics, the press and others who might have helped people highlight grievances or battle with authority prevented them developing the contacts that other communities have found so valuable and necessary when they lacked power and know how.

The Community Relations Commission (CRC, established in 1969 as part of James Callaghan's reform package) was also viewed with hostility by most Protestant workers. Not only did they cut themselves off from its potentially radicalising influence and ideas, they saw it as an extra reason to suspect any sort of community action activity. The CRC's aims, progress, problems and eventual demise have been extensively discussed elsewhere.[28] The main point here is that a lot of the theoretical arguments surrounding the CRC were irrelevant to Protestant workers: they tended to see it simplistically as a sop to Catholics (it was derisively labelled the Catholic Rights Commission). This response was influenced by the fact that initially, both Ministry and Commission did put most of their resources into especially violent and deprived (i.e. Catholic) areas. One ex-CRC fieldworker recalled that poor Protestants angrily claimed the CRC 'only helped you if you were destroying, or demonstrating about something. People said violence pays. I suppose if we burn down the area we'll get a new community centre.'

The second thing they knew about was the ill-disguised opposition to internment of many CRC workers and their work in emergency centres (ably chronicled by Darby and Williamson)[29] during the post-internment upheavals. They tended to interpret this (as, indeed, did some Unionist politicians!) as a sign that the CRC did not merely hand out cash to Catholics: it even supported the rebels who wanted to bring down the state.

So the actual theory of the community development programme launched by Maurice Hayes in early 1971 was little known and less understood. The strategy of placing fieldworkers within communities to help people identify local needs, strengthen community organisation and tackle statutory bodies effectively was potentially as useful and as applicable to Protestant areas as to Catholic ones. Acceptance of 'parallel lines' programmes in Protestant and Catholic areas was not a sectarian strategy: the aim was to 'raise local communities to a level of self-confidence whereby they could deal with other communities without a feeling of insecurity'. The challenge to a consensus model of society—the acceptance of inevitable conflict between different social groups—was as applicable to Protestants as to Catholics. But at this time loyalists either had no chance to perceive these points, or they were unable to do so.

So there were many reasons why people kept a tight rein on their social discontents. But the biggest general constraint was simply the state of the political system. After giving way to the reformers' demands (so Protestants felt) it faced only an escalation of attacks; unsatisfactory though it was, there seemed no obvious alternative: any social protest, however small, might hasten the downfall of this tottering structure.

Internment and its aftermath (including wholesale population movement and increased bomb attacks) laid important foundations for the growth of Protestant community action. Not that it brought new sympathy for the things Catholics had been saying: on the contrary, it polarised Protestants and Catholics dramatically. But it literally forced people to confront welfare problems like overcrowding, squatting, destruction of social facilities and transport difficulties. (The black taxi services in both Falls and Shankill were a response to the destruction of buses and disruption of bus services.) Existing authorities could not cope adequately with the emergency: as Darby and Williamson show, their failings reflected both overwhelming problems (like having staff threatened or shot) and poor planning.

Chaos and sectarian conflict also heightened the youth problem. Gangs like the Tartans[30] made the headlines with violence, especially in borderline areas like Ormeau Road and the 'Village' in the Donegall Road area. This caused great public anxiety and several of the community groups that emerged in 1972 had their origins in voluntary groupings specially set up to tackle the problems of youth (mainly via provision of leisure activities, organised sports, etc.). All this adversity pushed and prodded people into doing something novel: making demands on the political system. A Glencairn community worker describes the process that made people question traditional assumptions.

Before the Troubles, the Protestant people took things like housing and social benefits for granted. They saw RCs as experts at milking the system and rather despised them for it. People here were mainly uprooted from New Barnsley; there's little sense of community, few people to turn to for help.

With the bombing campaign there were even more problems affecting families: unemployment, injuries, squatting etc. and a lack of facilities the RCs seemed to be getting, such as community centres. And people began to say—just how are the Catholics getting all these things? How do you go about getting something from the system? Bureaucracy and officialdom were unknown and rather feared, but people were beginning to realise they'd have to find out how by knocking on their doors.

So the CRC fieldworker recalled: 'You take X [a leading member of a community group]; a more forceful and articulate man you couldn't see now. But I remember him in late '71 when his group had just started, going along to the Housing Executive absolutely terrified, literally cap in hand, apologising and saying, "yes sir, no sir"'. So the months before direct rule had galvanised less advantaged Protestants into at least thinking about the twin aspects of community action: pressurising the system, and taking up self-help. They were also starting to look about for advice and skills.

We have discussed the mental upheavals direct rule brought: how the bitter sense of betrayal, the loss of a whole structure finally convinced people their leaders had forfeited their right to loyalty. It was possible to admit that if Unionists had not looked after Protestants in one way, they had not cared for them in all the other ways either.

Once they stopped believing they should be grateful when politicians chose to bestow favours, they started to demand that these be responsive to citizens' needs. Anger also gave them the courage to take independent action themselves. Generally, the whole aura and mystique around official figures had evaporated. Challenge to authority was also eased by the fact that Ulster was now governed from Westminster. Many of the figures people had to confront were seen as part of an alien administration to which they felt no ties, even of familiarity. They included non-elected bureaucrats, people with a faceless image and little knowledge of local issues. Suddenly community workers, even CRC officials, began to find a tentative welcome. The reports of CRC fieldworkers[31] show the range of activities they were involved in from teaching people how to use printing presses, to arranging conferences and helping to found new groups.

The internment of Protestants and the upsurge of loyalist prisoners from early 1972 drew a wide network of people into routine self help activity like running buses to prisons, arranging help for fatherless families, fund raising, selling prisoners' handicrafts etc. But it also forced people to ask: how do you find out your legal rights, protest at brutality, negotiate with police and prisons, prepare a legal case? For neither the politicians nor the rest of the Protestant population seemed either sympathetic or interested. There was nothing for it but to seek and take help where it could be found—like among the students, intellectuals and civil liberties groups they suspected so deeply. Mutual prejudices were inevitably eroded as, for instance, legal advice centres were set up on the Shankill and law students gave their time free to help local people.

This increased the general know-how of communities, but did not alter political perceptions in the majority. Most saw the new knowledge as a way of protecting their own against the system. They still thought a future loyalist government could take action against the 'rebels', but leave them alone. Only a few made the crucial realisation that any government can abrogate civil rights against guilty and innocent alike unless certain liberties are enshrined in law. They were shaken into changing their minds about Catholic propaganda and realising that the two religious groups might have important common interests. The UVF and LAW members (page 135) explained their own mental upheavals: the UVF's political party (see below) stated unqualified opposition to internment and the non-jury Diplock courts. The Ulster Citizens Civil Liberties Centre, founded by UDA-linked people, also spoke out on human rights issues and advised on rights at arrest, interrogation procedures, etc. So, even within supposedly sectarian and hardline paramilitary circles, there was now at least a platform for the civil liberties lobby in working class Protestant districts.

But the involvement of paramilitants in welfare created its own controversy and problems. They were drawn in part from necessity because, as above, they had to look after their prisoners and internees—or because they got involved in thorny issues like squatting and lacked the knowledge and skills to tackle them except by brute force, which lost them community support.

They also got involved for tactical reasons. The UDA, of course, expanded enormously during the political upheavals of 1972, but so did the UVF on a smaller scale. Once the heady days of marches and rallies were over, the UDA badly needed to find something for its marginal members to do. They also needed to prove they existed to help people, not to prey on them. For allegations of racketeering and extortion had grown steadily while brutality like 'rompering' further lost them community support. Yet they needed support and finance ever more as increasing numbers of their men were sent to jail. This cost a lot of money, especially for family support. 'Going into welfare' was a means of restoring the group's image and legitimising its activities.

The UVF's involvement was less noticeable because of their smaller numbers but they were still keen to promote a 'pro-people' image, for three reasons. Prisoners and their families needed cash too: the UVF-linked Orange Cross was active in promoting their cause, and selling newssheets and prisoners handicrafts. The 'brigade staff' at the time were anxious to make social and political action part of their ideology, and when Gusty Spence was on the run during 1972 he pressed (often reluctant) young recruits to help repair people's houses, as well as train for military action. The UVF were also engaged in a constant propaganda battle with the UDA. They continually claimed to be the 'clean' force whose conduct set them apart from the 'Wombles' (UDA) who preyed on the people, robbed shops, demanded extortion money, etc. So they were always anxious to show off examples of constructive community activity.

But it was the UDA action which attracted most community attention and debate. Some people consistently opposed any sort of dealings with this group. Such opponents became strange bedfellows. Traditional bodies like the Orange Order were already alarmed that their control of the social order was slipping and were very concerned about the rise in teenage violence, under-age drinking, Sunday drinking in clubs, etc. They blamed paramilitary groups particularly for encouraging these trends. But the sort of people who looked with distaste on the Orange Order also objected to dealing with gunmen whom they saw as lawless and sectarian.

For instance in East Belfast—partly in response to Tartan gang excesses and heightened sectarian conflict—respectable groups like the Boys Brigade and WRVS had already mobilised to form the East Belfast Youth Council. This developed into the East Belfast Community Council, which organised events like the Ballynafeigh festival. These were inter-sectarian events, and concentrated on sports and games, with involvement of authority figures like the police.

In conversation, leading members of these umbrella groups tended to speak strongly against contacts with paramilitaries, and sought to exclude them from receiving any official funds. (They also tended to oppose the CRC, seeing it as political, left wing and bent on bringing down authority structures!) But the views of most local people were less dogmatic, and they often judged paramilitary groups by their record in the area, and their leading personalities. Militants themselves also got different things out of community work, depending on their own outlook and on the local situation. We can compare several examples.

In one loyalist area of South Belfast the local UDA took over a disused hut and decided to turn it into a youth club. They sought support and cash from the CRC fieldworker. He decided to give them a chance against the advice of the locals, who told him the men involved were well known bullies and wasters. Within a few weeks the 'youth club' had been turned into a drinking den, and the fieldworker faced criticism and disapproval.

In Glencairn there was a lot of concern that control of community projects should not pass into militants' hands, as this community activist put it: 'OK, there were a lot of strong loyalists here but still, some RC was always being found tied up shot or stabbed in an alley round Glencairn. This put some people off—they felt there must be a few psychopaths around—and it's hard to accept someone helping OAPs one night and putting on their killer's hat the next. We didn't want them taking over our community centre, though they could use it as individuals.' The campaign for the community centre was started by a couple of trade unionists, who went round canvassing opinion in the estate then put pressure on the authorities to help them convert an old hut into a social centre.

In Woodvale, the militants were seen like the curate's egg—good in parts. The WDA claimed to be the first defence group in the UDA: it had a sense of pride and a wish to show it stood up for the local community. It attracted some trade unionists and shopkeepers who were already respected in this skilled working class area. Some members were feared and disliked by local people; some were obviously involved in the many sectarian killings which happened in the vicinity. As a traditionally well-supported group, it was generally more representative of local people than a lot of other UDA branches.

The WDA ran a local newssheet which tried to canvass offerings from the locals and highlight community problems (it also contained sectarian jokes). Their activities in a club converted from a disused hut showed a mixture of self-interest and community concern. In 1973 they were doing a good trade in drink, but also letting rooms out for bingo, etc.

Some individuals who were interested in community work before the Troubles began to emerge again after 1972. For instance 'Bill', the 'amateur Freud' from Woodvale (page 83) responded to the UDA's glaring lack of welfare skills by going to community work conferences, reading the literature, talking to professional community workers and other activists, etc. He became visibly absorbed in this new, intense interest. 'It changed my life. I began to see that basic ways of thinking in this country had to be changed: the authoritarianism and the militaristic mania, the fear of doing things for yourselves and the stereotyping of the other side.' Paramilitary groups to some extent reflected these ways of thinking. So inevitably this man began to question his own involvement in the UDA. As he became more active in community work he started gradually to distance himself from the UDA.

Paramilitants and others co-operated with least friction in areas where conditions minimised the contradiction between military and community principles. Taughmonagh was one example. A strong sense of communal solidarity existed in this isolated area of prefab housing, which was squeezed into a prosperous middle class district of south Belfast. There was longstanding discontent about housing, amenities and neglect by the authorities: the UDA was drawn from the community and shared their feelings.

The fact that there was no republican threat to the estate also meant UDA men were confronted early on with their lack of a role, with a need to justify their existence. Finally, the UDA unit just happened to contain a few leading figures with a conspicuous talent for community work. These joined the Action Group which set up the Taughmonagh

Community Association in 1972. The idea of using cheap aluminium bungalows as social centres originated here, and was adopted by other community groups.

Two things were noticeable to visitors: first, there seemed far less friction among different factions of the community than elsewhere; there was a general sense of pride in shared community achievements. Secondly, the supposedly rigid values of paramilitants or, indeed of loyalist communities generally had not proved barriers to developing new ideas and interests. The idea that the UDA should use physical punishment, or foot patrols, to fight the major problem of vandalism was abandoned as a poor long term answer and energies were put into sports and leisure activities.

Individual outlooks were changed too: one youth, for instance, had joined the UDA because he was '17, unemployed and bored'. He was ordered to do community work against his will 'but it was very exciting watching things develop and seeing what happened when you went to the Council and the civil servants. Well I started writing down the minutes of our community association meetings and everything that happened. Now I've got books of them ... you'd have to take a whole day off [to read them] and I'd have to make sure you got everything understood.' Fired with confidence and enthusiasm, this boy seemed to have made the work his whole life.

In an important (but perhaps unpopular) paper Hywel Griffiths drew up a list of supposedly contradictory values, one set held by para-military groups, the other by advocates of community development.[32] He went on to question the existence of many of those distinctions in practice. Experience on the ground and some of the examples here also suggest that relationships could be varied and complex. Community work talent could emerge from extremist groups. Also the gap in values between such groups and local communities was often much smaller than is assumed (especially by counter-insurgency theorists). For instance, local people may have been shocked by brutal methods of law enforcement like kneecappings or beatings, but many of them shared a strongly punitive approach to lawbreakers, including support for corporal punishment.

Authoritarian structures, use of the threat of force and a clear sectarian rationale did of course conflict with community action values. A few paramilitants were able to see this and began questioning their organisation. But in their confusion, their lack of knowledge, skills and understanding, most militants were not that different from the general population (who had, after all, given birth to the UDA and UVF).

There are several dangers in drawing conclusions about the impact of the new community groups on working class Protestants. The first is to compare them too glibly with other groups of people, without making allowances for their own history. This leads people to dismiss the new developments as insignificant or unimportant. 'They say: After all, residents of Liverpool or Glasgow have been running playschemes for years; Belfast Catholics have long been organising advice centres or campaigning against bad housing. So what if the Prods began doing this too?' It did not seem to make them any less sectarian, more socialist, etc. etc.

But this ignores the overall picture. The fact that Shankill residents were learning about the legal system and how to challenge it at a new legal advice centre, that the Hammer Redevelopment Association was learning about and challenging state structures in their protracted battle with the housing executive,[33] did not mean they hung out the red flag next week. But it was a huge change in their experience and attitudes in a way that it simply was not for a Falls Road resident, whose community had a long tradition of opposition to the state. The second danger lies in going to the other extreme and over-romanticising community action. Here Protestant playgroups or bus services to Long Kesh help 'prove' Protestant workers were developing class consciousness, and discovering socialism and nonsectarian co-operation! The third danger lies in forgetting to compare Protestant workers with other groups of people. This can also result in a distorted perspective, and unrealistic expectations of the community being studied.

In Ron Wiener's book on the Shankill, we see time and again how hard it was for local people to work out their long term interests in their battles with the authorities over the motorway and housing development. Their own traditions undoubtedly formed an extra barrier to understanding. Yet their confusion, their absorption in minutiae and their campaign failures are familiar to any student of public policy as are the machinations of authority. The same old story emerges in studies of planning battles from Glasgow to Bristol.

So if we are to criticise Shankill people for not spotting the class interests of supermarket owners or property developers or politicians, we must make the same criticism of people in Govan or London's East End. The same debates that began emerging in Belfast feature in many other countries: Is community action about making the state more acceptable to dissidents, or should it actively challenge the state?

Should you refuse to work with groups like the police or, on the other hand, with lawbreakers from the community? Have X and Y sold out by accepting employment or funds from a Government social work agency? and so on.

No researcher working in an area like Shankill or Sandy Row could have dismissed the new growth in community groups as insignificant. This was because they had such a visible impact on the whole way people involved thought of themselves. Also, it became increasingly clear that if people were changing their political and social ideas at all, they were doing so as a result of involvement in such apparently small scale activities. They were not doing so by way of political parties nor, in most cases, by firing guns or planting bombs.

Running small groups on their own, learning about state structures, battling with them, accepting outside help, provided a launching pad for thinking about bigger political issues. Without that experience, it seemed, few people found the impetus to re-assess their beliefs or even begin to understand conflicts of interest between social groups. But the reverse of the coin was not necessarily true: having the experience did not automatically produce wholesale changes in political outlook. It was the start of a process, not the end. How it developed would depend on the wider political situation and especially on whether future events sharpened or obscured clashes of interest among different Protestant social groups.

Sectarian divisions, in particular, had hardly been dented by the new growth in community action at least, not in terms of mutual contact. More Protestants might say 'the Catholics were right about housing' or 'maybe they told the truth about paratroopers' behaviour'. But actual co-operation or exchange of ideas between Catholics and Protestant community activists was probably below the pre-1969 level. The security situation made such things virtually impossible. Amid the fear and tension generated by mass population movement, the bombing campaign and the sectarian killings, only the brave or foolish would cross the line. Community workers and members of mixed football teams were among those who died in the attempt.

By late 1973, then, most people in Protestant areas barely understood the theory of community development, nor had they considered what relationship, if any, existed between community politics and national politics, community activists and politicians. Nor had they thought about the links between community consciousness and class consciousness. The implications of their new actions and attitudes were clear neither to themselves nor to the politicians. Most community workers saw their field of concern as local, not national or universal. Like the paramilitary groups, the politicians and the general public, they saw the Assembly and Executive as the arenas where political energies would be concentrated in the months ahead.

PART FOUR

AFTER THE UWC STRIKE

In May 1974, a motley collection of Protestant industrial workers and paramilitants succeeded in toppling the power sharing government of Northern Ireland. For the two weeks of the Ulster Workers Council strike, effective political power was in the hands, not of Westminster nor of elected Ulster politicians, but of factory workers and labourers.

The strike was an extraordinary event, and seemed a yet more extraordinary achievement. The roots of its organisation lay in the efforts of a small group of workers in key industries to forge, from the ruins of LAW, a Protestant industrial machine with the muscle to directly influence the course of Northern Ireland politics.

The strategy of Hugh Petrie (ex-chairman of LAW's largest branch in Short and Harland) and his co-planners was threefold. The new group would rely not on mass membership but on key workers whose withdrawal of labour would bring maximum disruption to economic life. It would be distinct from the UDA and UVF but work with their leaders to enlist paramilitary support (thus intimidation by the UDA and UVF of people going to work was crucial in ensuring withdrawal of labour in the first days of the strike). It would maintain enough independence from loyalist politicians to be able to take action with or without the politicians' blessing.

In November 1973 Petrie and his colleagues held a meeting at Vanguard HQ, attended by trade unionists like Harry Murray and Bob Pagels who were to play a major role in the strike. Murray was made chairman of the group, then called the Loyalist Workers, which met regularly thereafter. Meanwhile UDA chiefs had been quietly approached and convinced that industrial stoppages might be used effectively to cripple the power sharing Executive (which took office in January 1974).

The Sunningdale proposals of December 1973—for a Council of Ireland involving government ministers from Ulster and the Republic—finally convinced the embryo group that they should call a strike to topple British proposals. Despite their secrecy, they did not consider themselves undemocratic because UUUC candidates (who opposed power-sharing and a council of Ireland) won 11 out of 12 seats at the February 1974 Westminster election; and because they felt their central demand for fresh Assembly elections to be a democratic one.

Now calling themselves the Ulster Workers' Council, the group formed a co-ordinating committee headed by Glen Barr, a Derry trade unionist with UDA and Vanguard connections. The Committee included UDA and UVF members and co-opted Ian Paisley, Bill Craig and Harry West but only Craig maintained a regular presence. Meanwhile Billy Kelly toured the province organising shop stewards and drawing up plans for electricity power cuts. Apart from this there was no publicity nor attempts to enlist mass Protestant support.

On 23 March 1974, the UWC issued its first public statement, threatening widespread civil disobedience unless fresh Assembly elections were held to test Protestant support for the British proposals being complied with by the chief executive, Brian Faulkner. But loyalist politicians remained unhappy about backing plans for a strike which lacked public support or even public knowledge. The UWC was not even invited to the Portrush conference of right wing Unionist parties in April 1974, and decided the politicians would have to be presented with a *fait accompli*.

They therefore made it known that if a motion condemning power sharing and the Council of Ireland was defeated in the Assembly on 14 May 1974, they would call a general strike with full support from Protestant paramilitary groups. This they duly did and on the fourteenth day of the stoppage Faulkner resigned, after Westminster had consistently refused to talk to the UWC.

The attention of commentators has mainly centred on the strike's technical preparations, on its day to day course (chronicled in admirable detail by Robert Fisk)[1] and on the potential for further loyalist strikes. (Again, that discussion has been dominated by technical rather than political considerations: 'Could they get the power workers out again' or 'Could someone else take over essential services' rather than: 'Would there be sufficient support or tolerance in key groups and among the Protestant population'). Little attention has been paid to how the strike affected those directly or indirectly involved in it, to what people did, and felt, when the dust cleared and the two week upheaval was over.

This section looks at the way different groups of people answered the question: where do we go from here, and what significance did the strike have for us? They made a range of choices: some strikers, including active UWC members, simply went back to their jobs and families, seeing their role as finished. Some, including members of loyalist political parties, sought to minimise (or reverse) the change in social power which the strike demonstrated, by trying to re-assert the authority of traditional and elected leaders in the Protestant community. But some tried to build on that new workers' power to plan new structures that would give the working class or the community a greater and more lasting influence in Northern Ireland politics. Or they made a new commitment to nonsectarian politics: Harry Murray ended up in the Alliance Party. Some groups, like the UDA, reacted in a confused way: the input of radical or anti-sectarian thinking grew, but reactionary or sectarian policies continued in tandem. If the strike created big waves, the UDA ship veered about rather wildly on them.

As we shall see, those who struck out for new alternatives were by and large defeated or failed to produce realistic policies. They then had to make more choices—like battling on alone, giving up altogether or (most often) diverting into low-profile community or peace work or the 'agreed independence' movement, where they could pursue at least some of their ideals.

The very fact that people turned in so many directions reflected the complexity of motivations among people who supported the stoppage originally: a complexity not acknowledged by British ministers or SDLP figures when they called all the strikers fascists. But the UWC and their paramilitary allies contained hardline loyalists, more conciliatory and socially radical elements, and people who had just not thought what they wanted to put in place of the power sharing government. There were some who detested power sharing and others who would have tolerated this, but opposed the Council of Ireland.

The UWC had never really existed as a coherent organisation with a political programme: originally a tiny group of key workers, it became a mere label for all the groups who hastily responded to the daily demands of the strike. Dissension and fragmentation was always likely when the group had to take a positive decision on where to go next. The belief even among the leaders that the strike was unlikely to succeed (and the amazement of many when it did) had further militated against careful planning for the future. Given the whole loyalist tradition, it was not surprising that many people simply went home afterwards. Loyalists had been familiar with halting or destroying change, but not with building something new: the belief that ordinary people like themselves did not or could not take part in politics (except in crisis) was also pervasive, and would take more than two weeks to overturn.

Some other UWC members were close in their views to loyalist politicians, the Orange Order and conservative paramilitaries like Down Orange Welfare. They were also prepared to work with these groups. When the strike ended, such people benefited from the willingness of influential groups to strengthen their position in the UWC. Two of the most powerful UWC members, Jim Smyth and Billy Kelly, were already known to be Paisley sympathisers. The UWC 'rump' increasingly expressed hardline, Paisleyite views.[2]

Another group within the UWC was prepared to consider Catholic participation in government and also felt—however incoherently—that they should keep some independence from politicians and help ordinary people after their strike achievement. Some who had become public figures came into contact with new people and groups, and with former opponents, at conferences or seminars. When several began to express more conciliatory views as a result they were edged out by hardliners or resigned in protest at the treatment they received.[3]

Yet another group, including Glen Barr and some UVF men, saw class dimensions in the strike victory and thought it should be the basis for some independent new movement; they also took a radical view of civil liberties issues. Immediately after the strike, the UWC issued a statement condemning internment: it was virtually unnoticed, except by right-wing loyalists to whom it was another alarming sign of the radicals' influence. Over the next few months strong pressures (largely successful) were exerted to neutralise these people. Radicals from groups like the UVF who remained in such bodies as the Ulster Loyalist Central Co-ordinating Committee (ULCCC) found they no longer spoke for any substantial element in the paramilitary or workplace groups. The UWC co-ordinating committee, renamed the ULCCC, was set up after the strike as a liaison body between militants and politicians. But only Craig among the politicians showed much enthusiasm for attending; conservative paramilitants like the Ulster Special Constabulary Association gradually withdrew, and the ULCCC became an unrepresentative group centred round Barr and John McKeague (whose political views had changed considerably since his spell in Long Kesh).

The strike also put some new ideas into the heads of the largest group, the UDA, and made them more aware of the need for some political programme in future. But the old problems of inconsistency and contradictory pressures continued. On the military side, the UDA declared a ceasefire in July 1974, partly for tactical reasons (to try and obtain the release of their remaining internees, and greater remission for sentenced men). But clearly some squads were allowed to remain in operation—there were 216 deaths related to the Troubles in 1974 and 247 in 1975, with many sectarian killings by Protestants.[4] The UDA appeared to grow more sensitive to accusations of sectarianism and the Protestant public's increasing reluctance to condone assassinations.

Several killings where the UDA was suspected went unclaimed, while with others the UDA went to great lengths to insist victims were in the IRA.

In early 1975 the paramilitaries also tried to resurrect an Ulster Army Council to draw up plans for another strike or a doomsday situation. The fact that neither doomsday nor a suitable occasion for another strike were apparent caused the initiative to peter out, as did personal jealousies (like the withdrawal of the UVF under its new, unpredictable leadership).

But the prospect of the Convention and a still unknown solution still gave the militants a sense of relevance. If the result was a sell-out, military or industrial actions could still save Ulster from a fate worse than death. If it resulted in a widely acceptable settlement, or even something which most people grudgingly accepted, Protestant paramilitary and industrial groups could start losing, perhaps for ever, all but their most committed members.

Perhaps UDA leaders showed a premonition of this fate in their enthusiasm for the organisation's social retrenchment via the expansion of Ulster Community Action Group, their community wing, and through involvement in business enterprises. This might ensure that, as one commander put it: 'You see, whatever happens, we'll just go on and on.' Like others who feared redundancy or popular rejection, he worried as much about himself as he did about those who wore his colours.

On the political as well as the military side, the UDA spoke with several voices. At times it found the courage (or the wish for one upmanship) to suggest talks with the IRA or SDLP.[5] At other times it drew back under grassroots pressure, or angrily accused the UVF of Communistic tendencies. The UDA's resentment against politicians, its wish to assert its right to take political action, its awareness that it must have more than a military role—all these things encouraged it to explore new choices. Organisational pressures, fears of a sell-out after the Feakle negotiations,[6] the creaming off of politically more articulate people into other groupings, all ensured that reactionary stances would re-appear and counterbalance the dabblings in radical politics.

The idea of an independent Northern Ireland was one radical notion that took root in various quarters after the strike, and the UDA were one important group involved in publicising the idea. They later developed it more formally in various statements and pamphlets. As the literature shows,[7] this was a very different concept from UDI and aimed to be a compromise for both communities, with Catholics no longer having to bow to British rule and Protestants free of domination from the Southern bogeyman.

There was doubtful evidence of the widespread Ulster nationalism referred to by the British Minister Merlyn Rees in his explanations of the UWC strike; nor is it likely that grassroots UDA men shared much of the conciliatory thinking being developed by Glen Barr and others. But willingness to discuss agreed independence did reflect more acceptance in the mainstream UDA that some alternative to civil war or total Protestant dominance must be found, and that any settlement must make some concession to the aspirations and fears of the minority. But as mentioned later, the idea failed to find appeal in substantial sections of either community: it was one of those schemes that, in the optimistic days after the strike, threw very diverse people together in animated debate in smoke filled rooms... like quite a few of the hopes and dreams we discuss in this part of the book.

The first section looks at how loyalist politicians reacted to the strike, and at how by and large they succeeded in keeping new hopes and dreams firmly in the world of fantasy. An examination of some UVF dreamers who tried to move from the military to the political world takes a case study approach to how the events came about, and how internal and external pressures defeated the reformers. The final section looks at the ideas some community activists got into their heads after the strike. Following such dramatic events, even a Community Government seemed possible now... at least, if your spectacles were sufficiently rose-tinted.

13

The Loyalist Parties
Hit Back

After the UWC strike, loyalist political parties had to think seriously about two major issues. First, their position within the Protestant community: should they try to reassert their social and political dominance, or seek a new role based on acceptance of the alternative community leaderships who had run the strike? Secondly, they had to decide what stance to take towards Westminster's new plans for an elected constitutional convention.

Loyalist parties were bound to have mixed feelings about the strike. It had achieved their political aims, yet it was a usurpation of their power and an indictment of their own failure to achieve those aims constitutionally. The power of workers' groups came as a shock, and largely an unpleasant one. For several reasons, these parties were more likely to try and defeat the new forces and seek constitutional change by alliances with each other, than to bow to workers' power or seek success by making links with those who used extra-constitutional methods.

Despite the undignified antics of some DUP men in the Assembly chamber,[8] constitutional respectability had been growing more important for most members of loyalist parties. It became more so after hardliners, led by Harry West, took control of the Unionist Party and pro-power sharing elements left to join Brian Faulkner's Unionist Party of Northern Ireland (UPNI). As powerful long term alliances now looked possible, loyalist politicians knew they would not woo conservative, law abiding rural Unionists by flirting with wild men or workers' groups.

Besides, they had seen the benefits of constitutional alliances when the UUUC won 11 out of 12 Westminster seats at the February 1974 election. For the first time in years they could feel very confident about their support among Protestant electors: it was moderates who began

161

doubting their future. The politicians felt they had an overwhelming mandate as legitimate community leaders. Thus, on the one hand, the UWC strike jarred: it seemed to reverse the tide that had been flowing for them in their own community. On the other hand, their sense of strength gave them the incentive to recover lost ground, with few doubts about rallying public support in any power battle with the militants and industrial workers.

The role of UWC activists who saw class dimensions in the strike and wanted the UWC to be a power base for Protestant workers also rang many alarm bells among the politicians. Old fears about a communist menace were realised when people saw suspect figures like Glen Barr actually running a campaign, taking decisions and becoming a media guru. Would the strike lay foundations for social and political demands the politicians could not control, especially as the radicals were articulate people who would probably not be bought off by political patronage?

Bill Craig, and a minority in both Vanguard and the DUP, favoured a conciliatory approach and efforts to keep a foot in both camps. But a more representative reaction was put by one leading member of Vanguard who had helped out at strike headquarters during the stoppage. He was so upset and angry that the strikers had usurped his role that he shook and had to be calmed by cups of tea: 'Who do these boys think they are? We're the politicians, not them. They need us.' He also believed Communism was rife among the strikers and paramilitaries, whose heads had been filled with left wing notions by 'outside influences and intellectuals'. Other, more temperate members of political parties felt the workers' groups had no experience of politics and did not understand its rules and procedures: they and the politicians were just too far apart for any long term alliance to be workable.

The fightback materialised quickly. In their 12 of July speeches to huge audiences, several Orange leaders explicitly warned of the dangers of Communism among Protestants. There was also evidence of a co-ordinated campaign by traditionalists in some working class areas to scare the population off new leaders (see Chapter 14).

In the battle for supremacy the loyalist parties could generally count on the support, both of the Orange Order and of home guard paramilitary groups like Down Orange Welfare, who were socially conservative and rural-based. Another advantage they had over the workers is that they had clear short term goals and could see the benefits of unity. Had the strike ended the search for political solutions, lack of a visible role might have fragmented the politicians and made the public disillusioned with their effectiveness.[9] But the prompt publication of a White Paper[10] with proposals for a Convention gave them a clear public role and concentrated minds on the policy issues: in contrast, workers' groups were uncertain or divided about their future political role, and even about what might signal an appropriate occasion for another strike. The politicians had also developed a UUUC committee for candidate selection, which reduced internal squabbling and enabled them to exclude undesirables (like gunmen or socialists!)

All these factors, along with their opponents' weaknesses, tended to reassert conventional parties' grip on the political world after their May 1974 setback. But politicians did not withdraw all contact with paramilitants and workers—rather, contact was limited and specific, more likely to be private soundings out than public agreements. Apart from a few VUP members, Unionist and loyalist politicians reduced or ended their representation on joint paramilitary–political committees (like the ULCCC). While Paisley's supporters appeared to gain control of the UWC rump, the UWC's general influence sank rapidly after the strike. This connection had more relevance for the abortive strike against direct rule, where Paisley joined forces with the UDA in May 1977.

The conventional loyalist parties also tended to move further away from the community groups, whose language and aims were growing less comfortable and comprehensible. We already saw how parties like the DUP lost members who found a new commitment to community action after the original upheavals of direct rule. As the DUP continued its move away from a populist role, the party's central and local representatives put more emphasis on national goals, or on the application of Protestant religious principles to social life. These could actually bring them into conflict with local community groups (e.g. when they tried to close leisure facilities on Sundays).

The British government's decision to hand back some community development functions to local councils after the Community Relations Commission was abolished had another effect: it put loyalist councillors and community groups in opposing camps. Councillors had to deal directly with the demands of such groups and face blasts of criticism about the failure of public representatives: this tended to increase mutual hostility and suspicion.

In discussing loyalist parties' reaction to the new grassroots power it is worth remembering the extent to which their feelings were shared by parties outside the loyalist spectrum. While there was no open alliance of political parties generally to 'do down' those groups who asserted themselves during the strike (or found new confidence, like community groups), the shared interests and fears of very diverse politicians certainly created a hostile climate for the intruders.

All political parties tended to see a threat in community groups and their more militant activists, fearing these undermined their own authority in the constituencies. The speech Ivan Cooper of the SDLP made to the Assembly when he abolished the Community Relations Commission made clear this resentment.[11] More obviously, the SDLP continued to share loyalist parties' hostility to paramilitants within their own religious community, with whom they vied directly for public support.

There were similar attitudes to the UWC strikers across the political parties—class hostility, forebodings about Communist revolution, and fears of a paramilitary takeover. An Alliance Party organiser recalled: 'The strike wasn't just a blow to everything we believed in and fought for. For a lot of people it was the last straw because they had to take orders from yobboes in the middle of the street. Some of the types I know thought there was a red revolution coming. Talk of a middle class exodus isn't fantasy—I know quite a few people who are packing their bags and quitting Northern Ireland.'

In the run up to the Convention, politicians from all parties would warn that the Convention was a last chance, that failure could open the door to a paramilitary *coup d'etat*. The Press often echoed these beliefs; they were all looking over their shoulders at the same spectre. Thus no political party at the time was able to provide an outlet for the new aspirations of some Protestant workers—nor did most of them wish to. Loyalist parties, in particular, did not seek to understand the new forces and demands which the strike symbolised and strengthened. Rather, they hoped the status quo could be restored without changes in their structures or policies.

They were largely successful in their efforts to neutralise political challenges from paramilitary, industrial or community groups. But their failure to come to terms with new aspirations and needs narrowed the area in which they were seen as useful or competent by at least the working class public. If the parties came to lose a significant political role in Northern Ireland's affairs for any length of time their relevance would be questioned still further, while what remained of their traditional prestige and status would be at risk of slipping away.

In contrast to the faction fighting that followed the imposition of direct rule in 1972, there was considerable co-operation and broad policy agreement among loyalist parties and the West-controlled Unionist Party in the period up to the Convention elections of May 1975. This was not just because they had a common interest in resisting intruders from the fringes, and felt they had a popular mandate for doing so. As politicians who naturally wanted office but who had been out in the cold since 1972, they also had a vested interest in the return of a majority rule provincial government that would guarantee them a job! They could see the merits in making a united push for that, even if it meant sacrificing some policies with which they had been identified.

The VUP, for instance, had realised that wild options like UDI had alienated Protestant public opinion and some loyalist groups: opinion poll support for it was consistently shown to be minimal.[12] The DUP realised the UWC strike had further reduced the credibility of direct integration, for it had angered and exasperated the British with Ulster Protestants. There were rumours of plans for British withdrawal rather than of a desire for closeness with people Harold Wilson had called spongers.

Optimism that the British might accept plans for a majority rule administration had several causes. Politicians hoped to play on British weariness with Ulster following the strike and the Convention was, after all, supposed to be about Ulster people choosing their own future. Plans for assemblies in Scotland and Wales could be used as another pressure point. British fears of a second strike might frighten them off saying no to loyalist plans even if these failed to include Westminster stipulations, like the need for consent by both religious groups.

There was also a feeling that there was all to be gained by pushing for as much as they could and trying their luck, because even if Britain rejected their plans, continued direct rule was preferable to power sharing with 'republicans' (i.e. the SDLP!) Time had largely healed the trauma and outrage that had fed the initial mass demonstrations: they knew the Protestant public was growing increasingly resigned to direct rule. So (though this was not admitted publicly) were some loyalist politicians: at least they had neither the willpower nor energy to go on battling against the British, just so long as they were not forced into power sharing or links with the Irish Republic. The lack of a 'do or die' quality about their deliberations, the very absence of those fears and tensions that had charged Protestant politics a few years before, also reduced the chance of cut throat faction fighting.

The UUUC called for the return of devolved government with full security powers and opposed power sharing or institutional links with the Republic. Like the Portrush conference declarations of April 1974 the proposals were conspicuous (opponents would say depressing) for their conservative and reactionary quality. It was as if seven years' events had not occurred, as if the status quo could be restored without concessions to opponents' grievances—the plans for opposition involvement in backbench committees apart. The UUUC policy programme again hinted at the extent to which the loyalist bloc had lost, or squeezed out, elements tinged with social radicalism or conciliatory views towards Catholics.[13]

But did broad policy agreement and good co-ordination in selecting candidates via joint committees therefore mean the parties were moving towards amalgamation? Things were not as simple as that. The VUP's future was bound to be in doubt once it shed its two distinctive Vanguard features: militant opposition to British domination and alliance with workers and paramilitants. As we have seen, the hard core of Vanguard, those who stayed while fringe elements drifted away or were kicked out, were disaffected Unionists who always hoped to return to the fold. With thoughts of fighting Britain or declaring UDI largely gone and the UP returning to a more hardline position, many VUP members were anxious for unity with the larger party. As VUP organisers pointed out, local branch members tended to go along to joint meetings when the UUUC was formed, so distinctive VUP organisation in the constituencies was neglected. In any case, a lot of VUP branches had originally consisted of the local UP branch, who had defected en masse.

The experience of UUUC co-operation simply increased the likelihood that VUP organisations would either disband or return to the official Unionist fold. But if that meant reluctantly accepting further direct rule if Britain rejected UUUC proposals, would not that come particularly hard to Vanguard members who saw an Ulster parliament as a vital expression of the Ulster identity?

Bill Craig's proposals for a voluntary coalition with the SDLP, made after the VUP won 14 seats at the Convention elections, were seen by some observers as an extraordinary change of heart. But they could also be seen as a way out of a dilemma for Vanguard activists who placed great importance on an Ulster parliament. Instead of sacrificing that parliament (perhaps permanently) they might win agreement for one from the British, at the price of some co-operation with their

Catholic constitutional opponents. The fact that Craig got the endorsement of the VUP's central council and some party branches suggests a surprising number of this hardline party were prepared to pay this price for the sake of another of their distinctive principles. But a majority of VUP Convention members, led by deputy leader Ernest Baird, broke from Craig on the voluntary coalition issue and were supported by most Vanguard branches west of the Bann. This division and disarray only hastened the end of the VUP as a separate party with distinctive policies.

The fact that Ian Paisley was instrumental in getting Craig expelled from the UUUC and temporarily removed from the Unionist–Orange mainstream emphases the DUP's return to a hardline role after its moderate phase as the voice of reason during the period of anti-British feeling in 1972 and 1973. The DUP might also have seemed in danger of disappearing into oblivion, because it had been losing a number of roles. As we have seen, more socially radical members were becoming disaffected with it or were being squeezed out, and the party had steadily lost its role as articulator of poor Protestants' social grievances. Its role as the voice of reason was superfluous now that Vanguard was no longer making noises about liquidating the enemy. fighting the British or declaring UDI; the direct integration policy had also lost most of its credibility.

But decline or amalgamation would have run counter to all the structural changes the DUP had been making. Paisleyite movements were traditionally more organised than baffled outsiders might acknowledge. The DUP based itself both on former UP branches and on local Free Presbyterian churches, but their structures still appeared esoteric and unconventional, as researchers who spent years looking for a headquarters or phone number for the DUP are aware. One engaging explanation is put by the Rev. William Beattie in the DUP *Yearbook* 1975/6: 'Prior to obtaining the new offices, we had no fixed abode and operated mainly from hotel rooms in various places.'[14]

However well this informal network had operated in the past, the DUP had been serving notice that it had every intention of sticking around and preserving its distinctiveness as a party by formalising its structures. In November 1973 it had held a conference to elect a national executive and draw up party rules and a constitution. Many new branches were formed in 1974 when the first party conference was held and new headquarters with fulltime staff were opened. The one distinctive role that was guaranteed to endure for the DUP was that of expressing the beliefs of people who felt Protestant religious principles should permeate social and political life. Through all the upheavals of recent years there had remained a substantial section of Protestant opinion who shared this view.

The likelihood that the DUP would return to its Paisleyite roots was strengthened just because members who had remained, and new recruits in rural areas where Paisley continued to open new churches were more conservative and fundamentalist than those who had left. And the more that religious issues dominated DUP thinking, the less palatable integration with other Unionist/loyalist parties would be, for the commitment of those parties to religious fundamentalist principles was viewed as highly dubious by the Paisleyite faithful. Party attitudes to any sort of co-operation with Catholic politicians or Catholic demands would also grow more hardline.

The expansion of the party and formalisation of its structures may have strengthened its position *vis-á-vis* other loyalist/Unionist parties. Its return to traditional roles may have ensured its long term survival, whatever constitutional proposals might be put forward in the future. But the effect on the DUP leadership was less clearcut. On the one hand, that leadership might seem to be strengthened: various troublesome dissenters had gone, there was no confusing multiplicity of roles, and recruits attracted by the messianic side of the DUP might, one could expect, be obedient to their messiah, Paisley. The fact that the same names kept reappearing on all the party committees listed in the DUP *Yearbook* (with Paisley and his deputy, Beattie, on all major ones) suggested that democratisation had not been a big part of the structural changes.

On the other hand, party expansion in the constituencies and a more vigorous and committed membership is always likely to bring constraints as well as advantages to any party leader. For Paisley, even though he had much trust and deference from his supporters, his political choices were narrowed: if he contemplated any form of compromise or conciliation there would be strong grassroots pressure to abandon it. Members of other parties commented on this influence in the run up to the Convention and during its deliberations, the more so because they often regarded DUP members as pliant and inactive ('organ grinder's monkeys') and found the change worthy of remark. Expansion also increased difficulties of monitoring and control from the centre.

This raised the question: Could more extreme or headstrong elements begin pulling Paisley along, reversing the usual way the wires were pulled? One interpretation of Paisley's involvement in the abortive 1977 strike against direct rule was that he was forced into supporting, against his better judgment, elements in his party who had started making links in certain local areas with the UDA, co-leaders of the strike. What one can say for certain is that conflicts and contradictions about internal democracy, which had always existed in Paisleyite movements, did not disappear with the departure of the social radicals, but reappeared under a different impetus, and were likely to prove as enduring as the party itself.

14

The UVF: From Soldiers to Politicians and Back

The months between the UWC strike and the second proscription of the UVF in November 1975 were turbulent ones for the group. Conciliatory political moves by leading UVF members led to meetings with republicans, socialists, peace groups and British civil servants. The UVF founded a political party whose candidates fought a Westminster election; then there was a coup by UVF hardliners and an orgy of sectarian killing and internecine feuding. After a particularly savage outburst of anti-Catholic violence, the UVF was once again banned.

These events give interesting insights into Protestant armed groups, the range of people they attracted, the constraints they operated under and the great problems members faced if they tried to break from their traditions. Some of these constraints and problems have also affected Catholic groups. The UVF's decline after the second ban also challenges a popular view of counter-insurgency theorists that armed groups win support from populations by terror alone. Instead it suggests that when these groups start behaving like 'Godfathers', that is precisely when the population is most likely to reject them.

The UVF turmoil also had a profound effect on the lives of one group of people caught up in the Ulster conflict. For some, their attempts to change the UVF needed a lot of commitment and courage. They experienced both great optimism and bitter disillusionment. Yet the events surrounding the launch and demise of the Volunteer Political Party have been almost ignored, even by the media and academic specialists in loyalist affairs. Perhaps this is because they challenge popular centrist and left-wing stereotypes of Protestant armed groups: but even in a land of bogs, inconvenient facts do not disappear.

The seeds of conflict about the UVF's political role were sown long before the VPP was formed. For several reasons, it was open to left of centre influence. We saw how the early UVF attracted people with social discontents, as well as 'Fenian-haters'. A secretive group where there was as much scope for dreaming as there was for fighting was always likely to draw in some politically unconventional people. One Belfast unit even picked up a couple of ex-communists when it was formed.

We also saw how the imprisoned Gusty Spence was attracted to aspects of Official IRA ideology, though he still rejected their aspirations for Irish unity. He spoke against the sectarian killings and voiced his wish for working class Ulster people to find common solutions to their social problems.[15] He also encouraged contacts between some UVF and Official IRA 'officers', who had sporadic political discussions. Though Spence became more of a figurehead than an active leader, his views and exhortations still commanded respect among old-guard straight militarists, as well as the politically minded.

We discussed how Spence's rhetoric and the disciplined, clean soldier image[16] the UVF tried to cultivate tended to attract what one barrister wryly called 'the better class of terrorist' as young men flocked to join Protestant armed groups during 1972. As the UDA quickly attracted a reputation for brutality and racketeering, more articulate or idealistic youths who wanted to believe their army would fight for the people as well as defeat the enemy found the UVF a much more enticing proposition. The barrister's observation tended to find support among local people in areas like Shankill or Sandy Row. Thus some of the young UVF prisoners would be talked of with respect as 'the good boys', 'the very best'—youths who had been promising at school and considerate to their families and community.

Informed sources suggest that, at this time, a number of more senior UVF men (at least in Belfast) were moving more firmly to the view that sectarian warfare was undesirable, that both 'extremes' might be involved in some political settlement and share certain social aims. Their existence and influence is at least strongly suggested by the UVF's low involvement in sectarian killings during 1972 and 1973. The internment of some leading UVF members in 1973 seemed to give this trend a big impetus. Not only did these internees see more clearly their conflict of interest with loyalist politicians (who gave them no support) but they came into contact with Catholics who had suffered the same fate as themselves.

Limited co-operation between religious factions in Long Kesh (especially during protests about conditions) brought new mutual respect among people who shared certain military codes and values, and who came from the same social background. This encouraged the belief that the two extremes must take part in any political settlement. It also brought some of the UVF much closer to republican views on civil liberties. At least three men who were later prominent in the VPP became outspoken opponents of internment and 'Diplock' (non-jury) courts. This position, put in the VPP manifesto,[17] was unusual for loyalists in that it was unequivocal—condemning use of special powers against republicans, as well as loyalists. The UVF ceasefire of November 1973 was not just a tactic for getting detainees released from jail: it also reflected the influence of the 'doves' at 'brigade staff' and 'officer' level. These men came mainly from Belfast and its hinterland: they were often skilled manual workers, though one of the internees was a university graduate and teacher. The UVF began putting out a stream of conciliatory political statements: the media, apart from the *Sunday News*, declined to publicise them. The statements called for, among other things, a forum where both UVF and republican groups could discuss political solutions.

The UVF also began publishing a magazine *Combat* which carried articles on Irish history as well as housing, jobs and other issues. The magazine and the public statements increasingly implied a tacit decision not to criticise the Official IRA, and there were several rumours of joint meetings. There was also the impression that UVF doves believed the Officials could somehow weaken or defeat the Provisionals, paving the way for reconciliation. The heady stuff grew headier, as the UVF told local units to hold political discussion meetings. Enthusiasts for this may have been in a minority but they were not confined to brigade staff. For instance one junior 'officer' in the Antrim area, a keen trade union shop steward, would round up reluctant or confused members and list an agenda for the evening's debate that ranged from trade union problems to Ulster's future relationship with the Republic. His optimism and obvious commitment was met by some bemused or embarrassed shuffling.

The idea of forming a political wing began to engross the 'doves'. The Ulster Loyalist Front (ULF) was formed in early 1974, but soon petered out: its National Front links caused confusion and alienation among most members. These links had largely been forged by one UVF man with NF connections, the editor of *Combat*[18] (of whom more later). While most other parties and groups shunned the UVF when it wanted advice about going political, the NF had been willing to help for its own reasons. Even the more politically minded UVF men were often surprisingly ignorant about the NF's philosophy: when this gradually sank in, they either felt hostile to it or saw no relevance to Ulster in its rantings about black immigrants. But at least the short-lived ULF familiarised UVF members with the idea of running their own political wing.

Then the British Government gave the 'doves' a further boost. Fired with one of their sporadic hopes about bringing gunmen in from the cold, and encouraged by recent UVF statements, they lifted the ban on the group in February 1974, along with Provisional Sinn Féin. Contacts with the UVF were made by British civil servants, who even encouraged UVF members to talk over their political ideas with academics. The Government saw further merit and urgency in encouraging political development after the UWC strike, which had brought home how much political power could be wielded by non-conventional Protestant groups. Indeed, the UVF began to be courted by so many suitors that some members were hardly out of one bus or plane before they were into another. For instance, one religious organisation took a party over to Scotland for a week of political discussion and education that included talks by an MP and a leading trade unionist.

Northern Ireland Labour Party members were often present on these parties, for the NILP had joined the queue of suitors. Motivations were mixed. Some influential members were genuinely concerned that their party no longer spoke for loyalist workers nor seemed relevant to them; the strike only rubbed this in, and had further divided their already weak party. They were anxious to listen to groups like the UVF and be more responsive to working class Protestants. More practically, they realised the NILP must attract that support or die. This realisation was shared by another group of NILP stalwarts, but they believed they would instruct and enlighten people like the UVF. As one NILP man put it, 'some of these fellas can be as thick as champ'.

One irony about this second group was that in their efforts to win support they tended to bend over backwards so far that UVF members actually accused them of being too sectarian. Uncertainty about just what the NILP believed caused visible suspicion. But the extent to which some members of the NILP did influence leading UVF members is shown in the VPP manifesto, much of which was very close to NILP policy.

By the summer of 1974 there were many auspicious signs for the launching of a conciliatory, anti-sectarian political wing in the UVF, including support from influential outside groups. There was also the important factor that the UVF happened to contain a number of articulate, committed people at influential levels, who had the tacit support of the UVF's overall commander (vital in a paramilitary group). Strong ties of loyalty and friendship among the group, cemented by years of secrecy and often by common deprivations and prison experience strengthened that commitment. The strike heightened their optimism: it seemed to show that ordinary working people could achieve change without the permission of politicians. Setting up their own independent political movement now seemed neither so frightening, nor so fraught with risk of failure.

[margin handwriting: between violence and straight politics]

At the same time, other influences and experiences militated against the political experiment. First, and most obviously, the UVF had always attracted numbers of people who felt particularly hostile and suspicious towards Catholics in general, and republicans in particular, who joined because they wanted to fight change and reform that would accommodate Catholic feelings.

To begin weeding these people out, the UVF leadership would have had to be united and very selective when recruits began queuing up to join after 1971, but the doves were only one element fighting for influence at that time. When Gusty Spence prompted a major recruiting drive during his four months of freedom in 1972,[19] he did indeed attract some idealistic youngsters. But the goal of numbers meant caution was sacrificed, and UVF sources claimed that some undisciplined hotheads, even young thugs were recruited. Spence, who had great faith in military groups for instilling discipline and idealism, also resurrected the Young Citizens Volunteers (YCV) who were, as in 1912, to be the UVF's junior wing. But if he expected them to behave as well-drilled boy scouts he was to be disappointed. Some YCVs, who had partial autonomy and a separate structure, were involved in sectarian violence and hooliganism: the UVF found it more and more difficult to control them.

One of the striking things about the UVF in 1974 was the apparent co-existence and social mixing of people with opposing views, who often visibly distrusted each other. In one drinking session I witnessed, an Antrim shop steward began singing a republican lament about a defeat in battle. He found it moving and interesting that both sides could feel these emotions. A young man who had joined up in 1972, and who came to prominence after the 1974 coup, at first grew disturbed and then angry, drowning out the singer with triumphal Orange chants.

Certain UDA stalwarts would probably have said the 'doves' were not ruthless enough with their opponents: that cut-throats only understand their own tactics. Because the radicals did not kill, injure or intimidate out the hardliners, they had to co-exist with them in this small, claustrophobic organisation, and simply try to change the views of the young man above by bringing him along to political seminars. Certainly an outside observer would have said that the radicals had a big handicap here: most were quite pleasant people, who found it hard to be ruthless. But even if they were, would they ever have got away with being tough on political hardliners? Ruthless UDA men found both members and populations would tolerate internal action against racketeers or 'head cases': even, sometimes, against mere personal rivals. But had they tried to 'take out' people whose sectarian militancy was part of the very ethos of Protestant paramilitary organisations, either they or their group might will have fallen apart.

Even the things which gave the progressives their strength and commitment could also undermine them. For instance 'Phil',[20] a teacher, felt that while internment radicalised leading UVF members it also took them away from the action. 'It put us out of the way, neutralised us and the hawks took advantage on the ground. We were doomed before we started our [party] campaign: even while we were canvassing for the VPP, some of our units were doing nasty bits of violence. I felt we'd have been better disassociating the VPP from the UVF—running as a separate party—but others wanted it to be this big UVF thing, they were sure the boys would be behind us and all that'.

Secondly, the very solidarity and friendship of the radicals caused jealousy. UVF hawks did not simply oppose their policies: they felt this clique who mixed with intellectuals and spouted big words looked down on the rest of the UVF. Such jealousies are, of course, common in political parties and even in community groups: the UVF could hardly hope to avoid them.

But the contradictions in the UVF as it built up to launching a political party were even more complicated than 'radicals versus hard-liners', or 'nice guys versus nasties'. Sometimes the contradictions could exist in one individual. For instance 'Richard', an ex-regular serviceman from the Antrim area, was prominent both in the UVF's politicisation and in the reactionary turn of the UVF after November 1974. Known as a 'spacer' or 'head case' by some of his colleagues, Richard's fulminations against popish doctrines earned him the nick-name 'Cromwell'. Catholic churches were sometimes blown to heaven in the area under his command. He liked to describe himself as a full time terrorist. Politically he was attracted to the National Front and maintained links with them.

But he also associated with some NILP members, and spoke enthusiastically of certain international socialist groups. He openly admired some of the policies and leaders of the Official IRA, joined in political discussions with them, read Irish history avidly and had a cassette of Irish nationalist songs in his car. He claimed this was in case he got caught in the Short Strand:[21] this might not have saved him, since he also kept a UVF jacket and hat under the front seat. Literate and well-read, his outpourings fill the pages of *Combat* and reflect all the contradictions of his political views.

Several lessons are suggested by Richard's case. First, while most Ulster paramilitarists have not been particularly eccentric or unstable members of society, armed groups, especially secretive ones, have always attracted a minority of such people. Once there, they can be hard to dislodge especially if they have real or imagined force behind them. If other members are themselves feeling confused politically, they will find it harder to decide what line should be taken with someone like Richard.

Secondly, people like him could give a distorted impression of the organisation to outsiders, particularly when they had such influence over a publication. Readers of *Combat* could easily have overestimated the extent of socialist thinking and interest in Irish identity among the UVF generally in 1973 and 1974. After the coup, they would certainly have overestimate the degree of right wing, pro-NF feeling in the organisation. Again, if the UVF as a whole had been less confused or divided politically they would have been more determined and better able to curb Richard's written excesses and make *Combat* a more accurate reflection of the wider group's thinking.

Thirdly, individuals can sometimes reveal in extreme form the confusion of a whole community at a time of change and uncertainty Gusty Spence showed some of these (though this is not to suggest he was either eccentric or unstable). Intellectually he understood the historic role of the Protestant working class under Unionism: his wish to change it, his hope for a more egalitarian and less sectarian society was gen-

uine. Intellectually too, he could realistically appraise British attitudes
to Ulster and had some sympathy with the left-wing, colonialist analysis of British relations with Ireland.

But in other ways he was still the ex-sergeant who found it hard to
break from the heroic loyalist ideology of the Somme and Korea. UVF
prisoners still held poppy day parades with hand-stitched emblems, and
were sent on ten mile route marches round the compound. Richard, in
a more bizarre way, showed the mental contradictions of many loyalist
workers who had been spurred into re-thinking their identity, into re-
assessing constitutional and social issues, but who found it hard to
reject lifelong beliefs or make sense of the new possibilities before them.

We have been talking about radicals and hardliners. But what about
the rest of the UVF, ordinary members who perhaps had not thought
very deeply about what they were doing or where they were going,
beyond vague ideas of fighting for Ulster and hitting back at the IRA?
They could presumably jump either way in the internal battle for
supremacy. With these people, the radicals had one or two advantages.
Several had gained respect and kudos as a result of being interned or
imprisoned: they had proved their loyalty to Ulster's cause, and it was
difficult for their opponents to challenge this. To some extent they
could get away with saying conciliatory things which would have
brought rejections or suspicion on others: respect carried over into a
willingness to listen. As an NILP man said in frustration to one of the
VPP founders. 'If I said what you said at some of your meetings, I'd be
called a Fenian lover.'

The radicals also tended to be respected as people by certain longstanding UVF men who were well regarded in their local communities
as basically honest characters, who helped out those communities and
wanted to keep the organisation 'straight'. Even if their ideas were ill
thought out, such men were prepared to give politics a try if the leaders
they trusted were keen and if it brought the organisation more respect.
Many volunteers took their cue from these middle ranking men. Besides, the hierarchal ethos of the UVF encouraged deference. (it was
convenient too e.g. volunteers could just be ordered to write envelopes
for election literature! If the boss of your unit said there would now be
political discussion meetings, then you accepted it.)

But several other things made the radicals task of converting the uncommitted a difficult and perillous one. Basically, they were caught up
in a vicious circle. The uncommitted had so many reasons for holding

back that most would only have thrown in their lot if the political experiment had already proved successful, had won wide support and gained kudos for the UVF. Yet the experiment had little chance of success unless everyone committed themselves before it was put to the test.

The chief problem was that the radicals were trying to impose a top down policy—not responding to a wave of grassroots feeling. This brought more than practical problems of control (e.g. inability to coerce unwilling leaders of peripheral units to start talking politics and keep the ceasefire properly). It also meant that the only teaching they were able to do was the least effective kind—lectures, exhortations and arguments which even the most willing might forget the next week. But as conflicts both in Ulster and elsewhere have suggested,[22] it is experience which is most likely to make people question lifelong beliefs, or change them. For instance, those loyalists who came to believe that internment was an unjust practice had usually been interned themselves, or had seen relatives interned.

By asking the UVF to enter the political world, the radicals were challenging much of the ideology, ethos and experience of UVF members. It was not just that their ideology had sectarian aspects, more basically, the UVF was not equipped to be or become a political movement. Despite Spence's efforts, there was no consistent tradition (in contrast with the IRA) which stressed that political and social programmes went hand in hand with military ones. Most members joined as a way of expressing disillusionment with politicians and constitutional methods, and the training they received did not equip them with political skills. their ethos, practices and even their language opened up a gap between themselves and politicians and, indeed, the Protestant electorate.

UVF men spent much of their time in the company of each other and like-minded people. Their world, which was dangerous and insecure in many ways, was still a protective cushion against other worlds, which demanded their own courage and stamina, especially if you belonged to a small minority party. As one NILP councillor remarked: 'Thirty years in the NILP and you know what failure is... you just have to have a good laugh and try again.'

The subjects UVF men talked about among themselves or to an interviewer show what was important to them, and what gave them personal fulfilment. Some things provoked animated discussion, like operations or gunbattles; military training and its problems (like having to wait for a night when a sympathetic UDR commander was on duty in a country area); resistance to interrogation; jibes at the UDA, whom they nicknamed 'the Wombles'; the fate of someone just up before the courts; home made guns and how to smuggle parts out of factories; prisoners' problems, etc.

There was a wealth of in-jokes about 'going for your tea', 'Mr Colt' etc, while reminiscences of bungled jobs caused great mirth. As others tittered over their holiday snapshots, the UVF (and UDA) cackled about the man who shot his own foot instead of an alleged IRA man.

Some members would affect speech reminiscent of Chicago gangsters: 'It's OK kid. I run East Belfast. No problem.' Even intelligent people who were by no means gangsters sometimes took part in play acting. One night at a social club in County Antrim, a group of UVF men came in bearing the proverbial sack of guns and surreptitiously put them inside the proverbial window seat. Another man carefully burned a photograph of UVF men in uniform, even though the picture was barely decipherable. Though some of this was obviously staged for the interviewers' benefit, certain people clearly enjoyed behaving in this kind of way. Lifting the ban did not fundamentally change the character of the UVF, with its atmosphere of secrecy and esoteric camaraderie.

The flippancies aside, memories of hardship and loyalty were an important source of solidarity but further cut them off from politicians and public, breeding a kind of elitism. 'We are the people who took the risks, did the real fighting, sacrificed our home lives and freedom' unlike the politicians in their comfortable existence, who disowned gunmen to avoid political embarrassment.

It is perhaps the esoteric nature of the activity and fulfilment which comes across most from this discussion. Such things did not con-cern the bulk of humanity, nor did they understand the importance of them. Other people were likely to find the uniform, the in-jokes and the military emphasis intimidating if not distasteful. They did not see that uniforms often served the purpose of reassurance, covering insecurity in settings (like press conferences) where UVF men might make fools of themselves.

Nor could most people see in the apparently callous humorising about killing and death a means of coping with the unpalatable and stressful. Many gunmen lived in regular fear of their own death, from internal as well as external enemies. Others knew the strain of being on the run while some had clearly been shocked by the experience of imprisonment, even if they put on a hard man act. Bouts of heavy drinking, practical jokes and other ways of 'acting daft' could all be cover ups for stress. Frank Burton's observations on the high tension some IRA men lived under would find parallels here.[23]

Republican militants would also understand the ethical distinctions that were important to many UVF men, but which were not accepted by most outsiders. UVF language distinguished between lawbreakers and active service units, criminals and prisoners of war, procurement operations and self gain robberies. UVF people would get angry and frustrated that outsiders would not acknowledge their code of ethics. They expected people to appreciate that they chose to rob banks instead of small shopkeepers!

The second point that emerges is the unpreparedness of most UVF men for their new political role and the barriers which would have to be overcome. Not only were their minds geared to military activity, but abandoning these activities would mean sacrificing excitement, fulfilment and a sense of competence. The earnest volunteer who felt 'I'd jump out of that window if my commander ordered me to' would less happily have obeyed an order to discuss politics from a soap box and would have found it more frightening than planting a bomb.

There is also the strong impression of a 'them against us' world, where politicians and authority figures in unfamiliar land beyond the pubs and clubs condemned people, hounded and interrogated them, tried and imprisoned them. With these people one engaged in a constant battle of wits, which often needed courage and daring (e.g. in springing a prisoner from hospital). But it did not teach the kind of skill, confidence and patience required to take on politicians on their own ground. There was also reluctance to 'play' a system which experience had taught them to suspect deeply, to fear that their own betrayal was inevitable. Even the VPP founders felt that reluctance about collusion and were ill prepared for any chill winds of political failure. The rest largely lacked the confidence or inclination to take the politicians on even once. If they were attacked after the VPP campaign started, they were likely to shrink back in greater alarm. They were particularly likely to take fright if politicians, other influential leaders and local people accused them of things they knew were especially bad news among loyalists... like being Communists or republican sympathisers.

Lastly, the UVF radicals faced a practical external problem in their efforts to win over the uncommitted to their new party. The problem was something they could do little or nothing about. Provisional IRA violence continued at a high level during 1974. It was very hard for UVF volunteers, even if they were not hardliners, to see what the UVF was getting for its new, conciliatory line. This was especially true in the troubled border areas. They couldn't see any hope in this idea of getting the extremes round a conference table. And though the UVF had pointedly stopped attacking the Official IRA physically or verbally, the average volunteer could not see that they were restraining the Provisionals in any way. Those who believed or hoped the Officials could do so felt let down, as if the other side had not reciprocated on the deal. Their hopes and beliefs may have been unrealistic but as we have said, they were not alone among loyalists in clinging to this idea. Its naivity bears witness to communal segregation and lack of mutual understanding about power structures and conflicts across the divide.

The VPP is launched

A journalist from a Belfast paper recalled the press conference which was called in one VPP member's house to launch the new party.[24] 'Very few reporters went or seemed to be interested. I listened to their views for a while and said: "That's socialism you're talking." You could see some of them taking fright—"oh, no, no" they said, "we're just for the working class people, that's all".'

That fright came mainly from their awareness of repercussions from hostile critics including some of the UVF if they were labelled socialist. This had been a continuing worry. Some weeks before, a group of UVF men who were preparing an article for *Combat* got into an intense discussion about whether use of the word 'exploitation' in reference to social conditions would have them labelled Communists by loyalist leaders. But in fact the VPP manifesto was, if anything, slightly left of the NILP position. It was written by an ex-internee, a skilled manual worker who had earlier been involved in Labour politics, and who stunned a NILP leading light for having 'written it all by himself'.

The first thing that distinguished the VPP from most loyalist workers was their conviction that an independent party was needed and should fight elections—whether or not it split the Protestant vote. In believing that the interests of paramilitants and others who had felt the weight of security force action should be articulated, they were also unusual in opposing internment and special powers against Catholics, as well as Protestants. They also spoke out on the damage that UDI would do to working class people on both sides, and warned that it could increase sectarian conflict. If they still ducked the issue of Protestant privilege in the workforce (and what Protestant-based party has not) their manifesto was clearly committed to a strong and expanding welfare state. If one could say (not entirely flippantly) that Protestant workers divided into two camps: those who felt welfare benefits were too high and those who thought wages were too low, the VPP belonged to the second.

The manifesto also pressed for more equitable distribution of resources to the deprived areas of the UK. Though it came out clearly in support of the Union, it was noticeable that more progressive-minded people in the UVF had for some time been interested in discussing the merits of other choices like agreed independence (which involved winning Catholic co-operation), or a federal Ireland. The former appealed to Phil, while Richard would indulge in flights of fancy about the union of the Celtic races. But the safe option was eventually chosen; it was the only one they could all accept, because the economic and other effects of different choices were far from clear, and on account of deference to feelings among the loyalist voters (plus the bulk of the UVF).

So the VPP manifesto was perhaps a pink shade of democratic socialism, tinged with a stronger libertarianism on legal issues. At first the VPP wanted to put up three Belfast candidates for the October 1974 Westminster election. But they lacked the organisational muscle and eventually entered only one, for West Belfast. Ken Gibson was another ex-internee and skilled manual worker, who had once been closely associated with Ian Paisley. His jail experience had made him a passionate opponent of internment, while the UWC strike filled him with confidence that working people would be prepared to break from traditional voting habits.

He was also keen that the VPP should not be seen as purely sectarian and hoped Catholics would read parts of the manifesto they could identify with, like the opposition to internment. He once tried to take his campaign car to canvass in the Lower Falls but was prevented by his friends, who feared this might invite attack from certain residents. After joining in a radio programme with other election candidates, he became very enthusiastic about how many policies he and the Official IRA seemed to share. It was a time for great optimism, which can, of course, often cloud realism.

The Campaign

When the VPP opened their campaign and began trying to win over the electorate and media, there were one or two points in their favour. They did not have to prove their loyalty in the diehard areas, because several were known to have been imprisoned and to have taken part in organising the UWC strike. The VPP's concern about the rights of prisoners and their families also struck a special chord in West Belfast from which a high percentage of both loyalist and republican prisoners have traditionally come. Politicians might have betrayed them, but the VPP's loudspeaker cars proclaimed that someone at least had not forgotten 'the boys'.

The VPP also had open support from Glen Barr, a popular figure among working class loyalists, and Hugh Smyth, an independent Shankill councillor respected locally for his redevelopment and civil liberties work. Barr's campaigning produced an 'Irish' situation for he also convassed for Bill Craig in East Belfast. The United Ulster Unionist Coalition had already rejected, as VPP leaders knew they would, the VPP's application to join their electoral coalition. Several loyalist figures canvassed openly against the VPP and Barr's appearances on the Shankill gave them some apoplectic moments. He was later suspended from the UUUC for supporting the VPP.

As we said, the VPP could partly compensate for its lack of a machine by commanding its ready made army to drive cars, distribute leaflets etc. But the disadvantages far outweighted the advantages. The UVF's internal ethos and experience could hamper their efforts to 'go political'. But external reaction was also very important. Groups across the political spectrum found themselves in an unusual alliance of hostility or suspicion towards the new party. This was very damaging, and calls in question one popular idea that in Ulster (or Ireland generally) people have found it easy to move between political and military roles. It suggests instead that most people remain unhappy about their soldiers becoming politicians, and vice versa.

We can consider first Catholic groups and electors, though these were obviously less important in the VPP's search for votes. The VPP had considerable sympathy and private best wishes from certain official republicans, from other socialist-inclined republican individuals, and from one leading member of the SDLP. But most left-wing Catholics felt bewildered, if not suspicious. They felt the VPP should prove its sincerity as openly as they themselves did. 'We want to be sympathetic but well, we're not sure ... are they socialists, can you tell me? If so, why don't they come out and say so? We know the problems, but we stick our necks out and get slammed by the priests, so why won't they do the same?' (Republican Clubs official).

The same situation viewed from inside a Protestant community was of course very different. VPP members felt they had already taken big risks (as indeed they had) which should surely have won the goodwill of people like the man above. Besides, they knew that open socialism might well be the kiss of death in their efforts to win Protestant votes. Left wing Catholics might well be slammed by traditional leaders, but at least they had a longstanding tradition to draw on.

The SDLP was not merely, like the Catholics it represented, suspicious and fearful of anything with a UVF tag. It was also a constitutional party who, like the Unionists and Alliance, felt very dubious about British enthusiasm for bringing gunmen in from the cold. Their interests lay in excluding the extremists. Some members, like the West Belfast MP Gerry Fitt, had had many acrimonious power battles with militant republicans and had to vie with them continually for Catholic allegiance. So the SDLP had more than one reason to oppose the VPP.

One example of their pre-election tactics was a newspaper advertisement asking ominously: 'Will the UVF and UDA be wearing their uniforms for the big occasion?' As paramilitants the UVF were very vulnerable to attack by suggestion, to accusations of violence and intimidation, and had little comeback against this. UUUC supporters also put it about that the VPP had threatened the life of their own candidate, Johnny McQuade.

Catholics generally found it almost impossible to believe a UVF-linked party would not be sectarian. The very record of loyalty that attracted a Shankill voter ensured Catholic alienation. Despite his bursts of optimism, Ken Gibson knew this in his heart: 'How can I expect Catholics to vote for me? What does the UVF mean to them?' Protestant voters were, of course the main problem. Like the official republicans, NILP supporters found it very hard to believe the UVF could really be socialists. NILP members who had discussions with the VPP said other NILP members attacked them for mixing with gunmen.

Other political moderates were worried that the VPP might indeed be some kind of socialists. They distrusted them not just because the UVF had a background of violence, but because social snobbery and class hostility also played a part in some moderates' attitudes to paramilitants. This could produce noticeably ambivalent views. Moderates, like certain Alliance members, seemed to believe armed groups were skilfully plotting to take over the country politically. Yet they also doubted that gunmen (or ex-gunmen) had the intellectual or moral capacity to take part in political programmes.[25]

As a result the VPP was denied even a neutral tolerance or suspension of disbelief from moderates. On the whole the media either ignored their political statements or interpreted them by imputing a range of sinister and sectarian motives to the UVF.[26] As for the Protestant public, they were more likely to be alarmed than reassured by what they could see of the VPP campaign. The advantage of being able to use a ready made army was double-edged and the disadvantage of not having a respectable-looking machine to draw on became obvious. Staid members of the public looked on with apprehension as enthusiastic, raucous YCVs in black jackets roared around in cars adorned with VPP stickers.

Meanwhile, voters in diehard loyalist areas were growing bewildered. Those most likely to feel sympathetic to a UVF party were militant loyalists and politically unsophisticated people who just knew they wanted to back the cause. But the VPP confused these very people by its departure from diehard loyalism. Visitors to the UVF-linked advice centre on the Shankill could be heard remarking that they found *Combat* too deep or hard to understand. Its articles on Irish history and discussions of economic exploitation also looked suspiciously republican-minded. People handed the VPP manifesto on their doorsteps would pore over it with visible bewilderment as they tried to grapple with its analysis of UK economic policy.

Besides, the UUUC candidate in West Belfast, John McQuade, was popular in the area: it seemed unkind to spurn him at the polls. More important, he was clearly working class, far removed from the affluent society, which the VPP seemed to be attacking. They did not find it easy to see that a person's policies might be equally, if not more, important than their social origins.

We can see what a vicious circle the VPP was in, even among potentially sympathetic local voters. For loyalists, its policies were too radical. For those (like former NILP voters) the VPP hoped to attract by its radicalism, a party linked to the UVF could not be trusted as radical. Most dramatic, perhaps, was the reaction of influential loyalists in Belfast. UUUC politicians, Orangemen and religious fundamentalists far from ignoring the VPP, like the media gave it attention out of all proportion to its size or strength. The orange elephant may have been looking at a pale pink mouse, but it seemed to see a bright red bear.

This loyalist alliance waged a campaign against the VPP which featured allegations of Communism, atheism, pro-republicanism, debauchery and all manner of vices. A virulent anti-VPP campaign was waged in the press via anonymous letters, which newspapers seemed only too eager to print. Traditional organisations were used to spread the word. Weary VPP canvassers would return to base and tell of their doorstep experiences: 'Time and again the same thing: "Are you communists? My husband's lodge was warned last night" or, "Have you had talks with the IRA?" and we'd be saying patiently "no, love," and seeing they couldn't quite believe us.'

Politicians and traditional leaders were articulate and skilful, had the ear of the media and were listened to with respect by ordinary working class voters. The VPP had few weapons with which to combat all this. It tended to provoke feelings of helplessness and frustration, increasing the hostility the VPP already felt towards loyalist politicians. The VPP members also became exasperated that local people could not see what was going on, and could not confront leaders who had duped them. Impatience was understandable but did not encourage reasoned argument with the voters. Close to tears of frustration, Ken Gibson was reduced to thumping the table one night: 'Scum, rats' [i.e. the politicians and Orangemen] 'I've told the people out there, but they're afraid. I've told them, you can run this country, you can have anything you want.'

In the run up to the election, then, the VPP lacked support from any significant social or political bloc. They also lacked the support of their larger paramilitary rival, the UDA, who had periodically accused the UVF of Communism and anti-Protestantism.

The Election

The VPP's eve of poll rally revealed some of the problems and dilemmas that had faced them throughout the campaign. It was a hopeful and enthusiastic group of supporters who gathered in the middle of the Shankill Road for the evening's events. There was a sense of strength, almost elation, at having taken on all the politicians and authority figures who had thrown mud at them up to the end. In that way the VPP campaign had been unique. It was rare indeed to see revered figures mocked in such areas, as when bystanders laughed uproariously to hear Hugh Smyth imitate Ian Paisley from a loudspeaker car.

But the small numbers also betrayed the lack of support for the party. Wives and children of VPP men jostled behind the campaigners, but few members of the public and fewer journalists joined in. A boys' band headed the parade, implicitly asserting its character as a familiar, working class loyalist event. Yet a non-sectarian party surely should not play the old songs. There was a lot of head scratching before the gathering moved off to the strains of the only neutral ditties they could think of—familiar, humorous songs like 'Is yer mammy in?'

Meanwhile, people on doorsteps took VPP leaflets with a mixture of goodwill and bewilderment. Any experienced political campaigner could see portrayed on their faces that when they reached the polling booth, they would not be voting VPP. The sparse audience on Highfield estate told the same story. Only small boys followed the VPP loudspeaker cars round the deserted streets. One verbal exchange, where both speakers had a good point, neatly exposed some of the party's dilemmas. One of their enthusiastic campaigners, a trade union shop steward whose prejudices about Catholic work habits had exasperated other VPP members during drinking sessions, had been shouting through the loudspeaker about loyalist prisoners and the cause in general. 'Sam', one of the party's founders, wound down the car window and pleaded: 'More on houses and jobs, eh? It sounds too sectarian.' 'That's what they want to hear, Sam' replied the shop steward: 'That's what they want.'

At the election, Ken Gibson polled 2,600 votes and lost his deposit. In fact, this was not at all a bad vote given the huge breakthrough problems of small minority parties in Ulster, and a NILP candidate—certainly at that time—might have done no better. Paramilitary-linked candidates have always had special problems in winning votes and during the current Troubles, Protestant ones have rarely attracted more than a few hundred.

But such rational considerations cut little ice, especially with people unused to reading history books of election statistics. It was widely regarded as a humiliating failure by the VPP stalwarts, by the uncommitted, and by the hawks. The very optimism and commitment that enabled the party to fight on in face of all the criticism had seemed to breed in some an unrealistic expectation of what could be achieved. The uncommitted tended to look at the list of voting figures and at the lost deposit, and feel the experiment had gone horribly wrong. The UVF had been made to look silly, it seemed and it had lost face and kudos. The hawks lost no time in making use of this reaction.

Aftermath

At a meeting of all UVF commanders in October 1974, a motion to end the ceasefire was narrowly defeated. But it was ended informally in some areas (and in more as time went on). The UVF violence began to increase and UVF statements—full of Richard's flowery phrases—emphasised the group's military role. The Official IRA reappeared on the list of dangerous enemies, while *Combat* attacked the menace of Communism and extolled the virtues of the National Front. But the heavies (with names like Nigger, Smudger and the Big Dog) who began replacing the radicals on UVF brigade staff understood less about right or left wing theory than their literate colleagues. They were more interested in military methods and, sometimes, in financial gain.

The UVF's overall commander, who had backed the VPP experiment, seemed powerless to prevent the changes, despite his unhappiness at what was going on. He kept contact with the new brigade staff but appeared to have little influence over their decisions.

The VPP was retained in name but was in fact disbanded. The new leaders kept Ken Gibson on as their political spokesman, perhaps because of his experience and because he was reasonably well known and accepted in the media. One can only speculate about the hold they had over him, since he had not lacked courage in the past in speaking out about his political beliefs. But now he was forced to lose face and compromise himself by contradicting his previous statements publicly. This only compounded the bitterness of an experience that had first fired him with visible enthusiasm and determination, then shocked him when the dream confronted failure. He never again played a prominent role in political or social movements, and eventually moved with his family to another part of Northern Ireland.

The others reacted in a variety of ways. 'Jim', author of the manifesto, whose calm shrewdness had contributed much to the VPP's survival in past months, refused to have any connection with the new leadership. But he felt bitter and disillusioned enough not to redirect his energies into any movement, opting out and concentrating on his job. He despaired that the UVF could become a radical movement of any sort, concluding angrily: 'Ask these fellas to rob a bank or kill a Catholic and you'll get 50 volunteers, but to do anything constructive? Not one. Gusty, X and Y [UVF prisoners near release] would be better staying where they are, writing their pamphlets and dreaming their dreams. Why should I try any more?'

'Sam' became involved in a (non-sectarian) internees' resettlement scheme and later in community development work. This also put him at some personal risk, since his background as an expert in 'hardware' was not unknown on both sides of the divide. Later he joined the lobby for agreed independence for Northern Ireland. This again had supporters from both religious groups. 'Phil' also became involved with this lobby after first avoiding attacks from UVF hit squads (or sending them back home—his physique and reputation were formidable.) By rejecting overtures from the UDA, who respected him and felt he could give them political direction, he also indicated that he no longer felt paramilitary groups were the vehicles for bringing about political change.

Other 'pink' activists were squeezed out of the UVF, tried to distance themselves from it, or took part in establishing groups like the East Antrim Workers Council. Though this was avowedly non-sectarian and aimed to promote working-class interests in the area, it seemed to fall more and more under Richard's influence. It began pushing a strongly anti-Communist line and called for the founding of a separate Ulster Trades Union Congress (TUC). After a few months, little was heard of it.

Decline

But if the VPP failed to persuade the UVF or the wider population that soldiers could become politicians, the new UVF leadership also managed to alienate many people. Relations with other Protestant paramilitaries also sank to an unprecedented low. This suggests that even in its familiar, military role, a group of this kind disobeyed unspoken rules of conduct at its peril. The time covered by this book ended with the UVF in disarray, with its membership, finances, prestige and popular support in a decline that was only accelerated by a crippling series of arrests.

First, their anti-Catholic violence was now unacceptable to any major section of the Protestant population. Many Protestants were uneasy about the IRA ceasefire agreement initiated at Feakle, the founding of Sinn Féin incident centres which kept contact with British civil servants,[27] and the phasing out of internment. Continued IRA violence also kept tension and resentment alive. But 1975 was not like 1972 in terms of violence, of Protestant alienation, or of fears about their constitutional future. Toleration of counter-terror was far more uneasy now. There was also a growing resignation to continued direct rule, and an almost tangible war-weariness.

It was not just that the UVF and its new front, the Protestant Action Force, carried out savage killings (like the Miami Showband murders) which shocked many people[28] but that it actually boasted about them.

Other armed groups felt these actions brought them unwanted security force attention, while loyalist politicians found their own credibility threatened by the violence. Secondly, some UVF men seemed to find fulfilment in other kinds of violence too. Casualties mounted as a feud escalated with the UDA; the abduction and murder of two UDA men strained relations to breaking point. In some areas local people spoke fearfully about the violence and unpredictability of certain characters in the UVF. Shootings and public brawls in social clubs grew almost commonplace.

But, as the UDA supreme commander Andy Tyrie put it: 'There's one rule in this game—you can't shoot your own. It's always somebody's friend or father or brother, and people who've done it end up shot themselves or in prison. It's the same with republicans: and the kiss of death to any organisation that tries it.' The UDA could probably speak with feeling: they knew the public credibility they had lost in earlier days by bitter faction fighting.

The UVF was also losing volunteers who killed themselves in bungled operations. In previous years such deaths had been rare. This caused ill feeling within the organisation and among relatives of dead volunteers: it also knocked holes in the UVF's efficient image. The new leadership was accused of racketeering and self-gain by other UVF men and by local people. These actions gathered their own momentum; Andy Tyrie again: 'You could watch this happening. At the start the UDA was picking up all the hoods, drunks, wild boys ... and the UVF was getting better people. Now it was the other way round—like atracts like.'

Many of the old straight militarists began to leave the UVF. The wife of one UVF-linked welfare worker summed up some general feelings. 'X and Y and Z, you've heard of them yourself ... I don't agree with everything they've done, they're not the world's greatest political thinkers, but they were straight and helped the [Shankill] people; they're sick now and just want to leave the UVF. They feel it's discredited with the people. As X said, whatever else I did, I never put someone else's money in my own pocket.'

The UVF's very lack of political direction now lost it credibility. The VPP had tried to impose policies, and many in the UVF tolerated their overthrow because their group had been made to lose face in an arena where they already lacked confidence. But lack of direction could also make them look foolish, especially if unpredictable behaviour went along with it. The pompous, flowery language of UVF statements at one extreme, and the behaviour of some UVF leaders at the other, just

seemed ridiculous and intolerable to many people—like the UDA delegate who watched a senior officer drawing moustaches on posters at a
loyalist co-ordinating committee. Where the average UVF volunteer
had been powerless to prevent the radicals disappearing to talk with
republicans or academics, he was now powerless to prevent his new
leaders from raising different sorts of antagonism in other groups and
in the population. If the radicals had made the UDA fearful of communism, they had at least not made the UDA fearful of landing a stray
bullet.

Gradually the disillusioned began to exert damaging pressures on the
organisation. The sea in which the fish swam started to turn sour. The
Orange Cross welfare organisation found with alarm that they could
no longer sell UVF prisoners' handicrafts, nor continue publishing
their longstanding fortnightly newspaper. The UVF found it ever more
difficult even to finance prisoners and their families. Information began
to flow from the public to the authorities about unpopular UVF
figures. Many were arrested and sentenced to long jail terms over the
next two years.

Influenced by these events and encouraged by the UVF prisoners
(several of whom had keenly supported the VPP) a group of long-
serving UVF men staged a counter-coup shortly after the UVF was
proscribed for the second time in October 1975. But while sectarian
atrocities were much reduced afterwards (with some isolated but
notable exceptions like the 'Shankill Butcher' killings) the latest
leadership failed to reassert control over, or gain recognition from,
certain UVF units. The group had lost its solidarity and was growing
more and more fragmented.

Politically. too, the reshuffled leadership understandably went for
caution and relative silence. Open support for ideas like agreed independence tended to be limited to the prisoners and ex-VPP members.

The prisoners were almost alone in clinging to the belief that the
UVF could be resurrected as a socially radical working class movement. This was partly because they were shielded from harsh realities
beyond prison gates, partly because their solidarity and heroic attachment to the group had been strengthened by their captivity and their
militaristic regime. So while they felt bitter about recent events in the
UVF, they still dreamed of a progressive, clean and moral organisation
which could show working class Protestants the way forward and help
to work out a settlement with their republican opposite numbers.

But the prisoners' belief that the extremes must be consulted in any future settlement was not shared by most of the population. The prisoners' absorption in issues of jail conditions, resettlement, civil liberties etc. cut them off further from the public, and reflected more closely the interests of IRA prisoners and their families. The gulf was likely to widen further into a positive conflict of interest as a war-weary population increasingly resigned itself to the direct rule solution, and accepted the need for an ever-tougher security policy by Westminster against disturbers of the peace on both sides of the religious divide.

15

Community Action: Dreams of Government by the Grassroots

The growth of community groups in Protestant working class areas received a major impetus from the political upheavals that followed direct rule. But with the advent of the power sharing administration, plans for a Council of Ireland and the bitter disputes that surrounded both, traditional loyalist voters' minds were absorbed with national rather than local political issues. Ron Wiener, for instance, has commented on how this political climate contributed to the temporary stagnation of the 'Save the Shankill' campaign.

On the other hand, a minority of people found their initial involvement exciting and thought-provoking enough to keep building, despite the political situation. They began going to conferences, learning about community development theory, discussing with professionals; some explored shared interests with Catholic community activists (e.g. in loose confederations like the Greater West Belfast Housing Association). This spread some radical political ideas about, but it also meant a gap was opening up between a minority in community groups, and local people on whom they relied for support.

So, before the strike even took place, leading activists of both religions were starting to become, if not an elite, at least a distinct group who often had more in common with each other than with their followers. The anger and frustration both had felt when the power sharing executive abolished the Community Relations Commission drew them closer together, as did the intense debates and negotiations over what was to take its place.[29] In contrast the uninvolved were often barely aware of these developments, or their significance.

So we cannot expect a single answer to the question: How did the UWC strike affect the views or activities of community groups? Various elements within them were at different stages of thinking, and might well react differently to the strike. The stoppage gave people at the grassroots several reasons to look much more positively at community action in the future. It removed most of the political grievances that had been absorbing their minds; it gave them a sense of political effectiveness they had not felt for many years: if they could bring down a Government, how much easier to stop a high rise block being built! A lot of previously uninvolved people had been faced with having to run emergency transport, help pensioners or organise supplies. They gained both confidence and enthusiasm from having done this.

It also seemed to make many Protestants feel able to meet Catholics (or tolerate others in their community doing this) with confidence in the equality of both parties. It was very noticeable how the atmosphere in loyalist areas after the strike was not one of hostility or gleeful vengefulness towards Catholics, but one of new willingness to make gestures of reassurance—there was a carefree, if undirected, feeling of generosity. The extent to which the strike had demoralised and frightened Catholics did not seem to be grasped at all.

Community workers in Shankill and East Belfast remarked how much easier it was to get volunteers for their organisations afterwards, or interest people in the social and housing issues they were fighting for. The message they took from the strike was that real power lay at the grassroots—politicians had been running behind the bus trying to jump on—so neither politicians, planners nor councillors looked so daunting now where local battles like 'Save the Shankill' were concerned. New confidence also further eroded the chip on the shoulder attitude to academics or the Press. The help offered e.g. by students who gave legal advice, or Queen's University academics who drew up alternative plans for the Shankill was not only welcomed but itself built up community strength and resources.

Change in the style of political and social protest was speeded up too. The patient, orderly inquiries and requests (seen, for instance, in the Hammer campaign)[30] increasingly gave way to techniques once seen as un-Protestant, if not positively republican. Giant graffiti proclaiming 'no to rent rises' began to obscure sectarian slogans in parts of the Shankill: that campaign also saw direct action methods like placarding, marches and demonstrations.

One group that moved more firmly into community activity after the strike was the paramilitary UDA. It established the Ulster Community Action Group (UCAG), a federation of community groups from Protestant areas, mainly in East Belfast and the northern suburbs. The blessing of Andy Tyrie and the UDA's inner council was crucial, though their support had more to do with tactical considerations than with ideological commitment to community development theories. It killed several birds with one stone; it was a way of diverting and keeping happy a growing minority in the UDA (especially ex-NILP and trade union members) who had become seriously interested in community work and unhappy at the overt sectarianism of the UDA. It might soak up some of the many people galvanised for the strike, who (as after the UDA's mass demonstrations of 1972) were now left without a role. It improved the UDA's image and hopefully, its influence, showed it had a useful function even in the quiet times, and held out hope that grant money might flow in from a direct rule government flushed with enthusiasm about bringing gunmen in from the cold . . . at least if the UCAG had a non-sectarian constitution and clear community aims. The UDA had already seen Provisional Sinn Féin-linked people branching out into co-operatives, etc.

So UDA chiefs responded positively when the initiative was taken by a UDA member who was also a trade union shop steward. He got a few colleagues together to set up a committee to found an umbrella community group, but had little idea where to go next. A leading member of the British and Irish Communist Organisation[31] who had issued daily strike bulletins during the stoppage offered help in planning and remained a few months as chairman of UCAG. He said he saw it as a step towards developing greater political awareness in Protestant paramilitary groups.

The UCAG was eventually invited on to the direct rule administration's Standing Conference of Community Organisations. In some areas it was accused of sectarianism and self gain activities;[32] in others, like Tullycarnett and Taughmonagh, the calibre of UDA-linked community activists impressed even their critics.

But it is doubtful how much impact UCAG had on the mainstream UDA. It attracted few militants or hardliners, nor did it succeed in getting the UDA to sort out its political contradictions (like allowing some members to have friendly dialogues with Southern politicians or community activists, while UDA units were still bombing Southern targets). It was more a step sideways for the organisation, which added another role to the confusing number it had already. It changed the lives of some individuals, but the result was often that they left the UDA. Over time, UDA representation on local UCAG committees, which had never been total, diminished further.[33]

But the existence of UCAG did at least encourage the UDA to think of ways of going political, and to discuss non-traditional ideas. The involvement in community work of UCAG activists like this man, a trade union shop steward, made them think seriously about how they could link their grassroots activity to higher levels of politics.

> Putting up candidates on a paramilitary ticket or even trying to get into official parties doesn't get us anywhere. What's the alternative? People aren't ready for new approaches to politics. But if you work on the ground, this educates them, they know your record for the community and that you'll be responsive to them if elected. A group like UCAG starts putting up candidates on an independent ticket. Eventually you get a number of 'community candidates' elected and if Catholics do the same, well and good—we'll have mutual interests we can get together on later.

This long term strategy had appeal for several elements in the UDA, not just those with a genuine commitment to community issues. It also looked attractive to those who were simply anxious to ensure a long term role for the UDA and enhance its kudos and respectability. It seemed a more workable alternative than the UVF's more direct venture into the political world, the disastrous results of which were not lost on nervous senior UDA men. In future years a number of UDA-linked people did try their luck in local or national elections on a community ticket, or under the banner of the UDA political discussion group who promoted the idea of an independent Northern Ireland.[34]

But the very fact that the strategy appealed for different reasons reduced the urgency of really hammering out a consistent political programme to underpin their electoral ventures. UCAG-linked people, or those who were pushing for the UDA to support agreed independence, lacked the clout to enforce their theories on the organisation. While the leadership took up their ideas and discussed them publicly, they did not go a stage further and resolve the contradictions that resulted— which would have meant taking on other powerful factions in the UDA. For instance, while they stressed publicly that ordinary Catholics had nothing to fear from the UDA either then or in a future agreed Northern Ireland, they continued a selective assassination and bombing campaign. This included victims who were clearly not involved in republican violence. Meanwhile the vanguard of the community movement on the Protestant side were also toying with ideas on how to enter the political world and in different ways, some of these were as confused or ill-thought out as the plans of the UDA.

By mid-1974, there was great disillusionment with traditional politicians among leading community activists on both sides of the divide. Repeated failure to find a solution had culminated in a strike where the most carefully-laid constitutional plans of politicians had been swept away. On top of the feeling that parliamentarians were useless and ineffectual there was growing hostility from a community work standpoint. The abolition of the CRC and the disputes that followed it brought home to activists that many local and national politicians had little understanding of, or commitment to community development, and saw community groups as a threat to their own power. Politicians had become a threat to such groups' most straightforward work in the community let alone to any of their more radical plans.

We might expect that community activists who supported the aims of power sharing, or who disliked sectarian aspects of the strike, might also have given up on the Protestant grassroots as a force for progressive change. But this seems not to have happened among most: despite doubts and fears, the lesson they tended to draw was that the people had shown their power, and if they could do it in one way they might do it in others. If anything, activists were swept away with the exciting potential especially when they saw several strike leaders making radical or conciliatory noises after the stoppage.

The strike had thrown traditional power structures into turmoil: if the time was ripe for radical change, for alternatives to traditional, sterile politics, for something that harnessed and gave voice to the grassroots, might not the community movement be a basis for it? That was the idea which increasingly took root among community activists after the strike.

In contrast to politicians who were obsessed with constitutional issues which divided people, the community workers had highlighted things people could unite on. Some activists thought constitutional divisions could become unimportant—secondary to economic or environmental issues. Others thought their movement would be able to solve national divisions more easily than politicians could: that is if two people could agree about housing, they could eventually come to agree on a constitution: a sort of solution by stages.

The formation of Community Organisations Northern Ireland (CONI) in February 1975 also offered a possible power base for the development of community politics. Its roots lay in the failure of attempts to establish a new, independent community development body after the CRC was abolished. So community activists had turned their attention to creating some kind of federation to safeguard their interests, educate the population and enable community groups to negotiate with politicians from a position of strength.

Several different ideas about making an impact on Northern Ireland politics began to be discussed seriously. There was the UCAG idea (mentioned earlier) of putting up community candidates in local elections (and later, perhaps, in provincial ones). There was Sam Smyth's scheme for establishing a Community Convention[35] with delegates from trade unions, voluntary groups, paramilitaries, etc. But its exact mandate, its means of decision-making and its relationship to the planned Northern Ireland Convention were not clearly spelled out. There was the idea of a quite different constitutional setup, an independent Northern Ireland, with continuing discussions about how the communities might set up political and financial arrangements which both could trust and work for.

The commitment and energy of the people involved in discussing and publicising these ideas was clear to anyone who attended meetings of community activists. But they faced enormous problems and obstacles, only some of which they might have been able to overcome with more foresight and political know-how.

First, they lacked support from powerful political groups and individuals in Northern Ireland, and even from the official trade union movement. Members of parties, trade unions, the churches and so on would come along to meetings and conferences to discuss Ulster independence, co-operatives, and many other idealistic things: but they either lacked major influence or, worse still, were regarded as mavericks by their own organisations. Some of the radical priests or progressive paramilitants who came along found friends at the conferences, but few beyond. All sorts of dreamers found encouragement and hope from huddling together but not the sort of strength they needed to dent the political system.

Secondly, their very hostility to politicians and their lack of experience of constitutional politics could work against hard-headed realism—about the need to build rival machines, or about popular willingness to reject the politicians. One might think community activists would be especially tuned in to grassroots feeling: but one irony was that the more theory they were learning about participation and community development, the more time they were spending with each other, or in negotiation with statutory authorities, and the less with their own grassroots. The conference circuit which now stretched from Galway to Holland was becoming a source of amusement or embarrassment: as one veteran traveller put it, 'You always meet the same people there'. One Shankill community worker commented wryly: 'We were in danger of becoming a clique, an elite, but that's not something people like to discuss at these conferences.'

Like the UVF's Volunteer Party, community activists tended to misjudge popular opinion in the sense of over-estimating public willingness to reject old leaders and embrace new ones. Because local people were disillusioned with politicians' responsiveness on constituency issues it was tempting to assume they would reject them in their other roles, and were prepared to see constitutional issues as secondary (which, by and large, they were not). People would accept community activists as grievance-mediators, but were less prepared to give them (or paramilitants) legitimacy as national politicians. Community workers' tendency to see constitutional divisions as sterile or outmoded encouraged a retreat from facing up to real, unsolved divisions: the 'donkey politicians' they berated had been elected by the population itself, and thus reflected, rather than created, the political impasse.

Community activists, like many before them, soon found how hard it was to settle anything without facing up to constitutional divisions: for instance, how did you plan for a future housing or jobs policy unless you fixed the geographical and political parameters of your future regime? Again, they found that personal contact with the other side did not necessarily lead to agreement: it could show up stark differences. This UDA man who attended a conference on co-operatives merely made his point more bluntly than community activists who would echo his theme: 'It was a shock to me, talking to the IRSP people,[36] to discover just how far apart we were on politics and how rigid, even fanatical, they were on some things. I thought, how we ever live together if us Protestants think one thing and they think the opposite?'

The proponents of agreed independence did confront the major divisions and try to find a third constitutional way. The problem here was not that they ran away from awkward questions, but that so many different political groups and segments of both communities refused even to contemplate the idea. Also, the theorists lacked the power or resources even to publicise their thoughts effectively. Nearly all Catholics were afraid to take the risk of independence; Protestant moderates saw it, ironically, as a plot by extreme loyalists; extreme loyalists did not want the sort of genuine compromise the agreed independence lobby were planning for. An even more basic problem was that the community lobby was divided in itself, a fact sometimes obscured when activists united to protest at political threat like the abolition of the CRC.

People had discovered that community groups, despite their ethos of egalitarianism and open decision-making, suffered just as many personality squabbles as other groups: even playgroups had their power struggles. Community activists also disagreed about the sphere of their work (was it just about leisure and recreation, or something much wider?); about youth policies; about the nature of inter-sectarian activity; about appropriate protest; about how far they should work with groups like paramilitants on the one hand, and establishment bodies on the other. Any reading of CONI's reports or of community work magazines shows how fundamental these differences were: and as CONI itself admitted, it got so bogged down in working out structures and a constitution that it lacked clarity on its role and aims.

On top of these problems was the issue of co-option by central or local government after direct rule was imposed. People were divided about whether they should accept posts on the various standing conferences and advisory bodies that were set up: those who did often found themselves with little new power, yet suspected by the radicals who felt they had sold out.[37] The increasing professionalisation of community work also caused debate and sometimes ill-feeling among those who felt more skills and resources should be offered to local people.

The disputes we have discussed here were not unique to Northern Ireland: they have tended to erupt in the community action field in Britain and many other countries. Nor were they somehow unhealthy or destructive, they were simply inevitable. The point is rather that they were bound to increase the difficulty in formulating any kind of agreed political programme, especially in a society that was already bitterly divided on major political issues.

They would probably have been able to agree on a programme only if they shared an analysis of society which had worked out the links between the micro and macro levels of politics. For instance there were some articulate elements in the community lobby, especially on the Catholic side, who wanted to promote a socialist society in Northern Ireland and hoped community action would encourage the development of socialist ideas among local people. But they were in a minority and did not even agree among themselves on the nature of that socialism. Indeed any attempt to agree an analysis of the situation facing the working class would have resurrected the old thorny disputes about the

Constitution that had always plagued Labour movements in the North. Some community activists were actually hostile to the idea that their activities had any connection with socialism, while others could not readily see any link.

The principles of community development might be called radical–liberal, and while they may lead to greater class awareness they do not automatically do so. Community action encouraged people to see divisions in terms of 'the small man/woman against the establishment' (from planners to politicians) which could often lead to a rather woolly form of populism. Even among the radicals not everyone had given thought to the structures within which their many and various opponents operated or how power and resources were distributed. Only a minority had gone on to consider that, while any authority may be forced to give small concessions (like houses instead of high-rise flats) it is a regime's whole ideological perspective which determines how much of the national cake is given to projects such as public housing and new job creation. Those who did realise ran headlong into that old intractable question: so what will the regime we want look like, and where will its allegiances lie?

But if community activists failed to provide a radical political alternative after the strike, if they only enabled people to see themselves in an extra role (like 'Glencairn resident') instead of supplanting their traditional identities with new ones, there were other, less dramatic spinoffs from their collective activity. The negotiations, battles and (sometimes unrealistic) discussions of the 1974–5 period produced a hard nucleus of experienced people within the Protestant community. They continued to provide a voice and a negotiating power for Protestant community interests vis à vis statutory authorities. They were not always successful or satisfactory and internal criticism remained: but they had established themselves, and they were also one channel of communication with Catholics who shared some of their basic aims.

The ideas of the dreamers also made an impact in a diffuse way. In a society where the same sterile views and cries often seemed to follow each other endlessly, any novel ideas or projects frequently had their roots in the community lobby. Community activists contributed to new thinking about intractable problems in the legal and police systems; they helped devise imaginative school and community education projects which encouraged people to take control over their own lives and use more personal choice. These apparently low level activities assumed more importance after the Northern Ireland Convention failed to reach agreement, major change at the higher levels of politics looked unlikely for the foreseeable future, and political parties began to lose their role. As it became harder to see ways of directly influencing what went on at the top, grassroots action kept alive some sense of political and personal effectiveness, some hope that not all was static and unchangeable.

Notes

INTRODUCTION

1. G. Bell (1976).
2. But the bias towards Catholics was partly a result of loyalists' own attitudes. In the early years of the conflict at least, they tended to be hostile and uncooperative towards journalists and researchers; cf. Max Hastings (1970); and further discussion of the issue throughout this book.
3. Cf. Richard Rose's definition of an ultra—'an individual who supports a particular definition of the existing regime so strongly that he is willing to break laws, or even take up arms, to recall it to its "true" way'; Richard Rose (1971) p. 33.
4. For a review of general explanations, cf. J. H.Whyte (1978).
5. Frank Burton, (1978), pp. 155–163.
6. Rosemary Harris (1972); cf. also Frank Wright (1973).
7. Cf., for example, Ian Budge and Cornelius O'Leary (1973); Emrys Jones (1960); Andrew Boyd (1969); J. C. Beckett and R. E. Glasscock (1967).
8. Thus guessing people's religion is a game almost everyone ends up playing in Ulster, consciously or otherwise: it does not mean people are prejudiced. So I would question the political importance Frank Burton (op. cit). places on the concept of 'telling'.
9. Cf. T. K. Daniels, 'Myths and the Militants', *Political Studies* 24, IV, pp. 455–461.

PART ONE

1. For detailed analysis cf. Sidney Elliot (1973).
2. Andrew Boyd (1969).
3. Useful historical studies include Peter Gibbon (1975); F. S. L. Lyons (1971); Ronald McNeill (1922); Patrick Buckland, vols 1 and 2 (1973); A. T. Q. Stewart (1967).
4. Cf. House of Commons debates (Northern Ireland), vol. 29 col. 655, 1945.
5. J. M. Sinclair, Minister of Finance, speaking November 1943, authorised by British Treasury.
6. On the role of the Catholic church in Irish politics, cf. J. H. Whyte (1975); K. B. Nowlan and T. D. Williams (eds). (1969).
7. Cf. J. H. Whyte (1979) p. 48.
8. F. S. L. Lyons (1971) p. 716.
9. The 'myth of 1641' claimed that 150,000 Protestants, the entire Protestant population at that time, had been slaughtered by the native Irish.
10. Cf. D. Kennedy, 'Catholics in Northern Ireland, 1926–39' in F. McManus (ed.) (1967); Michael Farrell (1976); J. L. McCracken, 'Northern Ireland 1921–66' in T. W. Moody and F. X. Martin (eds) (1967).

11. Cf. M. W. Dewar, J. Brown and S. E. Long (1967); David Roberts (1971); Rosemary Harris (1972).

12. e.g. the Longstone Road March affair, report in Farrell (1976) pp.' 207–208.

13. For fuller discussion of this tradition cf. Frank Wright (1973).

14. Cf. David Miller, (1978).

15. Basil Brooke, later Lord Brookeborough, made several such comments in 1933–4. They are chronicled in Frank Gallagher (1957), pp. 201–205.

16. Reported in *Northern Whig*, 15 October 1920.

17. Cf. John Harbinson (1973), appendix E.

18. Sam Kyle, MP, from Hansard (NI) vol 6 col 39.

19. described in Peter Gibbon (1969).

20. Harbinson, *op. cit.* ch. 10.

21. Ian Budge and Cornelius O'Leary (1973) Table 10.

22. Cf. P. Hillyard (1982), I. Budge and C. O'Leary (1973).

23. Harbinson, op. cit. p. 67.

24. See footnote 11.

25. Cf. D. Barritt and C. F. Carter (1962); Ruth Overy (1972); Sue Jenvey (1972).

26. Cf. J. H. Whyte (1975).

27. Cf. J. H. Whyte (1975); J. F. Harbinson (1973).

28. Cf. J. F. Harbinson (1966); J. Graham (1973).

29. Farrell, *op. cit.* p. 196.

30. Cf. for example Liam de Paor (1970); Owen Dudley Edwards (1970); David Boulton (1973).

31. Terence O'Neill (1969), expounds this kind of philosophy.

32. Cf. D. Birrell (1972).

33. Cf. Frank Wright, *op. cit.*

34. For a detailed look at the history of redevelopment in the Shankill area, Cf. Ron Wiener (1975).

35. David Boulton, *op. cit.* p. 31; Patrick Marrinan (1973) also discusses his early career, though no personal interviews with Paisley were carried out for this biography. Laim de Paor, *op. cit.* describes Paisley's involvement in counter-demonstrations against the civil rights movement.

36. Survey of Ulster political attitudes by National Opinion Polls published in *Belfast Telegraph*, 8, 9, and 11–16 December 1969.

37. Frank Wright, *op. cit.* gives a detailed analysis of the religio–political viewpoint.

38. David Boulton, *op. cit.* p. 31

39. Cf. Clifford Smyth (1970).

40. As in heroic songs, e.g. *Orange Cross Book of Songs and Verse*, 2nd ed. published by Orange Cross, available at Linenhall Library, Belfast.

41. Pioneers were members of a Catholic-based organisation who swore to abstain from alcohol. The incongruity of this account was pointed out to me by an amused Catholic reader. The speaker definitely said this—he may have been mistaken, or loyalist militants may indeed have unthinkingly entered Catholic pubs with Pioneer badges on!

42. Gusty Spence, whose brother was a Unionist Party election agent, himself worked sporadically for the party.

43. The literature of civil rights includes 'Campaign for Social Justice', *The Plain Truth*, 1969; Fermanagh civil rights association, *Fermanagh Facts*, 1969; Aidan Corrigan, *Eye Witness in Northern Ireland*, Voice of Ulster Pubs. 1969; also cf. Cameron Commission report, *Disturbances in Northern Ireland*, HMSO Belfast, Cmd. 523, 1969. On the refusal of Protestants to accept accusations of discrimination, cf. Richard Rose (1971), especially Q. 43 of the opinion survey. In answer to the question 'Do you think Catholics in Northern Ireland are treated unfairly' 74 per cent of Protestants said 'no' and an equal percentage of Catholics said 'yes'.

44. I use here the example of someone with whom I had extensive contact and discussions over a period of time, not as an interviewee but as a family acquaintance and whose reactions to political events, daily news bulletins etc. I was able to witness in an everyday fashion.

45. Here I am summarising some typical reactions of people living in loyalist areas. Some were interview respondents from loyalist groups, others were housewives, or friends and relatives of interviewees who joined the conversation in a house or a pub. In their general tone, all the comments were things one would hear from large numbers of people—sometimes to the extent that they became cliches.

46. For this and other examples of mutual misunderstanding, cf. Conor Cruise O'Brien (1974).

47. Cf. quote from Anselm Strauss (1959): '"And why do you not draw on us Croats for officials?" asked Valetta... "But how can we...?" spluttered Constantine [a Serbian] "you are not loyal!" "And how" asked Valetta... "can we be expected to be loyal if you always treat us like this?" "But" growled Constantine, "how can we treat you differently till you are loyal?"'

48. *Orange Cross Songbook, op. cit.*

49. For more detailed (if badly written and punctuated) analysis of Protestant reactions to the discrimination debate see Sarah Nelson (1975).

PART TWO

1. Cf. Bowes Egan and Vincent McCormack (1969). For further accounts of the period 1968–69 see Michael Farrell (1976); Richard Deutsch and Vivian Magowan, 1973–4, Vol. 1; Liam de Paor (1970).

2. Cf. *Violence and Civil Disturbances in Northern Ireland in 1969:* Report of Tribunal of Enquiry (Scarman Report) 2 vols. HMSO Belfast, 1972, Cmd. 566.

3. For instance see E. A. Aunger (1975).

4. Cf. discussion of ULA in John Harbinson (1973), especially pp 67–69; also Farrell, *op. cit.* pp. 106, 123, 363.

5. Cf. heroic and complimentary image in books like Hezlet (1972); Wallace Clark (1967).

6. I myself experienced several examples either of stark ignorance or of apparent failure to work out just what the constitutional arrangements were in Northern Ireland and Southern Ireland. I was often asked by British people if I travelled to Belfast by Aer Lingus, and during a bank strike in the Republic in the mid-1970s I was told in several British banks that they

could not handle my Ulsterbank cheques. After tortuous explanations and trips to see the manager, my cheques were then cashed. Years of TV coverage had apparently still not brought home to many British people that dispute over constitutional allegiances, and the division of Ireland, were part of what the conflict was about.

7. Government of Ireland Act 1920, clause 75.
8. On the night of 13 August 1969, with riots in Belfast, Derry and Dungannon, the Irish Prime Minister (Lynch) said on television: 'It is clear that the Irish government can no longer stand by and see innocent people injured and perhaps worse.' Some interpreted this as a threat of invasion. In the event Irish field hospitals were set up along the Border, Lynch called for a UN peacekeeping force in the North and for negotiations with Britain on the basis that unification 'can provide the only permanent solution for the problem'.

PART THREE

1. Cf. David Boulton (1973), pp. 148–149.
2. At a rally in the Ulster Hall on 3 October 1971, Paisley said Britain was about to introduce direct rule: this was quickly denied by Westminster.
3. Lisburn rally, 12 February 1972.
4. For details of these incidents see Boulton, *op. cit.* and Martin Dillon and Denis Lehane (1973).
5. Pamphlet, *Government Without Right*, Vanguard Pubs. (1972.)
6. From *Ulster a Nation*, Vanguard Pubs. 1972. This and other pamphlets from fringe groups and political parties should be available from the Linenhall Library, Belfast.
7. Israel was much admired by some loyalist groups; cf. alleged statement by Ulster Freedom Fighters in Dillon and Lehane, *op. cit.* p. 286: 'We have more in common with the state of Israel, the Star of David on our flag. These brave people fought and won their battle for survival.'
8. Pamphlet, *Speech by William Craig to Ulster Vanguard First Anniversary Rally* Vanguard Pubs. (1973.)
9. The range of constitutional alternatives discussed by Vanguard members can be seen in their publications, e.g. *Ulster a Nation,* Vanguard Pubs. (1972); *Community of the British Isles*, Vanguard Pubs. (1973); *The Future of Northern Ireland*, Vanguard Pubs. (1973); *Dominion of Ulster*, by Prof. Kennedy Lindsay, Vanguard Pubs. (1972).
10. Implied at points in Michael Farrell (1976); Geoffrey Bell (1976).
11. Implied at points in Dillon and Lehane, *op. cit.*
12. McKittrick, D. and Holland, J., unpublished manuscript.
13. Cf. K., Boyle T., Hadden P. Hillyard (1980).
14. Cf. Dillon and Lehane, *op. cit.* p. 272.
15. For details of speech and reactions to it, cf. Boulton, *op. cit.* p. 154.
16. Cf. Dillon and Lehane, *op. cit.* p. 285.
17. *Ibid* p. 71, description of Moane killing.
18. Letter quoted in Dillon and Lehane, *op. cit.* p. 56.
19. Cf. Farrell *op. cit.* p. 296.

20. Interview on 'World This Weekend', 17 December 1972.
21. Dillon and Lehane, and Boulton, give the flavour of UDA internal feuding at this time, even though the details are not always accurate.
22. See 'Murphy said to be prime mover in butcher death', David McKittrick, *Irish Times*, 17 November 1982, and 'Twentieth victim one too many for Shankill butchers', David McKittrick, *Irish Times*, 21 February 1979.
23. On 7 September 1972, the 1st battalion parachute regiment broke into and searched a UDA 'command post' on Shankill. As they left they were fired on; returning fire they killed two Protestant civilians. A pitched battle followed.
24. A community group 'is drawn together by shared concern over an issue or condition, presumed to have significance... for the community from which the group is drawn. It is the assumption by the group that it is responsible for the articulation of the common views of that community, from which it derives its authority... The first type of issue arises from the failure of public representatives... and other responsible institutions to perform those tasks... for which they acknowledge they have responsibility; the second... from the emergence of new needs... which no one has contracted to provide... the group may bring pressure to bear on those who claim responsibility, in order to get them to deal with the problem satisfactorily or... take action to meet the defined problem themselves.' Hywel Griffiths, (1975).
25. *Fortnight* no. 68, 21 September 1973, has a list of known community groups in Belfast and a useful survey of some reasons for their growth after 1969.
26. Cf. Ron Wiener (1975).
27. Cf. *Sandy Row at the Public Inquiry*, pamphlet, Sandy Row Redevelopment Assn., July 1972.
28. Cf. *Community Development in Northern Ireland*, NICRC 1974 (A selection of NICRC publications is available at Northern Ireland Council of Social Services, 2 Annadale Avenue, Belfast 7.); Louis Boyle (1976); *Fortnight* 19–3–71, 15–12–72.
29. J. Darby and A. Williamson (eds) (1978).
30. Protestant teenage gangs who adopted tartan scarves as a uniform. They were strongest in East Belfast.
31. E.g. Louis Boyle (1972, 1973).
32. Hywel Griffiths, *op. cit.*
33. Cf. Wiener, *op. cit.* chapter 6.

PART FOUR

1. Cf. Robert Fisk (1975).
2. Cf. David McKittrick, 'Hand of Paisley seen in UWC fragmentation', *The Irish Times* 11 November 1975.
3. For instance the UWC chairman, Harry Murray, signed an anti-internment petition at the British–Irish Association Conference in Oxford (July 1974) and resigned after criticism of his action by the UWC and loyalist politicians.
4. Figures from Richard Rose (1971) p. 25.

5. Cf. Deutsch and Magowan (1974) vol. 3, pp. 121–122.
6. Where a group of Protestant clergymen met IRA leaders on the clergymen's initiative in December 1974. This led to an IRA ceasefire on 22 December 1974 and the establishment of Sinn Fein incident centres to monitor the truce. Monitoring involved contact between Sinn Fein and British civil servants, and was denounced by the SDLP as well as by Protestant leaders.
7. For examples of thinking about agreed independence see *Your Future: Ulster can survive unfettered* ULCCC, 40 Albertbridge Rd Belfast 1; 'Glen Barr's Ulster', *Fortnight* 12.9.75; *What Price Independence*, New Ulster Movement 1976; Ulster Defence Association (1979); Ulster Independence Movement (1976).
8. Cf. Deutsch and Magowan (1974). vol. 3 p. 8
9. As, it could be argued, happened after the failure of the Northern Ireland Convention. The huge Peace Movement rallies in 1976 were very symptomatic of a war weary population who wanted the Troubles to end, did not want to think in detail how, and now looked outside conventional politics for some answer.
10. *The Northern Ireland Constitution,* published 4 July 1974; proposals detailed in Deutsch and Magowan (1974) vol 3 p. 112.
11. Cf. Northern Ireland Assembly, official report, vol 31, 3 April 1974.
12. Cf. R. Rose, I. McAllister and P. Mair (1978).
13. The UUUC demands included a majority rule parliament with full security powers and an increase in local government powers.
14. *Ulster DUP Year Book 1975–76,* p. 13. Published by DUP, 1A Ava Ave, Belfast 7.
15. Cf. for example Boulton (1973), pp. 166–173.
16. In the early 1970s the UVF also introduced a uniform of black berets or balaclavas, black jumpers, black leather jackets and badges modelled on those of the original UVF. Usually members only bothered with the black jacket part of the uniform, unless they were parading in jail or impressing authors and research students. Proscription till early 1974 also led to caution about wearing insignia.
17. *The Volunteer Political Party—a progressive and forward thinking unionist party*. Enterprise Printing Services Ltd, 1974. Copies should be available at Linenhall Library, Belfast.
18. The UVF's magazine, which first appeared in early 1974.
19. The circumstances of his jail escape and some of his activities on the run are documented in Boulton (1973).
20. All names, except that of the UVF's election candidate Ken Gibson, are pseudonyms.
21. A small Catholic enclave in the heart of Protestant East Belfast.
22. The shortcomings of get-togethers where various group techniques are used to change the outlook of political opponents are suggested in G. Boehringer, V. Zeruolis and J. Bayley, (1974) pp. 257–275.
23. Cf. Frank Burton (1978) especially pp. 109–118.
24. The UVF announced the formation of the Volunteer Political Party on 22 June 1974. It launched the manifesto at a press conference on 27 September 1974.

25. Cf. for instance the patronising tone of 'Calvin Macnee' writing on UVF initiatives in *Fortnight* no. 77. 8 February 1974.

26. After the UVF cautiously welcomed Desmond Boal's proposals for an amalgamated Ireland', politicians in both Ulster and the Republic described them as murderers and people who simply wanted to restore a Protestant ascendancy.

27. Cf footnote 6, above.

28. In which several members of a famous Irish showband (group) were killed on 31 July 1975 by a bomb planted in their van by the UVF.

29. Cf. 'Community relations: rest in peace?' *Fortnight* no. 82 26 April 1974; *Community Development in N. Ireland*, CRC; *Community Action: which way forward?* report of conference at Magee College, Aug/Sept 1974; *The Role of District Councils in Community Work*, NICSS 1976; *The Development of Community Work* DHSS circular HSS 15 (OSO 1/751 *Community, sporting and recreational provision by district councils*, Dept of Education circular, 1975/51; Lovett and Perceval in Curno ed. (1978); L. O'Dowd, B. Rolston and M. Tomlinson (1980).

30. Cf. Ron Wiener (1975) ch. 6.

31. BICO/Workers Assn, 10 Athol Street Belfast 12 have published many pamphlets and journals: best known for formulation of two nations theory.

32. Cf. Tom Lovett and Robin Perceval (1978).

33. Cf. Sarah Nelson, 'Gunmen and Community Groups' *The Irish Times* 13 July 1976; 'UCAG—what it does', *Scope* 16, May–June 1978.

34. Ulster Defence Association (1979).

35. Cf. *Community Convention,* pamphlet by Sam Smyth, 1975, published by North Belfast Resource Centre 359 Antrim Rd, Belfast; also debates in *Scope* March–April, November–December 1976.

36 The Irish Republican Socialist Party, which took a more militantly antiloyalist position than the Official IRA, from whom many IRSP members had broken.

37. Co-option problems are discussed in more detail by Lovett and Perceval (1978) and in L. O'Dowd, B. Rolston and M. Tomlinson (1980) especially ch. 6.

Select Bibliography

Akenson, D. H., *Education and Enmity—Control of Schooling in Northern Ireland, 1920-1950*, David & Charles, 1973.

Barritt, D. P. and Carter, C. F., *The Northern Ireland Problem: A Study in Group Relations*, Oxford University Press, 1962, 1972 (2nd ed.).

Beckett, J. C. and Glasscock, R. E., *Belfast: The Origin and Growth of an Industrial City*, BBC, London, 1967.

Bell, G., *The Protestants of Ulster*, Pluto Press, 1976.

Bew, P., Gibbon, P. and Patterson, H., *The State in Northern Ireland*, Manchester University Press, 1979.

Boulton, D., *The UVF 1966-1973: An Anatomy of Loyalist Rebellion*, Torc Books, Dublin, 1973.

Boyd, A., *Holy War in Belfast*. Anvil Books, Tralee, 1969.

Boyle, K., Hadden, T. and Hillyard, P., *Ten Years On: The Legal Control of Political Violence*, Cobden Trust, 1980.

Buckland, P., *Irish Unionism, vol. 1: Ulster Unionism and the Origins of Northern Ireland 1886-1922*, Gill & Macmillan 1973.

Buckland, P., *The Factory of Grievances: Devolved Government in Northern Ireland, 1921-39*, Gill & Macmillan, 1979.

Budge, I. and O'Leary, C., *Belfast: Approach to Crisis A Study of Belfast Politics 1613-1970*. Macmillan, 1973.

Burton, F., *The Politics of Legitimacy: Struggles in a Belfast Community*, Routledge and Kegan Paul, 1978.

Clark, W., *Guns in Ulster: A History of the B Special Constabulary in part of Co. Derry*, RUC Constabulary Gazette, 1967.

Cormack, R. J. and Osborne, R. D., *Religion, Education and Employment: Aspects of Equal Opportunity in Northern Ireland*, Appletree Press, Belfast, 1983.

Darby, John, *Conflict in Northern Ireland*, Gill & Macmillan, Dublin, 1976.

Darby, J. and Williamson, A. (eds.) *Violence and the Social Services in Northern Ireland*, Heinemann, 1978.

De Paor, Liam, *Divided Ulster*, Penguin, 1970.

Deutsch, R. and Magowan, V., *Northern Ireland 1968-73: A Chronology Of Events* (3 vols), Blackstaff Press, Belfast 1973 & 1974.

Dewar, M. W., Brown, J. and Long, S. F., *Orangeism: A New Historical*

Appreciation, 1688–1967, Orange Order, Belfast, 1967.

Dillon, M. and Lehane, D., *Political Murder in Northern Ireland*, Penguin, 1973.

Dudley Edwards, Owen., *Sins of our Fathers: roots of conflict in Northern Ireland,* Gill and MacMillan, Dublin, 1970.

Elliott, S., *Northern Ireland Parliamentary Election Results 1921–1972*, Political Reference Publications, 1973.

Farrell, M., *Northern Ireland: The Orange State*, Pluto Press, 1976.

Fisk, R., *The Point of No Return: The Strike that Broke the British in Ulster*, Andre Deutsch, 1975.

Gallagher, F., *The Indivisible Island*, Gollancz, 1957.

Gibbon, P., *The Origins of Ulster Unionism*, Manchester University Press, 1975.

Harbinson, J. F. *The Ulster Unionist Party 1882–1973*, Blackstaff Press, 1973.

Harbinson, R., *No Surrender: An Ulster Childhood*, London, 1960.

Harris, R., *Prejudice and Tolerance in Ulster*, Manchester University Press, 1972.

Hadden, T. and Hillyard, P., *Justice in Northern Ireland: A Study in Social Confidence*, Cobden Trust, 1973.

Hastings, M., *Ulster 1969: The Fight for Civil Rights in Northern Ireland*, Gollancz, 1970.

Hezlet, Sir A., *The B Specials: A History of the Ulster Special Constabulary*, Tom Stacey, 1972.

Heslinga, M. W. *The Irish Border as a Cultural Divide*, Van Gorcum, 1962.

Hillyard, P., *Rents, Repairs and Despair: A Study of the Private Rented Sector in Northern Ireland*, Bristol 1982.

Jones, E., *A Social Geography of Belfast*, Oxford University Press, 1960.

Kelly, M., Wickham, J. and O'Dowd, L., *Power, Conflict and Inequality*, Marion Boyers, 1982.

Lyons, F. S. L., *Ireland Since the Famine: 1850 to the Present*, Weidenfeld & Nicolson, 1971.

McCarthy, C., *Trade Unions in Ireland 1884–1960*, Institute of Public Administration, Dublin, 1977.

McCarthy, C., *The Decade of Upheaval: Irish Trade Unions in the 1960s*, Institute of Public Administration, Dublin, 1973.

McManus, F. (ed.) *The Years of the Great Test, 1926–39*, Mercier Press 1967.

McNeill, R., *Ulster's Stand for Union*, John Murray, London, 1922.

Marrinan, P., *Paisley, Man of Wrath*, Anvil Books, Tralee, 1973.

Miller, D., *Queen's Rebels: Ulster Loyalism in Historical Perspective*, Gill & Macmillan 1978.

Moody, T. W. and Martin, F. X., *The Course of Irish History*, Mercier Press, 1967.

Morgan, A. and Purdie, B., (eds) *Ireland: Divided Nation, Divided Class*, Ink Links, London, 1980.

Nowlan, K. B. and Williams, T. D., (eds) *Ireland in the War Years and After, 1939–51*, Gill & Macmillan, 1969.

O'Brien, C. C., *States of Ireland*, Hutchinson, 1972, Panther, 1974.

O'Dowd, L., Rolston, W. and Tomlinson, M., *Northern Ireland: Between Civil Rights and Civil War*, CSE Books, 1980.

O'Neill, Terence., *Ulster at the Crossroads*, Faber & Faber, 1969.

Patterson, H., *Class Conflict and Sectarianism: The Protestant Working Class and the Belfast Labour Movement 1868–1920*, Blackstaff Press, 1980.

Rose, R., *Governing Without Consensus: an Irish Perspective*, Faber & Faber, 1971.

Stewart, A. T. Q., *The Ulster Crisis*, Faber & Faber, 1967.

Strauss, A., *Mirrors and Masks*, Glencoe, Illinois, 1959.

van Voris, W. H., *Violence in Ulster: an Oral Documentary*, University of Massachusetts Press, 1975.

Whyte, J. H., *Church and State in Modern Ireland*, 1923–1970, Gill & Macmillan, 1975.

Wiener, R., *The Rape and Plunder of the Shankill*, Notaems Press, Belfast, 1975. Re-issued by Farset Co-operative Press, Belfast, 1980.

PAMPHLETS, JOURNAL ARTICLES, THESES ETC.

Aunger, E. A., 'Religion and Occupational Class in Northern Ireland', *Economic and Social Review*, 7 January 1975.

Bleakley, D., 'The Northern Ireland Trade Union Movement', *Journal of Social and Statistical Inquiry Society of Ireland* 19, 1953–4.

Boal, F. W. *et al. The Special Distribution of some Social Problems in the Belfast Urban Area*, N. Ireland Community Relations Commision 1974.

Boal, F. W., Campbell, J. and Livingstone, D. W., *Protestants and Social Change in Belfast*, (Dept. of Geography). Queen's University, Belfast, research in progress.

Boehringer, G. *et al.* 'Stirling: Destructive Application of Group

Techniques to a Conflict', *Journal of Conflict Resolution* 18, 2, 1974.

Boyle, J., 'The Belfast Protestant Association and the Independent Orange Order', *Irish Historical Studies* XIII, 1962–3.

British and Irish Communist Organisation, *The Two Irish Nations*, B & ICO, Belfast 1975.

Campaign for Social Justice in Northern Ireland, *The Plain Truth.* CSJ, Dungannon, 1972.

Community Relations Commission, *Flight: A Report on Popular Movement in Belfast during August 1971*, NICRC, 1971.

Craig, William, *The Future of Northern Ireland*, Styletype Printing 1973, Speech at Ulster Vanguard First Anniversary Rally, 12 February 1973. Vanguard Pubs. 1973.

Daniels, T. K., 'Myth and the Militants', *Political Studies* 24, IV.

Dewar, Rev. M. W., *Why Orangeism?* T. H. Jordan, Belfast, 1970.

Egan, B. and McCormack, V., *Burntollet*, ERS Pubs. London, 1969.

Fair Employment Agency, *An Industrial and Occupational Profile of the Two Sections of the Population in Northern Ireland*, F.E.A., Belfast 1978.

Fortnight, 'Community Relations—Rest in Peace?' 26 April 1974. 'The Paper War', 11 January, 25 January, 8 February 1974. 'Glen Barr's Ulster', 12 September 1975. 'Who are the Terrorists?' 7 May 1976.

Gibbon, P., 'Ulster: Religion and Class', *New Left Review* 55, 1969.

Graham, J., *The Northern Ireland Labour Party 1949–1967*, Unpublished MA Thesis, Queen's University, Belfast, 1973.

Green, A. J., *'Devolution and Public Finance: Stormont from 1921 to 1972'*, SPP no. 48, Centre for the Study of Public Policy, Strathclyde University, 1979.

Griffiths, J. H., 'Carrying on in the Middle of Violent Conflict' in Jones & Mayo (eds), *Community Work One,* Routledge and Kegan Paul, 1974.

——, 'Paramilitary groups and other community action groups in Northern Ireland today', *International Review of Community Development*, 10, 11, 1975.

Harbinson, J. F., *History of the Northern Ireland Labour Party 1884–1949*, Unpublished M.Sc. thesis, Queen's University, Belfast, 1966.

Jackson, H., *The Two Irelands: a Dual Study of Inter-group Tensions*, Minority Rights Group Report, No. 2, 1971.

Jenvey, Sue. 'Sons and Haters: Ulster Youth in Conflict', *New Society* 20 July 1972.

Lindsay, Prof. K., *Dominion of Ulster*, Ulster Vanguard Pubs. 1972.

Lovett, T. & Percival. 'Politics, Conflict & Community Action in N. Ireland' in *Political Issues and Community Work* (ed. Curno), RKP, 1978.

McCarthy, C., 'Civil Strife and Trade Union Unity: the case of Ireland', *Government and Opposition* vol. 8 no. 4.

McKee, A., *Belfast Trades Council: the First Hundred Years,* 1881–1981, Belfast Trades Council, 1983.

McAllister, Ian, 'The Legitimacy of Opposition: the Collapse of the 1974 Northern Ireland Executive', *Eire–Ireland* 12, IV.

McAllister, I. and Nelson, S., 'Developments in the Northern Ireland Party System', *Parliamentary Affairs*, 32, 111, 1979.

Nelson, S., 'Protestant Ideology Considered' *British Political Sociology Yearbook*, 11, Croom Helm, 1975.

New Ulster Movement, *What Price Independence?* NUM, 1976.

Overy, Ruth, 'Children's Play', *Community Forum* no. 2, 1972.

Oliver, J., 'Working at Stormont', *Institute of Public Administration*, 1978.

Patterson, H., 'Independent Orangeism and Class Conflict in Edwardian Belfast: a Re-Interpretation', Royal Irish Academy, vol. 80, C, no. 1, 1980.

Roberts, D. A., 'The Orange Order in Ireland: A Religious Institution?' *British Journal of Sociology* 22, 111, 1971.

Roden Street Residents Assn. *Roden Street: Death of a Community*, Greater West Belfast Housing Association, 1973.

Rose, R. *et al. Is there a Concurring Majority about Northern Ireland?* SPP no. 22. Centre for the Study of Public Policy, Strathclyde University, 1978.

Sandy Row Development Assn. *Sandy Row at the Public Inquiry*, July, 1972.

Smyth, Clifford, *Ulster Assailed*, Belfast, 1970.

Smyth, Sam., *Community Convention*, North Belfast Resource Centre, 1975.

Ulster Defence Association, *Beyond the Religious Divide:* Papers for discussion, Reprint, March 1979.

Ulster Independence Movement, *Towards an Independent Ulster*, Ulster Heritage Society, July 1976.

Ulster Loyalist Central Co-ordinating Committee, *Your future: Ulster Can Survive Unfettered,* Proposals for Ulster Independence, ULCCC, 1977.

Ulster Vanguard, *Ulster—a Nation*, Ulster Vanguard Pubs. 1972.

——, *Spelling it Out*, Ulster Vanguard Pubs. 1972.

——, *Community of the British Isles*, Vanguard Pubs. 1973.

Whyte, J. H., 'Intra-unionist disputes in the Northern Ireland House of Commons, 1921–72', Duplicated: Political Science Dept. Queen's University, Belfast.

Whyte, J. H., 'Interpretations of the Northern Ireland Problem: an Appraisal.' *Economic and Social Review*, 9, IV, 1978.

Wright, Frank, 'Protestant Ideology & Politics in Ulster' *European Journal of Sociology* 14, 2, 1973.

——, 'The Ulster Spectrum', *Contemporary Terror: Studies in Sub-state Violence.* eds. David Carlton and Carlo Schaerf, Macmillan, 1981.

GOVERNMENT REPORTS AND CONSTITUTIONAL PROPOSALS

Disturbances in Northern Ireland: Report of the Commission appointed by the Governor of Northern Ireland (Cameron Report), HMSO Belfast, September 1969, Cmd. 532.

Report of the Advisory Committee on Police in Northern Ireland (Hunt Report), HMSO Belfast, October 1969, Cmd. 535.

Report of the Enquiry into Allegations against the Security Forces of Physical Brutality arising out of events on 9 August 1971 (Compton Report), HMSO London, November 1971, CMD. 4823.

Violence and Civil Disturbances in Northern Ireland in 1969: Report of Tribunal of Enquiry (Scarman Report) 2 Vols. HMSO Belfast, April 1972, Cmd. 566.

Report of the Commission to Consider Legal Procedures to deal with Terrorist Activities in Northern Ireland (Diplock Report), HMSO London, December 1972, Cmd. 5185.

Report of the Tribunal appointed to Enquire into the Events on Sunday 30 January 1972 which led to Loss of Life in connection with the Procession in Londonderry on that day (Widgery Report), HMSO London, 1972, H.L. 101/H.C. 220.

Northern Ireland Constitutional Proposals, HMSO London, March 1973, Cmd. 5259, White Paper.

Report of a Committee to consider, in the context of Civil Liberties and Human Rights, Measures to Deal with Terrorism in Northern Ireland (Gardiner Report), HMSO London, January 1975, Cmd. 5847.

Index

Chapter   — Violence and Votes